Created for
Connection

ALSO BY DR. SUE JOHNSON

Love Sense: The Revolutionary New Science of
Romantic Relationships

Hold Me Tight: Seven Conversations for a Lifetime of Love

The Practice of Emotionally Focused Couple Therapy:
Creating Connection

Emotionally Focused Couple Therapy with
Trauma Survivors: Strengthening Attachment Bonds

Created for *Connection*

....

The "Hold Me Tight" Guide for Christian Couples

SEVEN CONVERSATIONS
for a LIFETIME of LOVE

Dr. Sue Johnson
with Kenny Sanderfer

Adapted from *Hold Me Tight*

Little, Brown Spark
New York Boston London

Little, Brown Spark
Hachette Book Group
1290 Avenue of the Americas, New York, NY 10104
littlebrownspark.com

Revised Edition: October 2016

Little, Brown Spark is an imprint of Little, Brown and Company, a division of Hachette
Book Group, Inc. The Little, Brown Spark name and logo are trademarks of Hachette
Book Group, Inc.

The publisher is not responsible for websites (or their content)
that are not owned by the publisher.

The Hachette Speakers Bureau provides a wide range of authors for speaking events. To
find out more, go to hachettespeakersbureau.com or call (866) 376-6591.

Copyright acknowledgments appear on page 311.

ISBN 978-0-316-30741-3
LCCN 2016937281

Text design by Meryl Sussman Levavi

Printing 9, 2020

LSC-C

Printed in the United States of America

To my clients and colleagues, who have helped me

to understand love.

To my partner, John, and my children, Tim, Emma, and Sarah,

who have taught me how to feel it and give it.

And to Father Anthony Storey, who constantly reminded me of my

connection to God as the ultimate source of light and love.

—Sue Johnson

To my partner in life, love, and faith—Suzette Comer Sanderfer;

to my children—Kody and Kate; and to the other members of my

wonderful family—my parents, Sandy and Rosemary; my sister,

Kathy; and my incredible grandchildren.

And to the two people who taught me the most about bonding

and loving—Auntie Leighla Carter and Marcelle Woods.

—Kenny Sanderfer

....

Dance me to your beauty
with a burning violin
Dance me through the panic
till I'm gathered safely in
Lift me like an olive branch
and be my homeward dove
Dance me to the end of love

—Leonard Cohen

I can see now, GOD, that your decisions are right;...
Oh, love me—and right now!—hold me tight!
just the way you promised.
Now comfort me so I can live, really live;
your revelation is the tune I dance to.

—Psalm 119:75–77 (The Message)

....

Contents

Contents

Created for
Connection

Introduction

Sue Johnson

This is an exciting time for anyone aspiring to understand and begin deliberately shaping their most important love relationship. The first, bestselling version of this book laid out the revolutionary new science of adult love and the couple therapy model, Emotionally Focused Therapy (EFT), based on this science. It also described the explicit map to lasting love that this science now offers us. The book was designed to reach a broad general readership. However, a trusted Christian colleague of mine, Kenny Sanderfer, recently asked me to consider writing a version of this book specifically for Christian couples. His rationale was compelling: Christians seeking guidance for their love relationships want to know not only that what they are reading is grounded in sound research, but also that this guidance is completely consistent with their faith and the Scriptures that guide them in their pursuit of divine wisdom. This made perfect sense. As Kenny and I placed the science of EFT alongside the ancient wisdom of the Christian Scriptures, clear and consistent parallels between EFT and biblical teachings about divine love and God's teachings about human love leapt out at us. It is not surprising that a system of understanding love relationships based on the best of modern research on adult love is so consonant with the wisdom of this ancient book of faith, which is bookended with images of marriage (Gen. 2 and Rev. 22) and emphasizes the centrality of love from beginning to end. Science and spiritual wisdom often teach us to see things that, once we are aware of them, seem obvious and mirror our own innate sense of truth.

The main reason for the revision of the original book, which is titled *Hold Me Tight,* is the passion that both Kenny and I share for helping couples—all couples. Kenny communicated to me that, as a Christian, his deep calling in life is to help couples of faith find the love they were created to experience, with God and with each other. I agreed that it would be difficult to find an institution more committed to the task of reconciliation and the restoration of loving relationships than the church. Kenny pointed out that, unfortunately, divorce statistics show just how much people of faith struggle in their marriages. It seems that there has never been a time in Western societies when the challenges to long-term relationships have been so great.

Over many long, fascinating conversations, Kenny helped me see the natural connection between what EFT has to offer and the urgent need of the church to help people of faith shape more positive and lasting relationships. He is passionate about bringing this powerful, effective system for helping couples to people of faith, and helping Christian readers connect with the insights offered by EFT from the vantage point of their own biblical worldview. Our conversations also explored the broadened application of attachment theory to man's relationship with God — the ultimate giver of secure connection and love. Christians believe, as do I, that we are indeed created for connection. The Bible teaches that as creatures made in the very image of God, we bear the likeness of the One who made us in love for love, and who, in and of Himself, dwells in a community of love: Father, Son, and Holy Spirit. I was touched and inspired by the realization that my work could guide readers back to the unhindered loving connection that we were created for and that the Bible refers to again and again.

For my part, I shared with Kenny how my obsession with the drama of close relationships came out of my childhood struggles with the everyday mayhem of my parents' marriage. Watching them felt like helplessly seeing a train wreck happen again and again. Still, I knew that my parents loved each other deeply. In my father's last days, he wept raw tears for my mother although they had been separated for more than twenty years. As an adult, I became obsessed with understanding this mysterious and powerful emotion that defeated my parents, complicated my own life, and seemed to be the central source of both joy and suffering for so many of us. I knew in my heart that there just had to be a path through the maze that could lead us all to more empowering, enduring love.

I followed this fascination into a career in counseling and psychology, and in the final phase of my doctorate studies I started to work with couples. I was instantly mesmerized by the intensity of their struggles and, at the same time, continued to feel completely lost and defeated in the face of these struggles, just as I did when I was a child.

So I decided to simply let my couples teach me about the emotional rhythms and patterns in the dance of romantic love. I began to tape my couple sessions and watch them over and over again. Slowly, I began to grasp the key negative and positive emotional moments that defined a relationship and started formulating a clear way of working with couples that was based on changing these moments. My colleagues and I decided to call it Emotionally Focused Therapy, EFT for short. This was a natural choice, as it became clearer and clearer that, more than anything else, it was partners' emotional signals that shaped the dance between lovers. Emotions communicate and organize our responses to our loved ones. They are the music of the dance. We discovered that changing the music changed the dance.

As we developed EFT, our work was constantly informed and refined by the emerging new science of adult bonding, created by leading developmental and social psychologists. My lab's research studies began to show conclusive evidence that we could indeed help distressed partners transform their relationships. The results of these studies were, and still are, positive, powerful, and convincing. In addition, with the help of bonding science, we began to understand why distressed partners seethed with such strong emotions as they struggled to get a loved one to respond, and how the new conversations we shaped with our couples—we call them Hold Me Tight conversations—made a lasting difference to these couples' love relationships.

Many years and studies later, it is perfectly clear that romantic love is all about attachment. Emotional bonding is a wired-in survival code designed to keep loved ones close so that they will be there when we are in need. In order to truly thrive, we all need someone to depend on, a loved one who can offer reliable emotional connection and comfort. This partnership is the natural antidote to humanity's greatest pain: being alone in the face of the uncertainty of life. I now have a spiritual perspective on this and can see bonding relationships as echoing what the Bible describes as "becoming one" with a loved one (Gen. 2:24; Mark 10:8). God responds to the pain of human isolation by giving man an intimate partner who shares his bone and flesh (Gen. 2:23). God actually announces Eve's role in Adam's life using the Hebrew word for *helper* (Gen. 2:18), which, in Scripture thereafter, is most often used in reference to the strength and comfort God Himself provides as He comes alongside humanity in the inevitable but frightening battles of life. The love between adult partners is indeed infinitely more than the way it is all too often described — as a slightly adolescent mix of sexuality and sentiment.

In my conversations with Kenny that inspired this book, I was reminded of sharing the new science on the nature of love with one of my dearest friends and mentors, Father Anthony Storey, a Catholic priest who befriended me when I was an undergraduate at the University of Hull in England. When, in a long, rambling letter to Father Storey, I shared what I thought to be new and revolutionary insights about love, he wrote back a simple reply: "Of course, Christians have always known that."

He followed up with a long epistle describing his bond with God and how his closeness to Christ was his home and safe haven. He urged me to remember that Christians have always referred to God as an attachment figure, as the "Heavenly *Father*." Just before he died, Father Storey impressed on me again that I should understand the Christian faith as a special bond with God that frees us from fear, generates kindness and compassion, and teaches us, above all, to connect with and love others. He did not speak to me of moral rules, but of relationships.

As Kenny and I talked, these earlier discussions about God and bonding came flooding back, and I reconnected with my sense that, for me, my relationship with loved ones is where I find my way to the sacred, to what is holy. I then went back to reread the studies on the natural links between attachment theory and religious faith that had fascinated me years before. I also began to tune in to my Christian couples with a new awareness about how they viewed relationships, and how their commitment to their faith played into their dance with their loved ones. Even though I still see myself as a seeker rather than someone who has truly found her spiritual home, I have learned much from Christian writings, my Christian clients, and my collaboration with my colleague Kenny as a result of rewriting this book. My appreciation for the teachings found in the Bible has also been renewed.

In the end, as a result of the process I just described, the book you are about to read was an absolute joy to write. It seemed to spring naturally into being.

Perhaps I should back up a little at this point and tell you a bit more about Emotionally Focused Therapy for couples (EFT). As a way of seeing and shaping love relationships, it is simple: Forget about learning how to argue better, analyzing your early childhood, making grand romantic gestures, or experimenting with new sexual positions. Instead, recognize and admit that you are emotionally attached to and dependent on your partner in much the same way that a child is on a parent for nurturing, soothing, and protection. Adult attachments may be more reciprocal and less centered on constant physical contact, but the nature of the emotional bond is the same. EFT focuses on creating and strengthening this emotional bond between partners by identifying and transforming the key moments and messages that foster an adult loving relationship: being open, attuned, and responsive to each other.

Today EFT is revolutionizing couple therapy. Rigorous studies over the past twenty-five years have shown that 70 to 75 percent of couples who go through this therapy are able to move out of distress and become closer and happier in their relationships, and as many as 86 percent report significant improvement in relationship satisfaction in just a few sessions. Study after study has demonstrated positive results for EFT, and studies also show that these results appear to last, even for couples who are at high risk for divorce. This model has long been recognized by the American Psychological Association as fulfilling the criteria outlined for a tested and proven form of couple therapy. The power of EFT comes, I believe, from its grounding in the new science of attachment that allows an EFT therapist to go to the heart of a couple's relationship and help them shape the loving bond we all long for.

There are now many thousands of EFT-trained therapists and over fifty EFT centers and communities that provide training to mental health professionals all over the world. In addition to the original version of this book, I also recently published *Love Sense: The Revolutionary New Science of Romantic Relationships* to further explain the exponential growth in our understanding of love and loving.

Even though I have felt for many years that my work and that of my team was making a real difference in the world, I was still surprised when Kenny first wrote to me about his personal introduction to EFT and how he responded as a man of faith. He told me, "The first time I was introduced to EFT and the bonding perspective, I remember saying to myself, 'This just makes sense!' Then, as a practitioner, I began to see incredible changes with my couples in my sessions. But what I wasn't expecting was the impact EFT would have on me personally. It gave me a new way of seeing my relationship with God and with others. It changed how I engaged with the ones I love most—friends, family, and God. The Scriptures are clear that God is love, and He wants more than anything to have an intimate relationship with us individually and as couples. I don't believe the Bible was intended to be a marriage book, but it sure is a beautiful love story. Our relationship with God colors how we connect with others, and this human connection also helps us develop closeness with God."

When Kenny then went on to tell me that he believed God's

intention is that we each experience a divine gaze when we look into our partner's eyes, a gaze that communicates the miracle of being truly known and deeply loved, his perspective began to make complete and perfect sense to me. How could I not respond to his passion to usher his fellow Christians into the dance of love and connection that he and I have seen a thousand times in EFT sessions? How could we not create this new edition together and, as Kenny puts it, "usher Christian couples into the house of love, as science sets out and God intended"?

Like the original version, this book is divided into three parts. Part One answers the age-old question of what love is. It explains how we often slip into disconnection and lose our love, in spite of the best intentions and the greatest insights. It also documents and synthesizes the massive explosion of recent research into close relationships.

Part Two is the streamlined version of EFT, presented in a way that ties EFT into Christian values and beliefs and also links to biblical wisdom. It presents seven conversations that capture the defining moments in a love relationship, and it instructs you, the reader, on how to shape these moments to create a secure and lasting bond. Case histories and Play and Practice sections in each conversation bring the lessons of EFT to life in your own relationships.

Part Three addresses the power of love. The chapter Our Bond with God lays out an attachment perspective on our connection with God and how human love opens us up to the divine just as God's love teaches us to reach for one another. Love also enhances our sense of connection to the larger world. Loving responsiveness is the foundation of a truly compassionate, civilized society.

To help you through the book, I've included a glossary of important terms at the end.

I owe the development of EFT to all the couples I've seen over the years, and I make liberal use of their stories, disguising names and details to protect privacy, throughout this book. All stories are composites of many cases and are simplified to reflect the general truths I have learned from the thousands of couples I have seen. They will teach you as they taught me.

I started seeing couples in the early 1980s. Over thirty years later, it amazes me that I still feel passionately excited when I sit down in a room to work with a couple. I still get exhilarated when partners suddenly understand each other's heartfelt messages and risk reaching out to each other. Their struggles and determination daily enlighten and inspire me to keep my own precious connection with others alive.

We all live out the drama of connection and disconnection. I hope this book provides some new understanding that will help you turn your relationship into a glorious adventure, an adventure that resonates with and enriches your life and your Christian faith. The journey outlined in these pages has certainly been such an adventure for me.

"Love is everything it's cracked up to be," Erica Jong has written. "It really is worth fighting for, being brave for, risking everything for. And the trouble is, if you don't risk anything, your risk is even greater." I couldn't agree more. For us, in the twenty-first century, it is the tender understanding of the human heart, found in spiritual teachings and also now in the science of human bonding, that shows us how to risk and make a deeply loving, lasting bond with our life partners.

Introduction

Kenny Sanderfer

As Sue mentioned, this book came together as a result of many conversations over quite a long period of time. Participating with Sue in writing it stretched and challenged me. Sue is a world-renowned couple therapist and researcher and a master of asking hard questions and seeking clarity. As we sat together around her table in Ottawa, I did my best to answer her questions. I became immediately aware of my own contradictions and sometimes less-than-clear answers. Our conversations caused me to revisit my beliefs at multiple levels. I feel honored to be on this spiritual journey with Sue and to be her partner in this project.

The main reason for this revision of the incredible book *Hold Me Tight* is the passion that Sue and I share for helping couples—all couples. As a Christian, I feel a deep calling toward helping couples of faith find the love they were created to experience, with God and with each other. It would be difficult to find an institution more committed than the church to the task of reconciliation and the restoration of loving relationships. Unfortunately, the divorce statistics indicate that as a faith community we have a lot of room for improvement. Just like other couples, we Christians struggle greatly in our marriages. I don't think there has ever been a time in our society when the challenges to long-term relationships have been so great.

When I began using EFT in my counseling practice, I easily saw the applications for Christian couples; and yet I could also see the need for a book that clearly spoke the language of the Christian faith—a vernacular that people of faith would easily understand and that would broaden the application of attachment theory to our relationship with God. I'll never forget the first time I was introduced to EFT. I remember saying to myself, "This just makes sense!" I've heard the same sentiment expressed a thousand times by both counselors and clients as they experience EFT for the first time. As a practitioner, I began to see incredible changes in my couples in therapy sessions. This is not surprising—there is a body of sound research to support EFT. But what I wasn't expecting was the impact EFT would have on me personally. It gave me a new map for guiding me in my relationship with God and others.

EFT changed how I saw and interacted with the ones I loved most—friends, family, and God. It is a therapy that builds loving connection and really gets to the heart of the matter. And for the Christian, at the heart of love is God. The Scriptures are clear that God is love, and He wants more than anything to have an intimate relationship with us, both individually and as couples. EFT helped me make sense of the deeper places of my being, the places where only God prevails/dwells.

I don't believe the Bible was ever intended to be a marriage book, but it is a beautiful love story — a story about a God in pursuit of His bride. We are the bride of Christ. God created us to have a relationship with Him and with others. God's very nature is relational, and we see this in the relationship of the Trinity — Father, Son, and Spirit. The Father gave his all to the Son, and the Son gave himself to the Father. The Bible says we were created in His image, and that God has created us as relational beings. Our relationship with God is essential to how we connect with others, and our view of God is influenced by our lifelong interactions with others.

The person who most influenced my view of God was my great-aunt and caregiver, Auntie. Auntie lived in a small run-down garage apartment in town and depended on a small grove of pecan trees for most of her existence. I have vivid memories of working long, hard hours with her in her vegetable garden, the black gumbo soil of southeast Texas burning my bare feet. She rested only long enough to make lye soap in a black washpot on an open fire in the shade. It was amazing to me that anyone could be so poor and yet so happy. She refused government assistance — too much Texas pride for that. She had her faith, and that sustained her through thick and thin. It was my relationship with Auntie that forever formed my image of God and influenced my relationships with others.

In Texas, football was king. As a boy, I spent every waking moment preparing for and fantasizing about playing football. I remember one fall night, when I was about twelve, walking home from an important game that my high school had won. I should have been happy, celebrating with the rest of the town — car horns were honking, the band was playing, and fans were cheering — but that wasn't the case. I had this sudden sick realization that the chances of my ever playing football weren't that good. I had the desire, but my body hadn't gotten the message! I was almost the smallest kid in town.

I walked into Auntie's house late that night as disappointed as I had ever been in my life. If I wasn't a football star, then I was nothing. When I entered the house, I saw Auntie half-asleep on the couch, holding a transistor radio up to her hearing aid. Over her smudged glasses, she looked deep into my eyes and said, "Y'all beat, huh? You won." She didn't know or care a thing about football, but she had listened because she knew that the game was important to me.

My sadness lifted almost instantly, as I realized that winning the game wasn't the point. I mattered to her and she cared about what was in my heart, and that's what counted. She had held on to that radio all evening, waiting to hear the final score, because she knew how much it meant to me. I'll never forget the way I felt as she looked into my eyes. It went straight to my heart. My disappointment was replaced by a sense of calm delight. This is what I would describe as a "divine gaze" of love. This experience changed me forever. It shaped the template of how I see myself, my God, my wife, my family, and others. God created us for connection — intimate connection — a special and unique intimate relationship with Him and with our life partner.

I am convinced that it is God's intention that we each experience a divine gaze when we look into our partner's eyes. I've seen this happen a thousand times in my sessions with couples.

Jesus encouraged us to move out of the house of fear and to make our home in Him (John 15:4). It is my prayer that this book will help usher you into the house of love with your partner, and that you both may experience the true love and intimacy God created us for.

PART ONE

A New Light on Love

Love—
A Revolutionary New View

"We live in the shelter of each other."

—*Celtic saying*

"How priceless is your unfailing love, O God!
People take refuge in the shadow of your wings."

—*Psalm 36:7*

L ove may be the most used and the most potent word in the English language. We write tomes about it, pen poems about it. We sing about it and pray for it. We fight wars for it (see Helen of Troy) and build monuments to it (see the Taj Mahal). We soar on its declaration—"I love you!"—and plummet at its dissolution—"I don't love you anymore!" We think about it and talk about it—endlessly.

Of course, the Christian knows, this word does not just encompass romantic love. Love in its purest form is also the central theme of the Bible from Genesis to Revelation. The central message of the Bible is that God *is* love. For people of faith, then, romantic relationships are part of this spiritual reality.

But what is love, really? And what does the church say about love and intimacy?

No institution has devoted more time and resources to helping people find and keep love than the church has—premarital counseling, marriage retreats, sermons, teachings—and yet marriages are in trouble and the divorce rate is the same inside the church as outside the church. The messages about love and intimacy have been emphasized, but Christian couples struggle, like everyone else, to make sense of how love plays out in relationships.

Scholars and practitioners have wrestled with definitions and ways of understanding love for centuries. To some cold-blooded observers, romantic love is a mutually beneficial alliance based on trading favors, a give-get bargain. Others, more historically inclined, regard it as a sentimental social custom created by the minstrels of thirteenth-century France. Biologists and anthropologists view it as a strategy to ensure the transmission of genes and rearing of offspring. Christian teachers have viewed loving one's partner as a moral imperative and have stressed the spiritual value and aspects of such a relationship.

But to most people, in the end, love has been and remains still a mystical elusive emotion, open to description but defying definition. Back in the 1700s, Benjamin Franklin, an astute student in so many areas, could only attest to love as "changeable, transient and accidental." More recently, Marilyn Yalom, in her scholarly book on the history of the wife, admitted defeat and called love an "intoxicating mixture of sex and sentiment that no one can define." My English barmaid mother's description of love as a "funny five minutes" is just as apt, if a little more cynical.

Today, though, we can no longer afford to define love as a mysterious force beyond our ken. It has become too important. For better or worse, in the twenty-first century, a love relationship has become the *central* emotional relationship in most people's lives.

One reason is that we are increasingly living in social isolation. Writers like Robert Putnam in his book *Bowling Alone* point out that we suffer from a dangerous loss of "social capital." (This term was coined in 1916 by a Virginia educator, who noted the continuous help, sympathy, and fellowship that neighbors offered each other.) Most of us no longer live in supportive communities with our birth families or childhood friends close at hand. We work longer and longer hours, commute farther and farther distances, and thus have fewer and fewer opportunities to develop close relationships.

Most often, the couples I see in my practice live in a community of two. The majority of folks in a 2006 National Science Foundation survey reported that the number of people in their circle of confidants was dropping, and a growing number stated that they had no one at all to confide in. As the Irish poet John O'Donohue put it, "There is a huge and leaden loneliness settling like a frozen winter on so many humans."

Inevitably, we now ask our lovers for the emotional connection and sense of belonging that my grandmother could get from a whole village. Compounding this is the celebration of romantic love fostered by our popular culture. Movies, as well as television soap operas and dramas, saturate us with images of romantic love as the be-all and end-all of relationships, while newspapers, magazines, and TV news avidly report on the never-ending search for romance and love among actors and celebrities. So it should come as no surprise that people recently surveyed in the U.S. and Canada rate a satisfying love relationship as their number one goal, ahead of financial success and satisfying career.

It is, then, imperative that we comprehend what love is, how to make it, and how to make it last. People of faith, knowing that we are created in love and for love, feel this imperative on a spiritual as well as a pragmatic level. God is love (1 John 4:16) and we are created in the image of God (Gen. 1:27). To be disconnected from an understanding of what love is and how to live it out is a threat to the most fundamental aspect of our humanity, namely our connection to God and to one another. When we lose the ability to create and hold on to romantic love, we lose the completeness that God created us for as his image bearers (Gen. 2:18–24). Thankfully, during the past two decades, an exciting and revolutionary new understanding of love has been emerging, and it is one that reflects, echoes, and supports the Christian view of the union between life partners.

We now know that love is, in actuality, the most compelling survival mechanism of the human species. Not because it induces us to mate and reproduce. We do manage to mate without love! But because love drives us to bond emotionally with a precious few others who offer us safe haven from the storms of life. Love is our bulwark, designed to provide emotional protection so we can cope with the ups and downs of existence. As Mozart noted, "Love guards the heart from the abyss." We are relational beings. God created us for relationship with Himself and with others. We are created for connection.

This drive to emotionally attach—to find someone to whom we can turn and say "Hold me tight"—is wired into our mind, soul, and spirit. It is as basic to life, health, and happiness as the drives for food, shelter, and sex. We need emotional attachments with a few irreplaceable others to be physically and mentally healthy—to survive. We will see below how recent research bears out the truth of Scripture and how "all truth is God's truth." Here we find that, by obeying God's basic command "Love one another," we actually determine our ability not only to survive but also to thrive—to live fully.

A NEW THEORY OF ATTACHMENT

Clues to love's true purpose have been circulating for a long time. Back in 1760, a Spanish bishop writing to his superiors in Rome noted that children in foundling homes, though they were sheltered and fed, regularly "die from sadness." In the 1930s and 1940s, in the halls of American hospitals, orphan children, deprived only of touch and emotional contact, died in droves. Psychiatrists also began identifying children who were physically healthy but who seemed indifferent, callous, and unable to relate to others. David Levy, reporting his observations in a 1937 article in the *American Journal of Psychiatry,* attributed such youngsters' behavior to "emotional starvation." In the 1940s, American analyst René Spitz coined the term "failure to thrive" for children separated from their parents and caught in debilitating grief.

But it remained for John Bowlby, a British psychiatrist, to figure out exactly what was going on. Let me be honest. As a psychologist and as a human being, if I had to give an award for the single best set of ideas anyone had ever had, I'd give it to John Bowlby hands down over Freud or anyone else in the business of understanding people. He grabbed the threads of observations and reports and wove them into a coherent and masterful theory of attachment.

Born in 1907, Bowlby, the son of a baronet, was raised, in the fashion of the upper class, primarily by nannies and governesses. His parents allowed him to join them at the dinner table after he turned twelve, and then only for dessert. He was sent off to boarding school and then attended Trinity College, Cambridge. Bowlby's life departed from tradition when he volunteered to work in the innovative residential schools for emotionally maladjusted children being started by visionaries like A. S. Neill. These schools focused on offering emotional support rather than the usual stern discipline.

Intrigued by his experiences, Bowlby went on to medical school and then took psychiatric training, which included undergoing seven years of psychoanalysis. His analyst apparently found him a difficult patient. Influenced by mentors like Ronald Fairbairn, who argued that Freud had underestimated the need for other people, Bowlby rebelled against the professional dictum that the crux of patients' problems lay in their internal conflicts and unconscious fantasies. Bowlby insisted the problems were mostly external, rooted in real relationships with real people.

Working with disturbed youngsters at the Child Guidance Clinics in London, he began to believe that blighted relationships with parents had left them with only a few, negative ways to deal with basic feelings and needs. Later, in 1938, as a beginning clinician under the supervision of the noted analyst Melanie Klein, Bowlby was assigned a young hyperactive boy who had an extremely anxious mother. He was not allowed to talk to the mother, however, since only the child's projections and fantasies were deemed of interest. That infuriated Bowlby. His experience spurred him to formulate his own idea, namely that the quality of the connection to loved ones and early emotional deprivation are key to the development of personality and to an individual's habitual way of connecting with others.

In 1944, Bowlby published the very first paper on family therapy, *Forty-Four Juvenile Thieves,* in which he noted that "behind the mask of indifference is bottomless misery and behind apparent callousness, despair." Bowlby's young charges were frozen in the attitude "I will never be hurt again" and paralyzed in desperation and rage.

Following World War II, Bowlby was asked by the World Health Organization to do a study of European children left homeless and orphaned by the conflict. His findings confirmed his belief in the reality of emotional starvation and his conviction that loving contact is as important as physical nutrition. He believed that keeping precious others close is a brilliant, built-in survival code.

Bowlby's theory was radical and noisily rejected. Indeed, it almost got him thrown out of the British Psychoanalytic Society. Conventional wisdom held that coddling by mothers and other family members created clingy, overdependent youngsters who grew up into incompetent adults. Keeping an antiseptic rational distance was the proper way to rear children. That objective stance held even when youngsters were distressed and physically ill. In Bowlby's era, parents were not allowed to stay in the hospital with their sick sons and daughters; they had to drop the children off at the door.

In 1951, Bowlby and a young social worker, James Robertson, made a movie called *A Two-Year-Old Goes to Hospital,* graphically showing a little girl's angry protest, terror, and despair at being left alone in a hospital. Robertson showed the film to the Royal Society of Medicine in London in the hope that physicians would comprehend a child's stress at separation from loved ones and need for connection and comfort. It was dismissed as a fraud and almost banned. Well into the 1960s in Britain and the United States, parents still typically were allowed to visit their hospitalized offspring for only one hour a week.

Bowlby needed to find another way to prove to the world what he knew in his heart. A Canadian researcher, Mary Ainsworth, who became his assistant, showed him how to do that. She devised a very simple experiment to look at the four behaviors that Bowlby and she believed were basic to attachment: that we monitor and maintain emotional and physical closeness with our beloved; that we reach out for this person when we are unsure, upset, or feeling down; that we miss this person when we are apart; and that we count on this person to be there for us when we go out into the world and explore.

The experiment was called the Strange Situation and has generated literally thousands of scientific studies and revolutionized developmental psychology. A researcher invites a mother and child into an unfamiliar room. After a few minutes, the mother leaves the child alone with the researcher, who tries to offer comfort if needed. Three minutes later, the mother comes back. The separation and reunion are repeated once more.

The majority of children are upset when their mothers walk out; they rock themselves, cry, throw toys. But some prove more emotionally resilient. They calm themselves quickly and effectively, reconnect easily with their mothers on their return, and rapidly resume playing while checking to make sure that their moms are still around. They seem confident that their mothers will be there if needed. Less resilient youngsters, however, are anxious and aggressive or detached and distant on their mothers' return. The kids who can calm themselves usually have warmer, more responsive mothers, while the moms of the angry kids are unpredictable in their behavior, and the moms of the detached kids are colder and dismissive. In these simple studies of disconnection and reconnection, Bowlby saw love in action and began to code its patterns.

Bowlby's theory gained still greater currency a few years later when he produced a famed trilogy on human attachment, separation, and loss. His colleague Harry Harlow, a psychologist at the University of Wisconsin, also drew attention to the power of what he called "contact comfort" by reporting his own dramatic research with young monkeys separated from their mothers at birth. He discovered that the isolated infants were so hungry for connection that when given the choice between a "mother" made out of wire who dispensed food and a soft-cloth mother without food, they would choose the squashy rag mother almost every time. Generally, Harlow's experiments showed the toxicity of early isolation: physically healthy infant primates who were separated from their mothers during the first year of life grew into socially crippled adults. The monkeys failed to develop the ability to solve problems or understand the social cues of others. They became depressed, self-destructive, and unable to mate.

Attachment theory, at first ridiculed and despised, eventually revolutionized child-rearing methods in North America. (Now when I get to sleep beside my child's bed as he recovers from an appendicitis operation, I thank John Bowlby.) Today it is widely accepted that children have an absolute requirement for safe, ongoing physical and emotional closeness, and that we ignore this only at great cost.

It is interesting, in this context, to read in Scripture how often Jesus uses touch in His acts of care and healing. In Mark 10:13–16, we read, "People were bringing little children to Jesus to have him touch them, but the disciples rebuked them. When Jesus saw this, he was indignant. He said to them, 'Let the little children come to me, and do not hinder them, for the kingdom of God belongs to such as these. I tell you the truth, anyone who will not receive the kingdom of God like a little child will never enter it.' And he took the children in his arms, put his hands on them, and blessed them." By reaching for those who are vulnerable, honoring this vulnerability, and offering loving visceral connection, Jesus sets out a clear model for human behavior.

LOVE AND ADULTS

Bowlby died in 1990. He did not live to see the second revolution sparked by his work: the application of attachment theory to adult love. Bowlby himself had maintained that adults have the same need for attachment—he had studied World War II widows and discovered they exhibited behavior patterns similar to those of homeless youngsters—and that this need is the force that shapes adult relationships. But again his ideas were rejected. No one expected a reserved upper-class conservative Englishman to solve the riddle of romantic love! And anyway, the general belief among many members of the public was that we already knew all there was to know about love. Love was painted as simply short-lived, disguised sexual infatuation, Freud's basic instinct dressed up. Something we simply fell into and then fell out of. Or a kind of immature need to rely on others. Only in spiritual circles have these popular views of love been routinely questioned. In such circles, love between partners has often been framed as a moral imperative, with a focus on selfless giving rather than needing or attaining emotional connection.

Most important, however, the attachment view of love was, and perhaps still is, radically out of line with our culture's established social and psychological ideas of adulthood: that maturity means being independent and self-sufficient. The notion of the invulnerable warrior who faces life and danger alone is long ingrained in our culture. Consider James Bond, the iconic impervious man, still going strong after five decades.

Psychologists use words like *undifferentiated, codependent, symbiotic,* or even *fused* to describe people who seem unable to be self-sufficient or definitively assert themselves with others. In contrast, Bowlby talked about "effective dependency" and how being able, from "the cradle to the grave," to turn to others for emotional support is a sign and source of strength. Christianity, too, has always viewed reliance on God's love, the union with a partner and with others in the community of faith, as a positive force. Both attachment science and Christianity teach that turning to others and acknowledging our vulnerability is admirable, and that responding with empathy and care to others is a key part of emotional and spiritual wholeness.

Research documenting adult attachment began just before

Bowlby's death. Social psychologists Phil Shaver and Cindy Hazan, then at the University of Denver, decided to ask men and women questions about their love relationships to see if they exhibited the same responses and patterns as mothers and children. They wrote up a love quiz that was published in the local *Rocky Mountain News*. In their answers, adults spoke of needing emotional closeness from their lover, wanting assurance that their lover would respond when they were upset, being distressed when they felt separate and distant from their loved one, and feeling more confident about exploring the world when they knew that their lover had their back. They also indicated different ways of dealing with their partner. When they felt secure with their lover, they could reach out and connect easily; when they felt insecure, they either became anxious, angry, and controlling, or they avoided contact altogether and stayed distant. Just what Bowlby and Ainsworth had found with mothers and children.

Hazan and Shaver followed up with serious formal studies that reinforced the quiz's findings and Bowlby's theories. They found that the key principles of attachment applied to adult relationships too, and not just to the bonds between children and parents. These key principles simply state that:

• Our deepest instinct all through life is to seek out and stay close to a few precious loved ones.
• Contact with these loved ones offers us a safe haven to go to and a secure base to go out from with strength and confidence. Secure connection makes us stronger as individuals.
• Loss of a felt sense of connection with such loved ones is painful and creates a disorienting sense of vulnerability. Disconnection at times of high need can be traumatizing for human beings.
• Emotional accessibility and responsiveness to another's signals and needs shape secure loving connection. The quality of our

emotional engagement is the key element that shapes our love relationships.

• There are only a few simple strategies that we use to connect and deal with perceived disconnection. When we feel safe enough, we can risk *reaching* for a loved one and asking for our needs to be met. When we feel unsafe, we resort to *demanding* and controlling or, if we truly expect rejection and desertion, we try to *turn away* and shut down our needs for connection. These negative strategies can shape the very disconnection we are trying to cope with or avoid.

• As adults we can hold loved ones in our minds and find comfort, and we do not always need physical closeness. Adult romantic bonds also have a physical—a sexual—element. Sexuality is part of adult bonding.

• The relationship between God and people of faith can be understood as an attachment bond, in which God is a safe haven, a secure base, and the ultimate source of comfort and care.

Hazan and Shaver's work set off an avalanche of research. Hundreds of studies now validate Bowlby's predictions about adult attachment, and you will find them cited throughout this book. The overall conclusion: a sense of secure connection between romantic partners is key in positive, loving relationships and a huge source of strength for the individuals in those relationships. Among the more significant findings in attachment studies are the following:

• When we feel generally secure, that is, we are comfortable with closeness and confident about depending on loved ones, we are better at seeking support—and better at giving it. In a study by psychologist Jeff Simpson of the University of Minnesota, each of eighty-three dating couples filled out questionnaires about their relationship and then sat in a room. The female partner had been warned she would soon be participating in an activity that made most people very anxious (the activity wasn't spelled out). The women who described themselves as feeling secure in love relationships on the questionnaires were able to share their unhappiness about the upcoming task openly and ask for support from their partners. Women who generally denied their attachment needs and avoided closeness withdrew more at these moments. Men responded to their partners in two ways: when they described themselves as secure with relationships, they became even more supportive than usual, touching and smiling at their partners and offering comfort; if they described themselves as uncomfortable with attachment needs, they became markedly less sympathetic when their partners expressed their needs, downplaying their partners' distress, showing less warmth, and touching less.

• When we feel safely linked to our partners, we more easily roll with the hurts they inevitably inflict, and we are less likely to be aggressively hostile when we get mad at them. Mario Mikulincer of Bar-Ilan University in Israel conducted a series of studies asking participants questions about how connected they felt in relationships and how they dealt with anger when conflicts arose. Their heart rates were monitored as they responded to scenarios of couples in conflict. Those who felt close to and could depend on partners reported feeling less angry with and attributing less malicious intent to their partners. They described themselves as expressing anger in a more controlled way, and expressed more positive goals, such as solving the problems and reconnecting with their partners.

• Secure connection to a loved one is empowering. In a group of studies Mikulincer showed that when we feel safely connected to others we understand ourselves better and like ourselves more. When given a list of adjectives to describe themselves, the more secure folks picked out positive traits. And when asked about their weak points, they readily said they fell short of their own ideals but still felt good about themselves.

Mikulincer also found, as Bowlby predicted, that securely bonded adults were more curious and more open to new information. They were comfortable with ambiguity, saying they liked questions that could be answered in many different ways. In one task, a person's behavior was described to them and they were asked to evaluate this person's negative and positive traits. Connected participants more easily absorbed new information about the person and revised their assessments. Openness to new experience and flexibility of belief seem to be easier when we feel safe and connected to others. Curiosity comes out of a sense of safety, rigidity out of being vigilant to threats.

• The more we can reach out to our partners, the more separate and independent we can be. Although this flies in the face of our culture's creed of self-sufficiency, psychologist Brooke Feeney of Carnegie Mellon University in Pittsburgh found exactly that in observations of 280 couples. Those who felt that their needs were accepted by their partners were more confident about solving problems on their own and were more likely to successfully achieve their own goals.

From the very first studies on the nature of attachment bonds, it has been clear that for people of faith, their connection with God is experienced as a potent source of attachment security. He is seen as the ultimate safe haven and refuge. His guidance also offers an anchor and a compass for believers as they face the uncertainties of life. Psychologist Lee Kirkpatrick of the College of William and Mary, in Virginia, consistently finds in his research that believers describe God and relate to Him as a reliable, responsive parent—a perfect attachment figure who is always there for His children. Scripture describes God as a "father to the fatherless" (Ps. 68:5). Mario Mikulincer also finds that, in general, people naturally turn to thoughts of God and His comfort when subjected to subliminal threats—for example, images of failure or of death. This spiritual bond is explored further in Part Three of this book, in the chapter "Our Bond with God."

A WEALTH OF EVIDENCE

Science from all fields is telling us very clearly that we are not only social animals, but animals who need a special kind of close connection with others, and we deny this at our peril. As we read in Genesis 2:18, "It is not good for man to be alone." Indeed, historians long ago observed that in the death camps of World War II, the unit of survival was the pair, not the solitary individual. It's long been known, too, that married men and women generally live longer than do their single peers.

Having close ties with others is vital to every aspect of our health—mental, emotional, and physical. Louise Hawkley, of the Center for Cognitive and Social Neuroscience at the University of Chicago, calculates that loneliness raises blood pressure to the point where the risk of heart attack and stroke is doubled. Sociologist James House of the University of Michigan declares that emotional isolation is a more dangerous health risk than smoking or high blood pressure, and we now warn everyone about these two! Perhaps these findings reflect the time-honored saying "Suffering is a given; suffering alone is intolerable."

But it's not just whether or not we have close relationships in our lives—the quality of these relationships matters, too. Negative relationships undermine our health. In Cleveland, researchers at Case Western Reserve University asked men with a history of angina and high blood pressure, "Does your wife show her love?" Those who answered "No" suffered almost twice as many angina episodes during the next five years as did those who replied "Yes." Women's hearts are affected, too. Women who view their marriages as strained and have regular hostile interactions with their partners are more likely to have significantly elevated blood pressure and higher levels of stress hormones compared with women in happy marriages. Yet another study found that women who had had a heart attack stood a threefold higher risk of having another if there was discord in their marriage.

In men and women with congestive heart failure, the state of the patient's marriage is as good a predictor of survival after four years as the severity of the symptoms and degree of impairment, concludes Jim Coyne, a psychologist at the University of Pennsylvania. The poets who made the heart the symbol of love would surely smile at scientists' conclusion that the strength of people's hearts cannot be separated from the strength of their love relationships.

Distress in a relationship adversely affects our immune and hormonal systems, and even our ability to heal. In one fascinating experiment, psychologist Janice Kiecolt-Glaser of Ohio State University had newlyweds fight, then took blood samples over the next several hours. She found that the more belligerent and contemptuous the partners were, the higher the level of stress hormones and the more depressed the immune system. The effects persisted for up to twenty-four hours. In an even more astounding study, Kiecolt-Glaser used a vacuum pump to produce small blisters on the hands of women volunteers, then had them fight with their husbands. The nastier the fight, the longer it took for the women's skin to heal.

The quality of our love relationships is also a big factor in how mentally and emotionally healthy we are. We have an epidemic of anxiety and depression in our most affluent societies. Conflict with and hostile criticism from loved ones increase our self-doubts and create a sense of helplessness, classic triggers for depression. We need validation from our loved ones. Researchers say that marital distress raises the risk for depression tenfold!

That's the bad news — but there is good news, too.

Hundreds of studies now show that positive loving connections with others protect us from stress and help us cope better with life's challenges and traumas. Israeli researchers report that couples with a secure emotional attachment are much more able to deal with dangers such as Scud missile attacks than other less-connected couples. They are less anxious and have fewer physical problems after attacks.

These studies about the power of positive connections resonate with Christian teachings. Christians often report that turning to their bond with a loving God helps them deal with distress. They find comfort in their sense of belonging with and to God. In his book on the spiritual nature of man, Alister Hardy recounts the story of how a woman who was crippled by despair and hospitalized for depression decided to pray. She told Hardy, "Suddenly, a voice said, 'Afraid or sane, you are still one of my sheep.'" This became the pivotal moment of her life and her healing.

Simply holding the hand of a loving partner can affect us profoundly, literally calming jittery neurons in the brain. Psychologist Jim Coan of the University of Virginia told women patients having an MRI brain scan that when a little red light on the machine came on, they might receive a small electrical shock on their feet — or they might not. This information lit up the stress centers in patients' brains. But when partners held their hands, the patients registered less stress. When they were shocked, they experienced less pain. This effect was noticeably stronger in the happiest relationships, the ones where partners scored high on measures of satisfaction and that the researchers called the Super-couples. Contact with a loving partner literally acts as a buffer against shock, stress, and pain.

The people we love, asserts Coan, are the *hidden regulators* of our bodily processes and our emotional lives. When love doesn't work, we hurt. Indeed, "hurt feelings" is a precisely accurate phrase, according to psychologist Naomi Eisenberger of the University of California. Her brain imaging studies show that rejection and exclusion trigger the same circuits in the same part of the brain, the anterior cingulate, as physical pain. In fact, this part of the brain turns on anytime we are emotionally separated from those who are close to us. When I read this study, I remembered being shocked by my own physical experience of grief. After hearing that my mother had died, I felt battered, like I had literally been hit by a truck. And when we are close to, hold, or make love with our partners, we are flooded with the "cuddle hormones" oxytocin and vasopressin. These hormones seem to turn on "reward" centers in the brain, flooding us with calm and happiness chemicals like dopamine, and turning off stress hormones like cortisol.

We've come a long way in our understanding of love and its importance. In 1939, women ranked love fifth as a factor in choosing a mate. By the 1990s, it topped the list for both women *and* men. And college students now say that their key expectation from marriage is "emotional security."

Love is not the icing on the cake of life. It is a basic primary need, like oxygen.

Attachment science and Scripture are coming together here to sing a hymn on the primacy and sanctity of loving connection.

The Hebraic word for *love* in the Bible, *ialeph,ayin,* is silent. It is actually just a sound—the sound of inhaling and exhaling.

Throughout Scripture this word is used to describe the intimate connection that God desires to have with us and that we can have with our life partners. This kind of love is one in which we are so close to our beloved that we breathe in the breath of the other. This closeness is described as *panim el panim,* which literally means face-to-face.

The Christian faith affirms that God desires a breath-to-breath and face-to-face relationship with us. This, then, is the model for our love with our partners.

Where Did Our Love Go?
Losing Connection

"To love at all is to be vulnerable."
— *C. S. Lewis*, The Four Loves

"Perfect love casteth out fear."
— *1 John 4:18 (KJV)*

T he basic issue is that Sally just doesn't know anything about money," declares Jay. "She is very emotional and she has a problem trusting me and just letting me manage it." Sally explodes: "Yeah, right. As usual the problem is me. Like you really understand money! We just went out and bought that ridiculous car you wanted. The car we don't need and can't afford. You just do what you want. My take on things never counts with you anyway. In fact, I don't count with you, period."

Chris is a "cruel, rigid, and uncaring parent," accuses Jane. "The kids need taking care of, you know. They need your attention, not just your rules!" Chris turns his head away. He speaks calmly about the need for discipline and charges Jane with not knowing how to set limits. They go back and forth arguing. Finally, Jane puts her face in her hands and moans, "I just don't know who you are anymore. You're like a stranger." Again, Chris turns away.

Nat and Carrie sit in stubborn silence until Carrie cracks and sobs out how shocked and betrayed she feels about Nat's affair. Nat, with an air of frustration, ticks off his reasons for the affair. "I've told you again and again why it happened. I've come clean. And jeez, it was two years ago! It's in the past! Isn't it about time you got over it and forgave me?" "You don't know the meaning of *clean*," shrieks Carrie. Then her voice falls to a whisper. "You don't care about me, about my hurt. You just want everything back the way it was." She starts to weep, he stares at the floor.

I ask each couple what they think the basic problem is in their relationship and what the solution might be. They dig a bit and offer up their ideas. Sally says Jay is too controlling; he has to be taught how to share power more equitably. Chris suggests that he and Jane have such different personalities that agreement on a parenting style is impossible. They could settle the issue by taking a parenting course from an "expert." Nat is convinced that Carrie has a sex hang-up. Maybe they should see a sex therapist so that they can get back to being happy in the bedroom.

These couples are trying hard to make sense of their distress, but their formulations are missing the mark. Their explanations are just the tip of the iceberg, the superficial tangible crest of a big block of trouble, many therapists would agree. So what is the "real problem" that lies beneath?

If I ask therapists, many would say these couples are caught up in destructive power struggles or caustic fighting patterns, and that what they need to do is learn how to negotiate and improve their communication skills. But counselors, too, are missing the crux of the issue. They've just worked their way down the iceberg to the waterline.

We have to dive below to discover the basic problem: these

couples have disconnected emotionally; they don't feel emotionally safe with each other. What couples and therapists too often do not see is that most fights are really *protests* over emotional disconnection. Underneath all the distress, partners are asking each other: *Can I count on you, depend on you? Are you there for me? Will you respond to me when I need, when I call? Do I matter to you? Am I valued and accepted by you? Do you need me, rely on me?*

The anger, the criticism, the demands, are really cries to their lovers, calls to stir their hearts, to draw their mates back in emotionally and reestablish a sense of safe connection.

A PRIMAL PANIC

Attachment theory teaches us that our loved one is our shelter in life. When that person is emotionally unavailable or unresponsive, we face being out in the cold, alone and helpless. We are assailed by emotions — anger, sadness, hurt, and above all, fear. This is not so surprising when we remember that fear is our built-in alarm system; it turns on when our survival is threatened. Losing connection with our loved one jeopardizes our sense of security. The alarm goes off in the brain's amygdala, or Fear Central, as neuroscientist Joseph LeDoux of the Center for Neural Science at New York University has dubbed it. This almond-shaped area in the midbrain triggers an automatic response. We don't think; we feel, we act.

We all experience some fear when we have disagreements or arguments with our partners. But for those of us with secure bonds, it is a momentary blip. The fear is quickly and easily tamped down as we realize that there is no real threat or that our partner will reassure us if we ask. For those of us with weaker or fraying bonds, however, the fear can be overwhelming. We are swamped by what neuroscientist Jaak Panksepp of Washington State University calls "primal panic." I think this is what David was experiencing in Psalm 38:10 when he vividly describes his state of loneliness, saying, "My heart beats wildly and my strength fails" (NLT). Once this primal panic has kicked in, we generally do one of two things: we either become demanding and clingy in an effort to draw comfort and reassurance from our partner, or we withdraw and detach in an attempt to soothe and protect ourselves. No matter the exact words, what we're really saying in these reactions is: "Notice me. Be with me. I need you." Or, "I won't let you hurt me. I will chill out, try to stay in control."

These strategies for dealing with the fear of losing connection are unconscious, and they work, at least in the beginning. But as distressed partners resort to them more and more, they set up vicious spirals of insecurity that only push them further and further apart. More and more interactions occur in which neither partner feels safe, both become defensive, and each is left assuming the very worst about the other and their relationship.

If we love our partners, why do we not just hear each other's calls for attention and connection and respond with caring? Because much of the time we are not tuned in to our partners. We are distracted or caught up in our own agendas. We do not know how to speak the language of attachment; we do not give clear messages about what we need or how much we care. Often we speak tentatively because we feel ambivalent about our own needs. Or we send out calls for connection tinged with anger and frustration because we do not feel confident and safe in our relationships. We wind up demanding rather than requesting, which often leads to power struggles rather than embraces. Some of us try to minimize our natural longing to be emotionally close and focus instead on actions that give only limited expression to our need. The most common: focusing on sex. Disguised and distorted messages keep us from being exposed in all our naked longing, but they also make it harder for our lovers to respond.

THE DEMON DIALOGUES

The longer partners feel disconnected, the more negative their interactions become. This negativity can destroy a relationship and erode partners' trust in connection altogether, leaving them in an emotional hell that echoes the images of pain and despair we see in Christian frescoes and paintings of people being literally assaulted by demons. Researchers have identified several such damaging patterns, and they go by various names. I call the three that I consider the most basic "Demon Dialogues." They are Find the Bad Guy, the Protest Polka, and Freeze and Flee, and you'll learn about them in detail in Conversation 1.

By far the most dominant of the trio is the Protest Polka. In this dialogue, one partner becomes critical and aggressive and the other defensive and distant. Psychologist John Gottman of the University of Washington in Seattle finds that couples who get stuck in this pattern in the first few years of marriage have more than an 80 percent chance of divorcing within four or five years.

Let's take a look at one couple. Carol and Jim have a long-running quarrel over his being late to engagements. In a session in my office, Carol carps at Jim over his latest transgression: he didn't show up on time for the home group that they host for their church. "How come you are always late?" she challenges. "Doesn't it matter to you that we have a commitment, that I am waiting and needing your help? You always let me down." Jim reacts coolly: "I got held up. But if you are going to start off nagging again, maybe we should just quit hosting this group." Carol retaliates by listing all the other times Jim has been late. Jim starts to dispute her "list," then breaks off and retreats into stony silence.

In this never-ending dispute, Jim and Carol are caught up in the factual content of their fights. When was the last time Jim was late? Was it only last week or was it months ago? They careen down the two dead ends of "what really happened"—whose story is more "accurate" and who is most "at fault." They are convinced that the problem has to be either his irresponsibility or her nagging.

In truth, though, it doesn't matter what they're fighting about. In another session in my office, Carol and Jim begin to bicker about Jim's reluctance to talk about their relationship. "Talking about this stuff just gets us into fights," Jim declares. "What's the point of that? We go round and round. It just gets frustrating. And anyway, it's all about my 'flaws' in the end. I feel closer when we make love." Carol shakes her head. "I don't want sex when we are not even talking!"

What's happened here? Carol and Jim's attack-withdraw way of dealing with the "lateness" issue has spilled over into two more issues: "we don't talk" and "we don't have sex." They're caught in a terrible loop, their responses generating more negative responses and emotions in each other. The more Carol blames Jim, the more he withdraws. And the more he withdraws, the more frantic and cutting become her attacks.

Eventually, the *what* of any fight won't matter at all. When couples reach this point, their entire relationship becomes marked by resentment, caution, and distance. They will see every difference, every disagreement, through a negative filter. They will listen to idle words and hear a threat. They will see an ambiguous action and assume the worst. They will be consumed by catastrophic fears and doubts, be constantly on guard and defensive. Even if they want to come close, they can't.

Partners sometimes can see glimpses of the Demon Dialogue they're trapped in — Jim tells me he "knows" he will hear how he has disappointed Carol before she even speaks and so has put up a "wall" to keep from "catching fire" — but the pattern has become so automatic and so compelling that they cannot stop it. Most couples, however, aren't aware of the pattern that has taken hold of their relationship.

Angry and frustrated, partners scrabble for explanation. They decide that their lover is callous or cruel. They turn the blame inward, on themselves. "Maybe there is something deeply wrong with me," Carol tells me. "It's just like my mom used to say, I am too difficult to love." They conclude that no one is trustworthy and love is a lie.

The idea that these demand-distance spirals are all about attachment panic is still revolutionary to many psychologists and counselors. Most of the colleagues who come to me for training have been taught to see conflict itself and couples' power struggles as the main problems in relationships. As a result they have focused on teaching couples negotiation and communication skills to contain the conflict. But this addresses the symptoms, not the disease. It's telling people caught in a never-ending dance of frustration and distance to change the steps when what they have to do is change the music. "Stop telling me what to do," orders Jim. Carol considers this for a nanosecond before angrily retorting, "When I do that, you do nothing and we are nowhere!"

We can come up with many techniques to address different aspects of couples' distress, but until we understand the core principles that organize love relationships, we cannot really understand love's problems or offer couples enduring help. The demand-withdraw pattern is not just a bad habit, it reflects a deeper underlying reality: such couples are starving emotionally. They are losing the source of their emotional sustenance. They feel deprived. And they are desperate to regain that nurturance.

Until we address the fundamental need for connection and the fear of losing it, the standard techniques, such as learning problem solving or communication skills, examining childhood hurts, or taking time-outs, are misguided and ineffectual. Happy couples do not talk to each other in any more "skilled" or "insightful" ways than do unhappy couples, Gottman has shown. They do not always listen empathetically to each other or understand how their pasts might have set up problematic expectations. And in my office, I see very distressed couples who are amazingly articulate and show exquisite insight into their own behavior, but cannot talk to their partners in a coherent way when the emotional tsunami hits. My client Sally tells me, "I am pretty good at talking, you know. I have lots of friends. I'm assertive and I'm a good listener. But when we get into these terrible long silences, trying to remember the points from our marriage training weekend is like trying to read a 'how to pull your parachute' manual when you are in free fall."

The standard remedies do not address yearnings for or threats to safe emotional connection. They do not tell couples how to reconnect or how to stay connected. The techniques they are taught may interrupt a fight, but at a terrible cost. They often further the distance between partners, reinforcing fears of being rejected and abandoned just when couples need to reaffirm their bond.

KEY MOMENTS OF ATTACHMENT AND DETACHMENT

The attachment view of love gives us a way of understanding toxic patterns. It guides us to the moments that break and make a relationship. Clients sometimes tell me, "Things were going so well.

We had a great four days. It felt like we were friends. But then that one incident happened and everything got bad between us. I don't understand."

Dramatic exchanges between lovers evolve so fast and are so chaotic and heated that we don't catch what's actually happening and can't see how we could react. But if we slow things down we see the turning points and our options. Attachment needs and the powerful emotions that accompany them often arise suddenly. They catapult the conversation from mundane matters to the issue of security and survival. "Johnny is watching too much TV" all at once mushrooms into "I just can't deal with our son's tantrums anymore. I am just a lousy mom. But you are not listening to me right now. I know, I know, you have to keep working, that is what is important here, isn't it? Not my feelings. I am all alone here."

If we are feeling basically safe and connected to our partner, this key moment is just like a brief cool breeze on a sunny day. If we are not so sure of our connection, it starts a negative spiral of insecurity that chills the relationship. Bowlby gave us a general guide to when our attachment alarm goes off. It happens, he said, when we feel suddenly uncertain or vulnerable in the world or when we perceive a negative shift in our sense of connection to a loved one, when we sense a threat or danger to the relationship. The threats we sense can come from the outside world and from our own inner cosmos. They can be true or imaginary. It's our perception that counts, not the reality.

Peter, who has been married to Linda for six years, has been feeling less important to his lady of late. She has a new job and they make love less often. At a party, a friend comments that while Linda is radiant, Peter seems to be losing his hair. As Peter watches Linda converse attentively with a stunningly handsome man—a man with lots of hair—his stomach churns. Can Peter calm himself with the knowledge that he is precious to his wife and that she will turn to him and be there for him if he asks? Perhaps he remembers a moment when this happened and uses this image to soothe his unease.

What happens, though, if he can't quiet his gut? Does he get angry, walk over to his wife, and make a cutting remark to her about flirting? Or does he throw off his concern, tell himself he doesn't care, and go off to have another drink, or six? Either of these ways of dealing with his fear—attacking or retreating—will only alienate Linda. She will feel less connected and less attracted to her mate. And that, in turn, will only heighten Peter's primal panic.

A second key moment occurs after the immediate threat has passed. Partners have the chance to reconnect then, unless their negative coping strategies kick in. At the party later in the evening, Linda seeks Peter out. Does he reach out to her, letting her see the hurt and fear he felt when he saw her talking so intimately with another man? Does he express these emotions in a way that invites her to reassure him? Or does he attack her for "whoring around" and demand that they immediately go home and make love, or remain silent and withdrawn?

A third key moment is when we do manage to tune in to our attachment emotions and reach for connection or reassurance and the loved one responds. Say Peter manages to pull Linda aside, take a deep breath, and tell her that he was having a hard time watching her talk to the handsome stranger. Or maybe he only manages to go and stand beside her and express his upset with a troubled look. Suppose Linda responds positively. Even if he can't quite express his feelings, she senses something is wrong, and she offers Peter her hand. She asks softly if he is okay. She is accessible, she is responsive. But does Peter see this, does he trust it? Can he take it in, feel comforted, move closer, and continue to confide?

Or does he instead stay guarded and push her away so as to avoid feeling so vulnerable? Does he even attack her to test if she "really cares"?

Finally, when Peter and Linda go back to their everyday way of connecting, is he confident that she is there as a safe haven in times of trouble or doubt? Or does he still feel insecure? Does he try to control and push Linda into more and more responses that assure him of her love, or does he minimize his need for her and instead focus more on distracting tasks and toys?

This drama has focused on Peter, but a scenario centered on Linda would reveal she has the same attachment needs and fears. Indeed, men and women alike, we *all* share these sensitivities. But we may express them a bit differently. When a relationship is in free fall, men typically talk of feeling rejected, inadequate, and a failure, women of feeling abandoned and unconnected. Women do appear to have one additional response that emerges when they are distressed. Researchers call it "tend and befriend." Perhaps because they have more oxytocin, the cuddle hormone, in their blood, women reach out more to others when they feel a lack of connection.

When marriages fail, it is not increasing conflict that is the cause. It is decreasing affection and emotional responsiveness, according to a landmark study by Ted Huston of the University of Texas. Indeed, the lack of emotional responsiveness rather than the level of conflict is the best predictor of how solid a marriage will be five years into it. The demise of marriages begins with a growing absence of responsive intimate interactions. The conflict comes later.

As lovers, we poise together delicately on a tightrope. When the winds of doubt and fear begin blowing, if we panic and clutch at each other or abruptly turn away and head for cover, the rope sways more and more and our balance becomes even more precarious. To stay on the rope, we must shift with each other's moves, respond to each other's emotions. As we connect, we balance each other. We are in emotional equilibrium.

Emotional Responsiveness — The Key to a Lifetime of Love

"[A person's] heart withers if it does not answer another heart."

—*Pearl S. Buck*

"I slept but my heart was awake. Listen! My beloved is knocking: 'Open to me, my sister, my darling, my dove, my flawless one. My head is drenched with dew, my hair with the dampness of the night.'"

—*Song of Songs 5:2*

Tim and Sarah are sitting in my office. Tim isn't sure why he's here. All he knows, he says, is that he and Sarah have had a brutal fight. She's accused him of ignoring her at a party and is threatening to take their child and move in with her sister. He doesn't understand. They have a good marriage. Sarah is just being "too immature" and "expects too much." She doesn't get how pressured he is at work and that he can't always remember the "hearts and flowers part of marriage." Tim turns in his chair and stares out the window with a "What can you do with such a woman?" expression on his face.

Tim's complaints awaken Sarah from a despairing trance. She announces in an acid tone that Tim is not as smart as he thinks he is. In fact, she tells him, he is "a communication cretin" who has "zero skills." In fact, she notes, things are so bad that she has stopped attending her women's Bible study group, because she doesn't want her friends to pick up on how unhappy she is and how her marriage is a failure. But then sadness overwhelms her and she murmurs, in a voice that I can hardly hear, that Tim is a "stone" who turns away when she is "dying." She should never have married him. She weeps.

How have they arrived at this point? Sarah, a small dark-haired woman, and Tim, a stylishly groomed man, have been married for three years. They have been successful work colleagues and happy play partners, well matched in skill and energy, and joined in their commitment to serve Christ. They have a new house and an eighteen-month-old daughter whom Sarah has taken time off from work to care for. And now they are sparring all the time.

"All I hear is that I am home too late and I am working too hard," Tim says in exasperation. "But I am working for us, you know." Sarah mutters that there is no "us." "You say that you don't know me anymore," Tim continues. "Well, this is what grown-up love is all about. It's about making compromises and being buddies. I haven't cheated. I don't drink or hit you. I am a good Christian husband and I provide for you."

Sarah bites her lip and replies, "You didn't even take time off to be with me when I had the miscarriage. It's all deals and compromises with you...." She shakes her head. "I feel so hopeless when I can't get through to you. I have worn out my knees praying about this but it doesn't change. I have never felt so lonely, not even when I lived alone."

Sarah's message is urgent but Tim doesn't get it. He finds her "too emotional." But that is the point. We are never more emotional than when our primary love relationship is threatened. Sarah desperately needs to reconnect with Tim. Tim is desperately afraid that he has lost that intimacy with Sarah—connection is vital to him as well. But his need for connection is masked by talk of compromise and growing up. He tries to dismiss Sarah's concerns to keep everything "calm and on track." Can they begin to emotionally "hear" each other again? Can they be tuned in once more? How can I help them?

THE BEGINNING OF EFT

My understanding of how to help couples like Sarah and Tim began slowly. I knew that listening to and expanding on key emotions was essential to change for the individuals who came to me for counseling. So when I began to work with distressed couples on hot summer afternoons in Vancouver, Canada, in the early 1980s, I recognized the same emotions and how they seemed to create the music for the dance between partners. But my sessions seemed to swing between emotional chaos and silence. Very soon, I was spending every morning in the university library searching for direction, for a map to the dramas that played out in my office. The material that I found mostly said that love was irrelevant or impossible to understand and also that strong emotions were obviously dangerous and best left alone. Offering insights to couples, as some of these books suggested, insights like how we seem to repeat our parental relationships with our lovers, didn't seem to change much. My attempts to get couples to practice communication skills sparked comments about how these exercises didn't really get to the heart of the matter.

They missed the point.

I decided that they were right—and that I was somehow

missing the point as well. But I was fascinated, so fascinated that I sat and watched hour after hour of videotaped sessions. I decided that I would watch until I really understood these dramas of love gone wrong. Maybe even until I understood love! Finally the picture began to develop.

Nothing brings people together like a common enemy, I remembered. I realized that I could help couples by helping them see their negative patterns of interaction — their Demon Dialogues — as the enemy, not each other. I started recapping couples' exchanges in my sessions, helping partners see the spiral they were caught in, rather than just focusing on the other's last response and reacting to it. If we compare it to tennis, this was like learning to see the whole game rather than just the serve or the volley on the last ball spinning across the net. Clients began to see the whole dialogue and how it had a life of its own and was hurting them both. But why were these patterns so strong? Why were they so compelling and so distressing? Even when both partners recognized their toxic nature, these dialogues kept repeating. Partners seemed to get pulled back in by their emotions, even when they understood their pattern and how it trapped them both. Why were these emotions so potent?

I would sit and watch couples like Jamie and Hugh. The angrier Jamie became, the more she criticized Hugh, and the more silent he became. After lots of gentle questions, he told me that underneath his silence, he felt "defeated" and "sad." Sadness tells us to slow down and grieve, so Hugh had begun to grieve his marriage. And, of course, the more he closed down, the more Jamie demanded to be let in. Her angry complaint cued his sense of silent defeat and his silence cued her angry demands. Round and round. They were both stuck.

When we slowed down the "spin" of these circular dances, softer emotions, like sadness, fear, embarrassment, and shame, always appeared. Talking about these emotions, maybe for the first time, and seeing how their pattern trapped them both, helped Jamie and Hugh feel safer with each other. Jamie didn't look so dangerous when she was able to tell Hugh how alone she felt. No one had to be the bad guy here. They began to have new kinds of conversations and their narrow exchange of blame and silent distancing slowed down. Sharing their softer emotions, they started to see each other differently. Jamie admitted, "I never saw the whole picture. I just knew he wasn't close to me. I saw him as not caring. Now I see how he was ducking my bullets and trying to calm me down. I shoot when I get desperate and can't get a reaction any other way."

Now I was getting somewhere in my practice. Couples were nicer to each other. The drama of painful emotions didn't seem to be so overwhelming. These negative patterns always started when one partner tried to reach for the other and could not make safe emotional contact. That was the moment when the Demon Dialogue began. Once a couple grasped that they were both victims of the dialogue and were able to show more of themselves, to risk sharing deeper emotions, then the conflicts calmed down and they felt a little closer. So everything was fine. Or was it?

My couples told me no. Jamie told me, "We are nicer to each other and we fight less. But somehow nothing has really changed. If we stop coming here, it will all start up again. I know it will." Others told me the same thing. What was the problem? As I replayed tapes, I saw that deeper emotions like sadness and straight "terror," as one client put it, still hadn't really been dealt with. My couples were still watching their backs.

Emotion comes from the Latin word *emovere*, to move. We talk of being "moved" by our emotions, and we are "moved" when those we love show their deeper feelings to us. If partners were to reconnect, they indeed had to let their emotions move them into new ways of responding to each other. My clients had to learn to take risks, to show the softer sides of themselves, the sides they learned to hide in the Demon Dialogues. I saw that when more withdrawn partners were able to confess their fears of loss and isolation, they could then talk about their longings for caring and connection. This revelation "moved" their blaming partners into responding more tenderly, and sharing their own needs and fears. It was as if both people suddenly stood face-to-face, naked but strong, and reached for each other. This parallels the description in Genesis 2:25, "Adam and his wife were both naked, and they felt no shame."

Moments like these were amazing and dramatic. They changed everything and started a new positive spiral of love and connection. Couples told me that these moments were life-changing. They could not only exit from the Demon Dialogue, they could move into a new kind of loving responsiveness, of safety and closeness. They could then create a new narrative and plan, in an atmosphere of easy cooperation, for how to care for their relationship and safeguard their new closeness. But I still didn't understand exactly why these moments were so powerful!

I was so riveted by this series of discoveries that I decided to do the first study to test this approach for my dissertation project and call it Emotionally Focused Therapy, or EFT. I wanted to show how certain new emotional signals changed the connection between lovers. The first study confirmed all my hopes that this way of working with relationships not only helped people step out of negative patterns, it also seemed to create a new sense of loving connection.

During the next fifteen years, my colleagues and I did more and more studies on EFT, finding that it helped over 85 percent of the couples who came to us to make significant changes in their relationship. These changes also seemed to last, even in couples who faced terrible stressors, such as a seriously and chronically ill child. We found that EFT worked for truck drivers and lawyers, for couples from many different cultures, for couples where women called their men "inexpressive" and men called their mates "angry" and "impossible." In contrast to other approaches to couple therapy, a couple's level of distress when they came into therapy didn't seem to make much difference in terms of how happy they were at the end. Why? I wanted to find out, but first there were other puzzles to solve.

What was this emotional drama all about? Why were the Demon Dialogues so common and so powerful? Why did those moments of connection transform relationships? It was as if I had managed to find a way through a strange land, but I still didn't have a map or really understand where I was. I had watched couples move from threatening divorce to falling in love again, and even found out how to encourage and direct this. But still the answers to these questions eluded me.

Small moments end up defining our lives, for couples in love relationships and for struggling therapists and researchers like me. When I answered a colleague's question, "If love relationships aren't bargains, deals about profit and loss—what are they?" I heard myself say, casually, "Oh, they're emotional bonds.... You can't reason or bargain for love. It's an emotional response." And suddenly my mind slid into a new place.

I went back and looked at my tapes, paying particular attention to the needs and fears people talked about. I looked at those dramatic moments that transformed relationships. I was looking at emotional bonding! Now I understood. I was seeing the emotional responsiveness that John Bowlby said was the basis of loving and being loved. How could I have missed it? It was because I had been taught that this kind of bond ended with childhood.

But this was the dance of adult love. I rushed back home to write and bring this insight into my work with couples.

Attachment theory answered the three questions that had tormented me. Very simply, it told me that:

1. The powerful emotions that came up in my couples' sessions were anything but irrational. They made perfect sense. Partners acted like they were fighting for their lives in therapy because they were doing just that. Isolation and the potential loss of loving connection is coded by the human brain into a primal panic response. This need for safe emotional connection to a few loved ones is a wired-in recipe for survival. Distressed partners may use different words but they are always asking the same basic questions: "Are you there for me? Do I matter to you? Will you come when I need you, when I call?" To feel suddenly emotionally cut off from a partner, disconnected, is terrifying. We have to reconnect, to speak our needs in a way that moves our partner to respond. This longing for emotional connection with those nearest to us is *the* emotional priority, overshadowing even the drive for food or sex. The drama of love is all about this hunger for safe emotional connection, a life-and-death imperative we experience from the cradle to the grave. Loving connection is the only safety nature ever offers us.

2. These emotions and attachment needs were the plot behind negative interactions like the Demon Dialogues. Now I understood why this kind of pattern was so compelling and never-ending. When safe connection seems lost, partners go into fight-or-flight mode. They blame and get aggressive to get a response, any response, or they close down and try not to care. Both are terrified; they are just dealing with it differently. Trouble is, once they start this blame-distance loop, it confirms all their fears and adds to their sense of isolation. Emotional edicts as old

as time dictate this dance; rational skills don't change it. Most of the blaming in these dialogues is a desperate attachment cry, a *protest against disconnection*. It can only be quieted by a lover moving emotionally close to hold and reassure. Nothing else will do. If this reconnection does not occur, the struggle goes on. One partner will frantically try to get an emotional response from the other. The other, hearing that he or she has failed at love, will freeze up. Immobility in the face of danger is a wired-in way to deal with a sense of helplessness.

3. The key moments of change in EFT were moments of secure bonding. In these moments of safe attunement and connection, both partners can hear each other's attachment cry and respond with soothing care, forging a bond that can withstand differences, wounds, and the test of time. These moments shape safe connection, and that changes everything. They provide a reassuring answer to the question "Are you there for me?" Once partners know how to speak their need and bring each other close, every trial they face together simply makes their love stronger. No wonder these moments create a new dance of trusting connection for couples in EFT. No wonder they make them stronger as individuals. If you know your loved one is there, that you are special to them and they will come when you call, then you are more confident of your worth, your value. Likewise, when we are confident in God's presence and love, we can be more confident in our other relationships. God has promised us, "Never will I leave you; never will I forsake you" (Heb. 13:5). And the world is less intimidating when you have another to count on and know that you are not alone.

With the first study of EFT, I knew that I had found a path to lead couples from desperate distress to happier connection. But once I understood that all the issues and drama revolved around attachment bonds, I realized that I also had discovered a broad map for love and could systematically plot out the steps of the journey to a special kind of loving connection.

Immediately, my sessions with my couples changed. As I watched partners demanding and withdrawing, I saw Bowlby's concepts of separation distress in action. Some partners shouted louder and louder to make the other turn toward them, others whispered softer and softer, so as not to disturb the "peace." I've jokingly asked Christian couples I counsel this question: If you are in the middle of conflict, which verse would you be more inclined to quote to your partner—"Do not let the sun go down while you are still angry" (Eph. 4:26) [We need to resolve this now] or "Blessed are the peacemakers" (Matt. 5:9) [Why can't we just stop this and get along]? I heard partners caught in the Demon Dialogues speak the language of attachment. A desperate need for an emotional response that ends in blaming and a desperate fear of rejection and loss that ends in withdrawal—this was the scaffolding underneath these endless conflicts. Partners' emotions now were easier to tune in to. I understood their urgency. As I reflected my new understanding to my couples, putting their emotions, their needs, their endless conflicts into an attachment frame, and directing them toward moments of connection, they told me that this fit for them. They told me they now understood their own unspoken longings and seemingly irrational fears and could connect with their loved one in a whole new way. They told me what a relief it was to know that there was nothing wrong or "immature" about these longings and fears. They did not have to hide or deny them. Now we could hone the EFT way of working with couples—we were not just in the right neighborhood, we had a direct map to home base. We could go to the heart of the matter.

Over the years, as scientific studies on adult attachment have continued and confirmed what I have learned in leading and watching thousands of couple therapy sessions, the key conversations that promote an emotional bond and a safe, secure connection have become clearer and clearer. We have shown in our studies that when they happen, couples recover from distress and build a stronger bond between them. This book is about sharing these conversations with you in a way that you can use in your own relationship. Until now this has been a process supervised by professionals trained in EFT. But it is so valuable and so needed that I have simplified the process so that you, the reader, can easily use it to change and grow your relationship.

A.R.E.

The basis of EFT is seven conversations that are aimed at encouraging a special kind of emotional responsiveness that is the key to lasting love for couples. Later, in Part Three of this book, we will see how this responsiveness is part of a Christian's bond with God and God's covenant with humanity. This emotional responsiveness has three main components:

Accessibility: Can I reach you?

This means staying open to your partner even when you have doubts and feel insecure. It often means being willing to struggle to make sense of your emotions so these emotions are not so overwhelming. You can then step back from disconnection and can tune in to your lover's attachment cues.

Responsiveness: Can I rely on you to respond to me emotionally?

This means tuning in to your partner and showing that his or her emotions, especially attachment needs and fears, have an impact on you. It means accepting and placing a priority on the emotional signals your partner conveys and sending clear signals of comfort and caring when your partner needs them. Sensitive responsiveness always touches us emotionally and calms us on a physical level.

Engagement: Do I know you will value me and stay close?

The dictionary defines *engaged* as being absorbed, attracted, pulled, captivated, pledged, involved. Emotional engagement here means the very special kind of attention that we give only to a loved one. We gaze at them longer, touch them more. Partners often talk of this as being emotionally present.

One easy way to remember these is to think of the acronym A.R.E. and the questions "Are you there for me, are you with me?" Scripture often refers to the accessibility, responsiveness, and active engagement that make up a secure bond. In John 15:7, Christ explicitly tells us, "If you make yourselves at home with me and my words are at home in you, you can be sure that whatever you ask will be listened to and acted upon" (MSG).

Christ offers a model of receptivity and responsiveness. This is captured in the story of the woman with an issue of blood who reaches for Him in a crowd and touches His garment (Luke 8:43–48). It was particularly brave of her to reach and touch Jesus since, because of her condition, she was considered unclean. She reached out in her vulnerability and Jesus immediately stopped and turned to her. He listened to her story. We are told that He was "moved by her strength, and vulnerability. He saw this as the ultimate act of trust." He tells her that her faith in Him will bring her peace and healing. Christ responds to her need for loving connection with tenderness. He shows us just what accessibility, responsiveness, and engagement look like!

THE SEVEN CONVERSATIONS OF EFT

Let's go back to the story of Sarah and Tim and see how EFT works. We can look at the first four conversations that transformed Sarah and Tim's relationship. This will help you understand the changes that Sarah and Tim made and use Part Two of this book to create these changes in your own relationship. Like Sarah and Tim, you can learn to stop the slide into emotional starvation and distance that plagues so many relationships. But more than that, you can learn the exquisite logic of love and the conversations that build it.

In the first conversation, Recognizing the Demon Dialogues, I encourage the couple to identify the damaging dance they get into, when this dance happens, and how each partner's moves escalate their confrontations. Once they are aware of their negative steps, I ask them to dig beneath the destructive remarks and to figure out what they are really saying. Sarah's attacks and demands are a desperate protest against the erosion of her bond with Tim, while Tim's defensiveness and cool rationality are expressions of his fears that Sarah is disappointed in him and that he is losing her. The more he tries to dismiss her concerns, the more alone she feels and the angrier she becomes. After a while, all they have left is accusations and defensiveness.

But now Tim and Sarah can have a new positive conversation, one that gives them power over this Protest Polka Demon Dialogue. Sarah is able to say, "I guess I do come on heavy. I do get hostile. I feel so let down. So I confront you to get you to see it. To see what is happening and come back to me. But it just drives you away and into justifying yourself. And I guess I seem pretty dangerous to be around then, so you retreat even more. Then I get even more upset. We are stuck. I never saw that before." Tim is able to see how his distancing sets Sarah up to become more demanding. They begin to see the pattern and to stop blaming the other for the steps. Now they are ready for a second conversation.

In Finding the Raw Spots, Tim and Sarah begin to understand their own and their partner's reactions and that the drama here is all about the safety of their emotional attachment. Each partner starts to look beyond immediate reactions, such as Sarah's rage and Tim's cool distancing. We begin to plug into the deeper current of softer feelings, feelings connected with attachment needs and fears. Tim turns to a calmer and very attentive Sarah and says, "You're right. Last night, at that moment, I could not hear your hurt. All I see is your anger at times like that. All I hear is that I have blown it again. Failed again. I just never can get it right." He brings his hands up to cover his face. He sighs and continues, "So I guess I just try to put a lid on everything. To stop the fight and the examples of how I have blown it yet again. But do you think I don't know that I am losing you?" He hangs his head. Sarah leans forward and puts her hand gently on his arm. It is not that he does not care for or need her; it is that he cannot deal with the fear of losing her.

Sarah and Tim begin to realize that no one can dance with a partner and not touch each other's raw spots. We must know what these raw spots are and be able to speak about them in a way that pulls our partner closer to us. Sarah and Tim now know the danger cues and sensitivities to certain events that spark off attachment fears. "I do get enraged when you are late," Sarah tells Tim. "It reminds me of my dad. After he left us, he would always call and say he loved me and tell me when he was coming to pick me up and then he'd never show. I'd hope—and then get that I was a fool to think I was important to him. This feels the same." Talking to Tim of her disappointment and longing rather than her anger at him gives Tim a new view of Sarah and what is at stake for her here. He listens more, and they begin connecting on a deeper emotional level.

In a third conversation, Revisiting a Rocky Moment, this couple replay a time when they got stuck in a demand-distance loop, acknowledging the steps each made and the emotions each felt. They now are in control of the momentum created by their dance. What does this look like?

SARAH: We got so caught up in it — that polka thing. Before I knew it, I heard myself threatening to leave. But this time, part of my head was saying "What am I doing? What are we doing? We are stuck in this again." I understand now that this need to get him to respond is just part of loving someone. I don't have to feel bad about it. But I get hot just talking about it. I was getting scared. He sounded like he was reneging on his promise that we would go away for that weekend together, and I just lost it. Then I realized, "Wait a minute. Here we are again. Let's slow down here." By that time he had left the room. [She turns to Tim.] So I came and found you and said to you, "Hey, we are caught in that polka thing. I am feeling let down, like you aren't going to keep your promise." [She beams.]

TIM: You're right. I had already shut down. Given up. But somewhere in the back of my mind, I remembered our talks. So when you came and found me, I was relieved. Then I could tell you that I did want to go on the weekend with you. We seemed to be able to step out of that dance and kind of grab hold of each other, calm each other down. It helped that I remembered you saying that you were scared that I would let you down and not take the time off for the trip. I didn't just hear you angrily telling me what a big disappointment I am.

SARAH: I never understood that it impacted you so much when I got angry. In fact, I thought it didn't get to you at all. So yes, I would get desperate, frantic, in fact. I couldn't get you to respond to me. It didn't help when you and your family would give me the message that I should just grow up and handle things on my own. I would feel even more alone then.

TIM: [Reaches for her.] I know. I didn't understand. We would just get caught in this thing — you hurting and lonely and me feeling like some kind of idiot. I couldn't figure out what was wrong with us, and the more I avoided and played it down, the worse it got. Sue says this happens a lot. Guess we never have talked that much about our emotional needs, what we need from each other.

SARAH: This dance we get stuck in is the problem, even though you are a space cadet sometimes as far as being close is concerned. [She smiles. He tips his head to acknowledge her point and smiles back.]

Tim and Sarah can now do what securely attached couples can do. They can recognize and accept each other's attachment protests. They have a safe place to stand to begin a new conversation to deepen their emotional bond.

These first three conversations de-escalate tension in the relationship and prepare the couple for the next dialogues, which build and strengthen the bond.

The fourth conversation, Hold Me Tight, is the one that transforms relationships. This is the exchange that moves partners into being more accessible, emotionally responsive, and deeply engaged with each other. The final three conversations, Forgiving Injuries, Bonding Through Sex and Touch, and Keeping Your Love Alive, all rest on the foundation of the intimate connection created in this dialogue. Once couples know how to have the fourth conversation, they have a remedy to the ups and downs of love and a way out of the snares of disconnection.

Hold Me Tight is a difficult but intoxicating conversation. The emotional bond forged here is something that many couples have never experienced, even in the midst of initial infatuation when their bodies were flooded with passion's hormones. It is similar to the joyous connection between parent and child, except that it is more complex, reciprocal, and sexual. As this conversation unfolds, partners see themselves and their lovers differently; they find themselves feeling new emotions and responding in new ways. They can now take more risks and reach for more intimacy.

Let's look at how this conversation goes for a couple like Tim and Sarah when everything clicks into place.

Tim can now tell his wife that he gets "crazy paralyzed" when he feels unable to please her. He ends up shutting down, but he doesn't want to do this anymore. Now he adds, "But I don't know how to be 'close.' I'm not sure I even know what it looks like. I can't do it, except to see if Sarah wants to have sex."

But attachment responses are wired in, and when I ask Tim how he shows his little daughter how much he loves her, his face lights up. "Oh, I whisper to her and hold her, especially at night before bed," he offers. "And as she smiles at me when I come home, I have little phrases to let her know I am glad to see her. She likes when I kiss her cheek and tell her that she is my sweetie forever. And I play with her, give her my undivided attention just for those special moments." Then his eyes go wide; he knows what I am going to say. "Oh, so when you feel safe, you are pretty good at love and closeness. In fact, you know how to tune in to your loved ones. You know how to respond tenderly and how to connect." Tim smiles, unsure but hopeful. We then talk about what blocks him from being this responsive and tender with his spouse. He turns to Sarah and tells her that often he is too "on edge," too afraid to play and tune in to her.

This is a defining moment in Tim and Sarah's relationship.

He stops briefly, then continues. "I know I have neglected you," he confesses. "I know I have let you down. I get so caught up in proving myself at work—and to you. Then when I hear you are angry in spite of all my efforts, it kills me. I can't take it, so I shut down. But I want us to be together. I need you. I want you to give me a chance here, to stop watching for the slipup, and to hear that you are very important to me. I want us to be together. I don't always know how to do it." Sarah's eyes go wide and her brow furrows as she weeps.

Tim has become accessible. He can tell his wife about his attachment needs and vulnerabilities. He is emotionally engaged. It is this that matters, not exactly what he says. But Sarah at first does not know how to handle this stranger. Can she trust him? In just a short time, he has changed the music in the relationship from a polka to a tango, a dance of intense connection. So she lapses back into a testing hostile comment. "And when you 'don't know,' as you put it—you will dash off to work where you are the 'expert,' no?"

Gradually, as Tim continues to express his needs, Sarah sees "the man I fell in love with, the man I always wanted." It is then Sarah's turn to move into a new dance where she can soften her angry stance. She can tell him about her fear that he had "abandoned" her and her longing for his reassurance. I encourage her to ask specifically for what she needs to make her feel safe. "It's such a risk, like leaping from a great height in the hope you will catch me," she says, hesitantly. "I have built up so much distrust." "Ask me," he whispers. "I am here." She replies, "I need your reassurance. I need your attention. To know that I come first, even if just for moments. I need you to see and to respond if I hurt, if I am scared. Can you hold me?" He stands and pulls her up into an embrace.

I know from watching thousands of couples that these are the key moments that move relationships from shaky to solid ground, that help couples find a lifetime of love. In these moments Tim and Sarah create that trust, that secure connection we all long for.

PLAY AND PRACTICE

The questionnaire and the exercises below will help you begin to see your relationship through the attachment lens.

The A.R.E. Questionnaire

This questionnaire is a great way to begin applying the wisdom in this book to your own relationship. Simply read each statement and circle T for *true* or F for *false*. To score the questionnaire, give one point for each "true" answer. You can complete this questionnaire and reflect on your relationship on your own. Or you and your partner can each complete it and then discuss your answers together in the way described after the questionnaire.

From your viewpoint, is your partner accessible to you?
1. I can get my partner's attention easily. T F
2. My partner is easy to connect with emotionally. T F
3. My partner shows me that I come first with him/her. T F
4. I am not feeling lonely or shut out in this relationship. T F
5. I can share my deepest feelings with my partner. He/she will listen. T F

From your viewpoint, is your partner responsive to you?
1. If I need connection and comfort, he/she will be there for me. T F
2. My partner responds to signals that I need him/her to come close. T F

3. I find I can lean on my partner when I am anxious or unsure. T F
4. Even when we fight or disagree, I know that I am important to my partner and we will find a way to come together. T F
5. If I need reassurance about how important I am to my partner, I can get it. T F

Are you positively emotionally engaged with each other?

1. I feel very comfortable being close to, trusting my partner. T F
2. I can confide in my partner about almost anything. T F
3. I feel confident, even when we are apart, that we are connected to each other. T F
4. I know that my partner cares about my joys, hurts, and fears. T F
5. I feel safe enough to take emotional risks with my partner. T F

If you scored 7 or above, you are well on your way to a secure bond and can use this book to enhance that bond. If you scored below 7, this is a time to focus on using the conversations in this book to strengthen the bond with your lover.

Understanding the bond between you and your partner, and sharing how you see it, is the first step to being able to create the connection you both want and need. Does your partner's perception of how accessible, responsive, and engaged you are fit with your view of yourself and how safe your relationship is? Try to remember that your partner is talking about how safe and connected he or she feels right now in your relationship, not about whether you are a perfect or imperfect partner. You can take turns talking about the question/answer that seemed most positive and important to you. It is best to keep this to five minutes each.

Now, if you feel comfortable, try to explore the question/

answer that seemed to bring up the most difficult emotions for you. Try to do this in the spirit of helping your partner tune in to your feelings. He or she will not be able to do this if you get caught up in being negative, so try to avoid criticism or blame. Again, it is best to keep this talk to five minutes each.

EXPLORING YOUR EMOTIONAL CONNECTIONS

Maybe you are more comfortable reflecting on general points rather than using the questionnaire. You can simply reflect on the questions below, or you might want to write your answers down in a journal and so deepen your exploration of them. You might also want to share and discuss your responses with your partner at some point.

• Did the story of Tim and Sarah make sense to you? Did it seem familiar? What part really seemed important to you, and how do you understand that?

• What messages about love/marriage did you get from your parents? Your community? Your church? Was being able to reach for and trust others seen as a strength and a resource?

• Before your present relationship, did you experience a safe, loving relationship with someone you trusted, felt close to, and could turn to if needed? Do you have an image of what this looks like in your head, a model that can help you as you create your present relationship? Think of one good time or typical moment that captures this relationship and share it with your partner.

• Did your past relationships teach you that loved ones were unreliable and that you had to be vigilant and fight to be seen and responded to? Or did you learn that depending on others is dangerous and it is best to distance yourself, to not need others and avoid closeness? These basic strategies often switch on when we feel that our lover is distant or disconnected. Which strategy did you use in past relationships, say, with your parents, when things started to go wrong?

• Can you remember a time when you really needed to know a loved one was with you? If he or she was not, what was that like for you and what did you learn from it? How did you cope? Does this have an impact on your relationships now?

• If it is hard for you to turn to and trust others, to let them close when you really need them, what do you do when life gets too big to handle or when you feel alone?

• Name two very concrete and specific things that a safe, accessible, responsive, and engaged lover in a relationship with you would do on a typical day and how those things would make you feel at that moment.

• In your present relationship, can you ask your partner, let him or her see, when you need closeness and comfort? Is this easy for you or difficult to do? Perhaps you wonder if this is a sign of weakness, or maybe it seems too risky for you. Rate your difficulty in doing this on a scale from 1 to 10. A high score means this is very difficult for you to do. Share this with your partner.

• When you feel disconnected or alone in your present relationship, are you likely to get very emotional or even anxious and push your partner to respond? Or are you more likely to shut down and try not to feel your need to connect? Can you think of a time when this happened?

• Think of a time in your relationship when questions like "Are you there for me?" were hanging in the air unanswered and you wound up getting into a fight about a mundane problem. Share this with your partner.

• Can you think of bonding moments in your relationship when one of you reached out and the other responded in a way that made you both feel emotionally connected and secure with each other? Share this with your partner.

* * *

Now that you have a sense of what love and the creation of positive dependency are all about, the transforming conversations in the following chapters will show you how to create this kind of bond with your partner. The first four conversations teach you how to limit negative spirals that leave you both disconnected and how to tune in to each other in a way that builds lasting emotional responsiveness. The next two conversations demonstrate how you can promote emotional bonding through forgiving injuries and sexual intimacy. The final conversation shows you how to care for your relationship on a daily basis and link this relationship to your spiritual life.

PART TWO

Seven Transforming Conversations

Conversation 1: Recognizing the Demon Dialogues

"Strife is better than loneliness."

—Irish proverb

"The tongue is a small part of the body, but it makes great boasts. Consider what a great forest is set on fire by a small spark."

—James 3:5

For all of us, the person we love most in the world, the one who can send us soaring joyfully into space, is also the person who can send us crashing back to earth. All it takes is a slight turning away of the head or a flip, careless remark. There is no closeness without this sensitivity. If our connection with our mate is safe and strong, we can deal with these moments of sensitivity. Indeed, we can use them to bring our partner even closer. But when we don't feel safe and connected, these moments are like a spark in a tinder forest. They set fire to the whole relationship.

This is what has happened in the first three minutes of an explosive session with Jim and Pam, a long-married couple who were experiencing a serious downswing in their relationship, though they still noted each other's appealing qualities. Jim had told me several times in previous sessions that Pam's golden hair and blue eyes "entranced" him, and Pam often observed that he was a good husband and father and even a "little bit" handsome himself.

The session starts innocently enough, with Pam saying she and Jim had a pleasant week together and that she had decided to try to comfort Jim more whenever she saw that he was feeling stressed by his work. She also says that she would really like him to be able to tell her when he needed emotional support. Jim snorts, rolls his eyes, and swivels his chair away from his wife. At that moment, I swear I could feel a hot wind rush through my office.

Pam blasts: "What on earth do you mean by that, that ridiculous expression? I have tried a lot harder to be supportive in this relationship than you have. Here I am offering to support you, but you would rather act superior, as always." "Look at you ranting away," Jim fires back. "I will never come to you for support. And the reason is right here. You would just berate me. You have done that for years. It's the reason we are in this mess to begin with."

I try to calm them down, but they are shouting so loudly that they don't hear me. They finally stop when I say that it seems a little sad that this interaction started out with Pam being positive and offering an image of being loving. Pam then bursts into tears and Jim closes his eyes and sighs. "This is what always happens with us," Jim says, and he is right. And this is where they can start to change what always happens. Change starts with seeing the pattern, with focusing on the game rather than the ball.

We get stuck in three basic patterns—I call them the Demon Dialogues—when we cannot connect safely with our partner. Find the Bad Guy is a dead-end pattern of mutual blame that effectively keeps a couple miles apart, blocking reengagement and the creation of a safe haven. Couples dance at arm's length. That's what Jim and Pam are doing when they fall into blaming each other for their distressed relationship. Many couples lapse into this pattern for short periods, but it is difficult to maintain over time. For most, Find the Bad Guy is the brief prelude to the most common and entrapping dance of distress. Marriage researchers have labeled this next dance demand-withdraw or criticize-defend. I call it the Protest Polka because I see it as a reaction to or, more accurately, a protest against the loss of the sense of secure attachment that we all need in a relationship. The third dance is Freeze and Flee, or as we sometimes call it in EFT, withdraw-withdraw. This usually happens after the Protest Polka has been going on for a while in a relationship, when dancers feel so hopeless that they begin to give up and put their own emotions and needs in the deep freeze, leaving only numbness and distance. Both people step back to escape hurt and despair. In dance terms, suddenly no one is on the floor; both partners are sitting out. This is the most dangerous dance of all.

All of us get caught in any one or all of these negative interactions at some point in our love relationships. For some these are brief, though risky, dances in otherwise secure connections. For others, less securely connected, they become habitual responses. After a while, all it takes is a hint of negativity from a lover to set off a Demon Dialogue. Eventually the toxic patterns can become so ingrained and permanent that they totally undermine the relationship, blocking all attempts at repair and reconnection.

We have only two ways of protecting ourselves and holding on to our connections with those we love when we do not feel safe and responded to. One route is to avoid engagement, that is, to try to numb our emotions, to shut down and deny our attachment needs. The other is to listen to our anxiety and fight for recognition and response. People of faith will recognize this in their connection with God, the one who is loved most of all. When we are disappointed in life or feel distant from God, we often deal with our emotions in the same ways. In prayer, we can rail against God, begging or even demanding that He respond to us, or we can try to turn away and dismiss our need for His grace.

In our human relationships, which strategy we adopt when we feel disconnected—becoming demanding and critical or withdrawing and shutting down—partly reflects our natural temperament, but mostly it is dictated by the lessons we learn in the key attachment relationships of our past and present. Moreover, because we learn with every new relationship, our strategy is not fixed. We can be critical in one relationship, and withdraw in another.

If I had not intervened with Jim and Pam during the session, they would probably have raced through all three Demon Dialogues; collapsed, exhausted, alienated, and hopeless; and then returned to the dialogue that they knew best. Inevitably, they would have made damning judgments about their relationship, judgments that would cloud future interactions and eat away at their trust in each other. Each time they do this and cannot find a way through into safe connection, the relationship becomes more and more tenuous. As it is, all we have done in the session is slow things down a little. Jim and Pam suggest that I fix the problem. Of course, to each of them, that means fix the *other* partner. The respite lasts for only thirty seconds before they launch again into Find the Bad Guy.

DEMON DIALOGUE 1—FIND THE BAD GUY

The purpose of Find the Bad Guy is self-protection, but the main move is mutual attack, accusation, or blame. The Bible tells us that Adam and Eve reacted just this way after eating from the tree in the Garden of Eden. The starting cue for this pattern of responses is that we are hurt by or feel vulnerable to our partner and become suddenly out of control. Emotional safety is lost. When we are alarmed, we use anything that promises to give us back this control. We can do this by defining our partner in a negative way, by shining a black light on him or her. We can attack in reactive anger or as a preemptive strike.

Find the Bad Guy could just as easily be called It's Not Me, It's You. When we feel cornered and flooded with fear, we tend to see and go with the obvious. I can see and I can feel what you just did to me. It's much harder to see the impact of my responses on you. We concentrate on each step and how "you just stepped on me," not the whole dance. After a while, the steps and pattern become automatic.

Once we get caught in a negative pattern, we expect it, watch for it, and react even faster when we think we see it coming. Of course this only reinforces the pattern. As Pam says, "I don't even know what comes first anymore. I am waiting for his put-down. I have my gun ready. Maybe I pull the trigger when he isn't even coming for me!" By being wary and anticipating being hurt, we close off all the ways out of this dead-end dance. We cannot relax with our partners, and we certainly cannot connect with or confide in them. The range of responses becomes more restricted, slowly deadening the relationship.

Jim puts it this way: "I don't know what I feel in this relationship anymore. I am either numb or seething mad. I think I have lost touch with all kinds of feelings here. My emotional world has gotten smaller, tighter. I am so busy protecting myself." This reaction is especially typical of men. Many partners, when they first come to see me, answer the question "What do you feel right now as you see your wife cry?" with a simple "Don't know." When we are attacking or counterattacking, we try to put our feelings aside. After a while we can't find them at all. Without feelings as our compass in the territory of close relationships, we are effectively lost.

We begin to see the relationship as more and more unsatisfying or unsafe and our partner as uncaring or even defective. So Jim says, "I keep remembering my mother telling me that Pam just wasn't mature enough for me and I guess, after these spats, I begin to think my mother was right. How can you have a relationship with someone who is so aggressive? It's hopeless. It might be better for both of us to just give it up, even if it's hard for the kids."

People of faith may even use their religious code as a source of reproach, accusing each other of betraying the principles of their religious commitment. In heated moments, partners might find themselves chastising their loved ones with phrases like "What kind of a Christian are you, anyway?" or "How can you act like this and call yourself a Christian?" These bullets are particularly painful because they imply that one's partner is failing not only in this relationship but in their relationship with God, too.

When partners do the Find the Bad Guy dance only occasionally and loving ways of connecting are still the norm, they can reach out to each other after they've cooled down. Sometimes they can see how they've hurt each other and apologize. They can even laugh about the "silly things" both said. I remember once screaming at my husband, John, "You big Canadian male, you," and then bursting into laughter because that is exactly what he is! However, once the patterns we've talked about here become rooted and habitual, then a powerful, regenerating feedback loop is set up. The more you attack, the more dangerous you appear to me, the more I watch for your attack, the harder I hit back. And round and round we go. This negative pattern has to be shut down before a couple can build true trust and safety. The secret to stopping the dance is to recognize that no one has to be the bad guy. The accuse-accuse pattern itself is the villain here, and the partners are the victims.

Let's look again at Jim and Pam in Find the Bad Guy and see how they can get out of this destructive pattern by using a few simple pointers and new responses.

PAM: I am just not going to sit here and listen to you tell me how impossible I am anymore. According to you, everything that ever goes wrong between us is my fault!

JIM: I never said that at all. You just exaggerate everything. You are so negative. Like the other day when my friend came over and everything was going fine, but then you turned and said...

Jim is off and sliding down what I call the Content Tube. This is where partners bring up detailed example after detailed example of each other's failures to prove their point. The couple fight over whether these details are "true" and whose bad behavior "started this."

To help them recognize their Demon Dialogue, I suggest that they:

- Stay in the present and focus on what is happening between them right now.
- Look at the circle of criticism that spins both of them around. There is no true "start" to a circle.
- Consider the circle, the dance, as their enemy and the consequences of not breaking the circle.

Here is what happens:

JIM: Well, I guess that's right. We do get caught in that, both of us. But I never really saw it before. I know I get so riled up that after a while I will say anything to get at her.

SUE: Yes. The desire to win the fight and prove the other is the bad guy has such a pull. But in fact, nobody wins this one. Both lose.

PAM: I don't want to fight like this. It kills me. And you are right, it is destroying our relationship. We are more and more on guard with each other. What does it matter who is "right" in the end? We are both more and more unhappy. I guess I keep it spinning by trying to show him he can't put me down. I try to make him feel smaller.

SUE: Yes. And do you know what you do, Jim? [He shakes his head.] Well, just a few minutes ago, you said, "I won't come to you, won't trust you, because you are dangerous for me sometimes." And then I think you accused her of being the problem, yes?

JIM: Yes, it's like I tell her, "You can't get me." And then I put her down.

SUE: And after all this sniping at each other, both of you go off, more and more defeated and alone, yes?

JIM: Right. So this circle, cycle, loop, dance, whatever it is, has us stuck. I see that. But how to stop it, that is the point. The incident that we are discussing now, I never said anything to her; she did start this cycle!

SUE: [I raise my eyebrows. He stops.] Well, first you have to see the circular pattern of responses and really understand that proving the other wrong just pushes you further and further apart. The temptation to be the "winner" and to make the other admit she is at fault is just part of the trap. Then you begin to pin down this dance, as it is happening, rather than getting meaner and meaner or searching for proof in endless versions of facts or incidents. If you want to, both of you can come together to stop this enemy taking over your relationship.

JIM: [Looking at his wife.] So, right now, I don't want to go into this attack thing. We are caught in this loop. Maybe we could call it the "Who is lousy?" loop. [They laugh.] This is killing us. So let's try stopping it right now. You were trying to tell me that you wanted to be supportive. So why was I going on about you ranting? I want you to support me more!

PAM: Yes, I think if we can stop and say, "Hey, we are in that loop again. Let's not keep turning up the heat and hurting each other," then we could be better friends and maybe even a little more than that! Perhaps a little like we used to be. [She tears up.]

Pam is right here. Being able to stop the Find the Bad Guy dance is a way to be friends. But couples want much more than friendship between them. Getting this attack-attack dance under control is just the first step. We have to go on to look at other places we get stuck in love relationships. But first you can try some of the exercises below.

PLAY AND PRACTICE

These questions and reflections can help you think about how you and your mate move in the dance when both of you get caught in fight-to-win mode. You can ponder them, write them down, read them aloud, and, of course, share them with your partner.

Most of us are good at blaming. As far back as the Garden of Eden, Adam blames Eve and Eve blames Adam. Both of them tell God, "It's not my fault. The other one is the bad guy." More recently, Frank McCourt in his book *Teacher Man* noted how easy it is to get kids to write if you let them pen excuse notes explaining why they have not done their homework; they are brilliantly inventive in blaming others for their own inaction. So, think of a time when you clearly were at fault in creating a minor problem.

For example, I went to a friend's house for a dinner party and dropped the entrée on the kitchen floor while trying to help. Now think of your actions in your situation and four different ways you could have made someone else the bad guy. (*But the dish was heavy and she had not told me!*) Find out how good you are at it. Imagine three ways a companion might respond negatively to your remarks. What would have happened then? Do you get into a loop?

Now see if you can remember a similar incident with your spouse. What did you use to "win" the fight and prove your innocence? How did you accuse your partner? What are your usual comebacks when you feel cornered?

Can you sketch out the circle of hostile criticism and labeling that trapped you both? How did each of you begin to define the other? How did each of you wound and enrage the other? Was there a "winner"? (Probably not!)

What happened after your Find the Bad Guy fight? How did you feel about yourself, your partner, the connection between you? Were you able to go back and talk about the fight and console each other? If not, how did you deal with the loss of safety between you? What do you think might have happened if you had said, "We are starting to label each other, to prove the other one is the bad one here. We are just going to get hurt more if we get stuck in this dance. Let's not get caught in an attack-attack dance with each other. Maybe we can talk about what happened without it being anyone's fault."

DEMON DIALOGUE 2 — THE PROTEST POLKA

This is the most widespread and ensnaring dance in relationships. Studies by psychologist John Gottman of the University of Washington, Seattle, indicate that many of the couples who fall into this pattern early in marriage do not make it to their fifth anniversary. Others are mired in it indefinitely. This "forever" quality makes sense because the main moves of the Protest Polka create a stable loop, each move calling forth and reinforcing the next. One partner reaches out, albeit in a negative way, and the other steps back, and the pattern repeats. The dance also goes on forever because the emotions and needs behind the dance are the most powerful on this planet. Attachment relationships are the only ties on earth where *any* response is better than none. When we get no emotional response from a loved one, we are wired to protest. The Protest Polka is all about trying to get a response, a response that connects and reassures.

Couples have a difficult time recognizing this pattern, however. Unlike the obvious attack-attack pattern of Find the Bad Guy, the Protest Polka is more subtle. One partner is demanding, actively protesting the disconnection; the other is withdrawing, quietly protesting the implied criticism. Dissatisfied partners, missing each other's signals, often complain of a fuzzy "communication problem" or "constant tension."

Let's take a look at how couples do the Protest Polka.

I ask Eva and Chuck, the young couple sitting in my office, "What seems to be the problem? You have told me that you love each other and want to be together. You have been together for six years. What is it that you would like to change about your relationship?"

Eva, small, blond, and intense, stares at her husband, Chuck, a tall handsome man who is still and silent, seemingly mesmerized by the rug at his feet. She lets out a big sigh. Then she looks at me, gestures toward him, and hisses, "This is the problem, right here. He never talks, and I get sick of it! I just get enraged at his silence. I am the one carrying the burden of this relationship. I 'do' it all, and I do more and more. And if I didn't..." She throws up her hands in a gesture of resignation. Chuck exhales deeply and looks at the wall. I like it when the picture is so clear and the polka is so easy to grasp.

This instant snapshot of their relationship tells me each partner's basic position in the dance of distress. Eva is hammering on the door, protesting her sense of separateness, while Chuck holds the door firmly shut. Eva tells me that she has left Chuck twice, but relented when he called and begged her to return. Chuck says that he just doesn't understand what is going on, but he feels pretty hopeless about their situation. He tells me that in his mind he has decided that it is either his fault—perhaps he was never meant to be married—or it's just that Eva and he don't fit together. Either way, he isn't sure there is any real point in coming to see me. They have tried counseling before.

I ask if they fight, and Chuck says that they hardly ever have a real fight. They do not get caught in Find the Bad Guy. But then there are the times when Eva says she is leaving, and Chuck says, "Fine." These moments feel pretty bad. And, he tells me, she does try to "coach" him. As he says this, he winces and laughs.

Eva and Chuck then tell me a story. If you ask most couples, they can tell you of a seminal incident, a small moment that captures the essential nature of the connection between them. If these moments are good, they bring them up on anniversaries or in tender moments. If they are bad, they puzzle over them, trying to figure out what the moment says about their relationship.

CHUCK: I think a lot about pleasing her. I do want her to be happy with me. But it just doesn't work. She really wants everything to be perfect when we go to church on Sunday. So I try. I help with getting the kids cleaned up and all. But then it just all falls apart anyway. Somehow it's never perfect enough. And the house has to be perfectly clean before we leave, too. Like that time a few months ago when, by the time we got to church, we weren't even speaking to each other!

EVA: We weren't speaking because you don't listen — you were out cleaning the garage when I needed help. Who cares about the garage?

SUE: And what did you do, Eva?

EVA: I went out to the garage and yelled at him to get back in the house and make himself useful. We were going to be late for church.

CHUCK: [Shaking his head.] I just needed to get away from your constant badgering. Maybe clear my head before we went to church.

EVA: Yeah. And if I hadn't gone out there to yell at you, you would have stayed there hiding in the garage, leaving me by myself to handle everything alone. Like last month when I gave up and just took the kids and went to church by myself. If I don't make you do it, nothing will happen. And that is the same for the whole relationship. If I don't make it happen, nothing will happen. [She turns to me.] He just doesn't take his part.

SUE: So this is what goes wrong between the two of you and not just on Sundays. This pattern of you wanting Chuck to respond and Chuck getting quiet and disappearing. This kind of way of relating keeps you demoralized and feeling unsafe with each other.

EVA: Right. And, I can never hear him. He mumbles a lot. So I was trying to get him to speak more clearly the other day. And then he won't talk to me at all!

CHUCK: So I mumble sometimes. You were screaming at me in the car on the highway. As I am driving, you are telling me to enunciate my words louder and louder!

SUE: Eva, it's kind of like you have become the dance instructor, telling Chuck how to move and speak. And you do it out of fear that he will stay distant and there will be no dance between you. No help with the family, and no connection. [Eva nods emphatically.] You keep waiting for Chuck to come and connect with you and respond when you need support, and when this doesn't happen, you feel really alone. And so you try to fix it, to teach him how to respond. But this gets rather pushy, even critical. Then Chuck hears that he is blowing it—how he talks is wrong, how he cleans the house is wrong—and he does even less.

CHUCK: That's it. I freeze up is what I do. I can't do anything right. She doesn't even like the way I eat.

SUE: Aha. And the more you freeze up, I guess the more Eva tries to instruct you.

EVA: I get so frustrated. I prod him, I poke him, that is what I do. I prod him to get a response. Any response.

SUE: Right, so let's track this. You prod and poke, Chuck freezes and responds less and less. You shut down, Chuck? [He nods.] And the more you shut down, the more Eva feels shut out and the more she pokes. It is a circle that just spins and spins and it has taken over your relationship. What is happening for you, Chuck, when you "freeze up"?

CHUCK: I get so that I am afraid to do anything, sort of paralyzed. Whatever I do will be wrong. So I do less and less. I go into a shell.

EVA: And then I feel so alone. I just try to get a rise out of him any way I can.

SUE: Right. This spiral has really taken over. One freezes up, feels paralyzed, shuts down into a shell, the other feels shut out and pokes harder and harder to get a response.

EVA: This is sad for us, for both of us. How can we stop it then, this spiral?

SUE: Well, we have pretty much set it out. These steps are like breathing for you now. You don't even know you are taking them.

You need to get real clear about how this cycle is creating a mine-field in the middle of your relationship. It is making it impossible for you to feel safe together. If I was Chuck here, I would mumble in case what I said was wrong. If I was Eva, I would push and prod because inside I would be pleading, "Listen to what I need, come and help, come and talk to me. Come and be with me."

EVA: I do feel like that. That is what I am trying to do, to reach him. But I know my calling has an edge to it. I get frustrated.

SUE: That's true. Many of us get stuck like this when we can't quite find a way to feel safe and connected with each other. The way I see it, you are so important to Eva that she cannot just wait you out or turn away. And you are freezing up because you are so worried about doing the "wrong" thing with her, upsetting her and shaking up the relationship again. The old axiom "When in doubt, say or do nothing" is terrible advice in love relationships. The question is, can you help each other stop this "spiral"? Can you see when you are caught in it and move together to take your relationship back?

CHUCK: Maybe we can!

In the following sessions, Chuck and Eva go over their polka again and again. They discover that their "spiral," as they call it, occurs specifically when attachment cues come up, when Eva needs help in a task or wants to connect and when Chuck hears that he is failing and disappointing her. Protest moments occur in all marriages, but when the basic bond is secure, these events can be canceled out or even used as springboards to reinforce the relationship.

For example, in a happy marriage, Eva would still protest at moments when she felt emotionally separated from Chuck, but in a lower key. Being less worried about the connection between them, she would express herself in a softer and clearer way. And

Chuck, in turn, would be more receptive and responsive to her appeals. He would not hear her distress or disappointment as a sentence of doom for him as a lover or for their relationship, but as a sign of her need for support and closeness with him.

In an insecure relationship, however, the Protest Polka speeds up and gets more intense. It eventually creates such havoc that partners cannot resolve problems or communicate clearly about anything. Then disconnection and distress infuse more and more of the relationship. It's important to note, however, that no relationship is entirely suffused with the destructive pattern I talk about here. There are still moments of closeness. But they do not occur frequently enough or with sufficient strength to counter the harm caused by the Protest Polka. Or the type of closeness isn't the one a partner craves. For instance, men with a tendency to withdraw from confrontations do initiate sexual intimacy in the bedroom, but for most women arousal is linked to emotional connection and sexual relations are not enough to fulfill their attachment needs.

For years, therapists have misguidedly viewed this pattern in terms of disputes and power struggles and have attempted to resolve it by teaching problem-solving skills. This is a little like offering Kleenex as the cure for viral pneumonia. It ignores the "hot" attachment issues that underlie the pattern. Rather than conflict or control, the issue, from an attachment perspective, is emotional distance. It is no accident that Chuck is "stonewalling," as his wooden lack of response is called in the research literature, and that this sparks off rage and aggression in his wife. An aggressive response seems to be wired into primates when a loved one on whom an individual depends acts as if the individual does not exist. An infant human or monkey will attack a stonewalling mother, in a desperate attempt to obtain recognition. If no response occurs, "deadly" isolation, loss, and helplessness follow.

What we have seen above is just one instance of the Protest

Polka. Not every distancing, defensive partner talks of "freezing" like Chuck does. But I've found that pursuing and distancing partners each tend to use characteristic expressions when describing their experiences. Let's listen in; you may hear some of your own patterns and moves here.

Partners who follow in Eva's steps often use these statements:

- "I have a broken heart. I could weep forever. Sometimes I feel like I am dying in this relationship."
- "These days he is always busy, somewhere else. Even when he is home, he is on the computer or watching TV. We seem to live on separate planets. I am shut out."
- "Sometimes I think that I am lonelier in this relationship than I was when I lived by myself. It seemed easier to be by myself than living like this, together but separate."
- "I needed him so much during that time, and he was just so distant. It was as if he didn't care. My feelings didn't matter to him. He just dismissed them."
- "We are roommates. We never seem to be close anymore."
- "I get mad, sure I do. He just doesn't seem to care, so I smack him, sure I do. I'm just trying to get a response from him, any response."
- "I am just not sure I matter to him. It's like he doesn't see me. I don't know how to reach him."
- "If I didn't push and push we would never be close. It would never happen."

Examining these statements closely reveals a wealth of attachment themes: feeling unimportant to or not valued by a partner; experiencing separateness in terms of life and death; feeling excluded and alone; feeling abandoned at a time of need or being unable to depend on a partner's support; longing for emotional connection and feeling anger at a partner's lack of responsiveness; experiencing the other as a friend or a roommate; and feeling the loss of the loved one as a fellow spiritual traveler and partner in Christ.

When these partners are encouraged to focus on the negative dance and describe just their own moves, instead of their partner's mistakes or faults, they often use the following verbs: *push, pull, slap, attack, criticize, complain, pressure, blow up, yell, provoke, try to get close,* and *manage.* Sometimes it is hard to see how your feet move in the dance. At those times, when we are caught in the pattern of pursuit and protest, most of us talk simply of being frustrated, enraged, or upset, and this is what our partner sees. But it is only the first, most superficial, layer of what is going on in the polka.

Partners who follow in Chuck's footsteps usually speak this way:

- "I can never get it right with her, so I just give up. It all seems hopeless."
- "I feel numb. Don't know how I feel. So I just freeze up and space out."
- "I get that I am flawed somehow. I am a failure as a husband. Somehow that just paralyzes me."
- "I shut down and wait for her to calm down. I try to keep everything calm, not rock the boat. That is my way of taking care of the relationship. Don't rock the boat."
- "I go into my shell where it's safe. I go behind my wall."
- "I try to shut the door on all her angry comments. I am the prisoner in the dock and she is the judge."
- "I feel like nothing in this relationship. Inadequate. So I run to my computer, my job, or my hobbies. At work, I am somebody. I don't think I am anything special to her at all."

- "I don't matter to her. I am way down on her list. I come somewhere after the kids, the house, and her family. Even the dog comes before me! I just bring home the money."
- "I end up feeling somehow empty. You never know if the love will be there or not."
- "I don't feel that I need anyone the way she does. I am just not as needy. I was always taught that it's weak to let yourself need someone like that, childish. So I try to handle things on my own. I just walk away."
- "I don't know what she is talking about. We are fine. This is what marriage is all about. You just become friends. I am not sure I know what she means by 'close,' anyway."
- "I try to solve the problem in concrete ways. Try to fix it. I deal with it in my head. It doesn't work. She doesn't want that. I don't know what she wants."

There are themes here, too: feeling hopeless and lacking the confidence to act; dealing with negative feelings by shutting down and numbing out; assessing oneself a failure as a partner, as inadequate; feeling judged and unaccepted by the partner; trying to cope by denying problems in the relationship and attachment needs; doing anything to avoid the partner's rage and disapproval; using rational problem solving as a way out of emotional interactions.

When partners like Chuck describe their own moves, they use the following terms: *move away, shut down, get paralyzed, push the feelings away, hide out, space out, try to stay in my head,* and *fix things.* What they usually talk about in terms of their feelings is depression, numbness, and lack of feeling, or a sense of hopelessness and failure. What their partner usually sees is simply a lack of emotional response.

Gender plays a part here, though the roles vary with culture and couple. In our society, women tend to be the caretakers of relationships. They usually pick up on distance sooner than their lovers, and they are often more in touch with their attachment needs. So their role in the dance is most often the pursuing, more blaming spouse. Men, on the other hand, have been taught to suppress emotional responses and needs, and also to be problem solvers, which sets them up to withdraw. Men of faith, in particular, often feel responsible for providing leadership in the family and keeping the family safe. They then become very focused on problem solving and very sensitive to messages that they are failing their partner in any way.

If I appeal to you for emotional connection and you respond intellectually to a problem, rather than directly to me, on an attachment level I will experience that as "no response." This is one of the reasons that the research on social support uniformly states that people want "indirect" support, that is, emotional confirmation and caring from their partners, rather than advice. Often men say that they do not know how to respond on an emotional level. But they do! They do it when they feel safe, most often with their children. The tragedy here is that a man may be doing his best to answer his wife's concerns by offering advice and solutions, not understanding that what she is really seeking from him is emotional engagement. This engagement is most often the solution she is seeking.

Jesus offers us examples of recognizing the emotional needs of others and responding to these needs with loving compassion. At one point He insists, putting all else aside, that the children in the temple be allowed to come to Him for a blessing (Luke 18:15–17). I see this as being about his welcoming love for children as much as about our need for a childlike faith. At another time, a blind man is calling loudly to Jesus, seeking His attention. Many people tried to quiet him but he shouted louder. Jesus stopped and responded to the man's emotional calls. He heard this man's need and invited him to come close. At the end of the story, this connection with Jesus results in the man being healed (Mark 10:46–52). Christ responded to emotional need with emotional presence and loving concern.

In our society, both men and women are inculcated with social beliefs that help ensnare them in the polka and make the expression and recognition of emotional needs problematic. Most destructive is the belief that a healthy, mature adult is not supposed to need emotional connection and so is not entitled to this kind of caring. Clients tell me, "I cannot just tell him that I am feeling small and need his arms around me. I'm not a kid," or "I can't just ask to come first, even sometimes. I have never asked for that. I don't feel entitled. I shouldn't need that." If we cannot name and accept our own attachment needs, sending clear messages to others when those needs are "hot" is impossible. Ambiguous messages are what keep the polka going. It is so much easier to say, "Why aren't you more talkative? Don't you have anything to say to me?" than to open up and ask that our need for loving connection be met.

The Protest Polka is danced not just by lovers, but by parents and children, brothers and sisters, indeed by anyone with close emotional ties to another. Sometimes it is easier for us to see ourselves performing it with our siblings or our kids than with our partner. Is it that the vulnerability is less obvious? I ask myself why my adolescent son, sighing and dismissing my comments about his being late, sends me over the edge into critical blaming, even when we have a loving bond between us. The answer is easy.

Suddenly I hear a message that vibrates with scary attachment meanings. He rolls his eyes at me. His tone is contemptuous. I hear that my concerns or comments do not matter to him. I am irrelevant. So I turn up the music and I criticize him. He retreats and dismisses me again. We are off. The polka music plays on. But suddenly I recognize the music. So I step to the side and invite him to look at the dance. "Wait a minute. What is happening here? We are getting caught up in a silly fight and we are both getting hurt." This is the first step in stopping the polka: recognize the music.

What have I learned in twenty years of watching partners take back their relationships from this dance? My couples have taught me so many things.

First, they have taught me that you have to see it. The whole enchilada. You have to see the *how* of the dance between you and your partner and what it says about the relationship, not simply the content of the argument. You also have to see the *whole* dance. If you just focus on specific steps, especially the other person's, as in "Hey, you just attacked me," you will be lost. You have to step back and see the entire picture.

Second, both people have to grasp how the moves of each partner pull the other into the dance. Each person is trapped in the dance and unwittingly helps to trap the other. If I attack you, I pull you into defense and justification. I inadvertently make it hard for you to be open and responsive to me. If I stay aloof and apart, I leave you separate and alone and pull you into pursuing and pushing for connection.

Third, the polka is all about attachment distress. It cannot be stopped with logical problem solving or formal communication skill techniques. We have to know the nature of the dance if we are to change the key elements and return to safe connection. We have to learn to recognize calls for connection and how desperation turns into "I push, I poke, anything to get him to respond," or "I just freeze, so as to stop hearing more and more about how flawed I am and how I have lost her already." These patterns are universal because our needs and fears, and our responses to perceived loss and separation, are universal.

Fourth, we can know the nature of love, tune in to these moments of disconnection and the protest and distress that are the key parts of the polka. We can then learn to see the polka as the enemy, not our partner.

Fifth, partners can begin to stand together and call the enemy by name, so they can slow the music down and learn how to step to the side and create enough safety to talk about attachment emotions and needs.

When Chuck and Eva can do this, they begin to have hope for their relationship. As Chuck says, "When we start to get into that thing, you know, the spiral we talk about here, we don't get so sucked down into it. I said to Eva yesterday, 'We are getting stuck here. I am getting more and more distant and frozen up, and you are getting all upset. These are the times when you feel shut out, right? We don't have to do this. Let's stop. Come over and just let's have a hug.' And she did. It felt great." I asked Chuck what it was that helped him most to defeat this polka. He replied that it helped him to realize that Eva wasn't "the enemy" and that she was "fighting for the relationship" when the polka started, not trying to "do me in."

Being able to recognize and accept protests about separation and exit the Protest Polka is crucial to a healthy relationship. If a safe, loving bond is to stay strong and grow, couples have to be able to repair moments of disconnection and step out of common dead-end ways of dealing with them, ways that actually exacerbate disconnection by destroying trust and safety.

PLAY AND PRACTICE

Does the story of Chuck and Eva seem familiar to you? Do you recognize parts of this dance in your own relationship? Can you think of the last time this polka took over your relationship? Can you put on your attachment glasses and see past the argument about facts or problems to the struggle over the connection between the two of you? For example, was the argument really about whether to rebuild the cottage, where one partner likes to go and paint, or was it about attachment security? Perhaps the partner who is left behind is just that—left behind. Maybe one of you was really talking about the lack of secure connection and closeness between the two of you or trying to get reassurance from the other, but the conversation stayed focused on pragmatic issues.

In your present relationship, what do you tend to do when you feel disconnected or unsafe? Try to think about which person you identified with in the stories of the couples given in this chapter. You can also think of the last argument or hurtful episode in your relationship. If you pretend you are a fly on the wall reporting on the incident to the *Fly Gazette,* what does the dance look like and what are your main moves? Do you protest or withdraw? Do you find yourself getting critical and trying to change your lover? Or maybe you shut down and tell yourself that any longing for reassurance is risky stuff and should not be listened to. All of us do all of these things at times.

Flexibility and being able to see your own moves and their impact on others is the key here. I am encouraging you to be courageous, look hard, and identify your usual response. It's the one that pops out before you have taken a breath. This is the response that can trap you in a vicious cycle of disconnection with the person you love best. These responses can also be different in different relationships. But for now, just think of your most significant connection and how you respond to this person at times when attachment uncertainties and issues come up.

The distancing stance is sometimes the one that is hardest for us to really grasp if we are the person doing the distancing. Perhaps your style is to retreat into yourself and try to calm yourself by shutting the world out? This can be very useful. Unless you start doing it automatically and find it harder and harder to stay open and responsive. Then this withdrawal sets you up to spin into the Protest Polka. Pretty soon, your partner will need you and feel shut out, abandoned, and excluded.

Can you think of a specific incident when withdrawing and not responding worked for you in a relationship? What happened after your withdrawal? We most often think of this strategy as preventing a fight that we fear will escalate and threaten the relationship. Now, can you think of times when moving away and shutting down did not seem to work? What happened after this withdrawal, to you and in your dance with your partner?

If you feel comfortable, see if you can share your responses to some of these questions with your partner. Are there times when the two of you get stuck in the polka? See if you can pin down each person's moves. Can you see the whole feedback loop? Describe it very simply by filling in the blanks in the following sentence with one word.

The more I _____, the more you

_____ and then the more I

_____, and round and round

we go.

Come up with your own name for this dance and see if you each can share how it erodes the sense of safe connection in your relationship. How does it change the emotional music between you?

For example, Todd talks about how his main way of connecting is through sex. He is much more sure of himself in bed than when he is discussing feelings with his wife. He spots his main move in the polka: "I chase you for sex. But it's not just for my own physical pleasure. It's the way I know to be close. When you turn me down, I chase you more and 'badger' you for explanations. The more I do this, the more you move away and guard your space."

His wife, Bella, replies, "Yes, and the more criticized and demanded from I feel, the more overwhelmed I get. So I turn away from you more and more. And you get more pushy and desperate, and this goes on and on. Is that it?" Todd agrees that this is the outline of the polka for them. They decide to call it the Vortex. For them the name expresses how obsessed Todd gets with his wife's sexual availability and how obsessed she becomes with guarding her space. Todd is then able to share that he feels more and more rejected and frantic, and Bella states that she feels "frozen" and lonely in their marriage. What is it like for you and your lover to talk about your own moves in your Protest Polka?

Even if you get stuck in the Protest Polka, are there times when you can step out of it, shut it down, and move into another way of interacting? Are there times when you can risk openly asking for closeness and comfort or disclose your feelings and needs to your spouse rather than withdrawing? What is it that makes these times possible? What do you do to keep the polka at bay? See if you can figure this out together. Is there a way to help each other feel safer so that a sense of disconnection does not immediately lead into this dance? Often this comes down to recognizing the attachment signals hidden in the polka. For example, Juan found that just telling his wife, Anna, "I see that you're really upset and need something from me but I don't know what to do here," was enough.

DEMON DIALOGUE 3—FREEZE AND FLEE

Sometimes, when a couple comes to see me, I do not hear the hostility of Find the Bad Guy or the frantic beat of the Protest Polka. I hear a deadly silence. If we think of a relationship as a dance, then here both partners are sitting out! It looks like there is nothing at stake; no one seems to be invested in the dance. Except that there is a palpable tension in the air, and pain is clear on the couple's faces. Emotion theorists tell us that we can try to suppress our emotions but it just doesn't work. As Freud noted, they seep out of every pore. What I see is that both partners are shut down into frozen defense and denial. Each is in self-protection mode, trying to act as if he or she does not feel and does not need.

This is the Freeze and Flee dance that frequently evolves from the Protest Polka. This is what happens when the pursuing, critical partner gives up trying to get the spouse's attention and goes silent. If this cycle runs its course, the aggressive partner will grieve the relationship and then will detach and leave. At this point, partners typically are very polite to each other, even cooperative around pragmatic issues, but unless something is done, the love relationship is over. Sometimes the usually withdrawn partner finally tunes in to the fact that even though things look more peaceful, there is now no emotional connection of any kind, positive or negative. This partner frequently then agrees to seek out a counselor or to read books like this.

The extreme distancing of Freeze and Flee is a response to the loss of connection and the sense of helplessness concerning how to restore it. One partner will usually tell a story of pursuing the mate, protesting the lack of connection, and mourning alone. This partner describes himself or herself as now unable to feel, as frozen. The other partner is often trapped in the withdrawal that has become the default option, and attempts to deny the unfolding detachment. No one is reaching for anyone here. No one will take any risks. So there is no dance at all. If the couple doesn't get help and this continues, a point comes when there is then no way to renew trust or revive the dying relationship. Then this Freeze and Flee cycle will finish the partnership.

Terry and Carol, they admitted to me, had never been what's called a "close couple." But Carol, a subdued, intellectual woman, insisted that she had tried repeatedly to talk to her husband about his "depression." This is the way she understood their emotional estrangement. Terry, a quiet, formal man, noted that his wife had been finding fault with him for years, especially around parenting issues. They had come in to see me because they had gotten into a fight, a very rare event for them. It started when Carol picked out a pair of pants to wear to a party that Terry disliked. Terry had declared that if she wore those particular pants it meant that she did not love him and they should divorce! Then on the way to the party, Terry had told her that he was on the verge of starting an affair with a work colleague, but he assumed that this did not matter to Carol as they never had sex anyway. Carol in turn had disclosed that she was infatuated with an old friend and pointed out that Terry never touched her for affection or sex.

In our session, they talked of lives so swamped with career duties and parenting responsibilities that finding time for personal closeness and lovemaking had become harder and harder. Carol claimed that once she had recognized that they were becoming "strangers," she had tried to "shake Terry up" so he would talk to her more. When this didn't work, she had become very angry. Terry noted that Carol had indeed been very "judgmental" for a number of years, especially about his parenting, but then, about a year ago, she had just become distant. Carol explained that she had finally decided to "swallow" her rage and to accept that this was the way marriage was. She concluded that her husband no longer found her attractive or interesting enough to capture his attention. In response to this, Terry spoke sadly of Carol's deep connection to their two children and told me that he somehow seemed to have lost his spouse. She was a mother but not a wife. He wondered if it was because he was simply too serious and "in his head" to be with a woman.

The real problem with the Freeze and Flee cycle is the hopelessness that colors it. Both of these partners had decided that their difficulty lay in themselves, in their innate flaws. The natural response to this is to hide, to conceal one's unlovable self. Remember that a key part of Bowlby's attachment perspective is that we use the eyes of those we love to reflect back to us a sense of ourselves. What other information could possibly be as relevant in our daily framing of who we are? Those we love are our mirror.

As Carol and Terry felt increasingly disconnected and helpless, they had hidden from each other more and more. The basic attachment cues that we see in infants and parents and in lovers, such as prolonged gazing and physical caressing, had become first muted and then nonexistent. Terry and Carol never made eye contact during our session and noted that spontaneous touching had disappeared from their lives long ago. Being very intellectual had enabled them to rationalize their lack of sexual connection and deny, at least most of the time, the pain of not feeling desired by their spouse. Both talked about the symptoms of depression, and indeed, depression is a natural part of losing connection with a lover. Over time, the gap between them widened, and it seemed more and more risky to reach out to each other. Carol and Terry described the themes, moves, and feelings that withdrawers in the Protest Polka reveal, but they had deeper doubts about their lovability. This doubt paralyzed both of them and "froze" the protest that usually draws attention to this kind of destructive distance.

When we began to delve into their pasts, they both talked of growing up in cold, rational families where emotional distance was the norm. When each felt disconnected, they automatically withdrew and denied their needs for emotional closeness. Our past history with loved ones shapes our present relationships. In moments of disconnection when we cannot safely engage with our lover, we naturally turn to the way of coping that we adopted as a child, the way of coping that allowed us to hold on to our parent, at least in some minimal way. When we feel the "hot" emotions that warn us our connection is in trouble, we automatically try to shut them down and flee into reason and distracting activities. In this dance of distance, avoiding these emotions becomes an end in itself. As Terry explains, "If I stay cool, we never talk about feelings. I don't want to open that Pandora's box."

These ways of coping with our emotions and needs become default options; they "happen" so fast that we have no sense of choosing them. But when we see how they lock us into self-defeating dances with our lovers, we can change them. They are not indelible parts of our personality, and we do not need years of therapy and insight to reshape them. Terry spoke of having an older, hostile father and a mother who was a famous politician. He looked blank when I asked him when he felt close to his mother. He said that all he remembered was watching her on the TV screen. He had no choice but to learn how to tolerate distance and numb his needs for comfort and closeness. He had learned his lesson well. But his childhood survival strategy was disastrous for his marriage. Carol, too, saw how she had begun to "wither inside" when she had "shut down" her need for touch and connection.

As with the other dances, once Terry and Carol understood the steps they were taking that isolated them from each other, they began to feel more hopeful and to reveal their feelings to each other. Carol was able to admit that she had "given up" and "built a wall" between herself and Terry to blunt her sense of rejection. She confessed that she had turned to the children to fulfill her longing for touch and connection. Terry divulged how shocked he was to hear this and how he still very much wanted his wife. They both began to uncover the impact each had on the other, and they realized that they were still important to each other. After a few new risks, and a few fights, Carol was able to tell me, "We both feel safer. Fights are hard, but they are so much better than the icy emptiness, the careful silence." Terry observed, "This vicious cycle we have been in, I think we can beat it. We both get hurt and scared and shut each other out. But we don't have to do that." New beginnings start with knowing how we create the trap that we are caught in, how we have deprived ourselves of the love we need. Strong bonds grow from resolving to halt the cycles of disconnection, the dances of distress.

PLAY AND PRACTICE

Does the Freeze and Flee pattern seem familiar to you? If so, where did you learn to ignore and discount your needs for emotional connection? Who taught you to do this? When do you feel most alone? Can you dare to share the answers to these questions with your partner? Learning how to take risks and initiate this kind of sharing is like taking an antidote to numbing or running away from your attachment needs. Is there any way your partner can help you with this?

Can you share with your partner one cue that sparks the distancing dance? It can be as simple as a turn of the head at a particular moment. Can you also identify exactly how you push your partner away from you or make it dangerous for him or her to come closer?

What do you tell yourself once you have emotionally withdrawn to justify separation and to discourage yourself from reaching out to your partner? Sometimes these are pronouncements about what love is and how we ought to act in love relationships that we have been taught by our parents or even our culture. Can you share these with your partner?

Can you make a list of all the things this dance has taken away from you? We usually have glimpses of emotional closeness when we first become infatuated with a person and are willing to take any risk to be by his or her side. We will remember those moments just as we remember our hopes and longings. How has this negative dance eroded them?

As a final exercise for this chapter, can you identify which of the three patterns—Find the Bad Guy, the Protest Polka, Freeze and Flee—most threatens your current love relationship? Remember that the facts of a fight (whether it's a fight about the kids' schedule, your sex life, your joint commitment, your spiritual life, your careers) aren't the real issue. The real concern is always the strength and security of the emotional bond you have with your partner. It is about accessibility, responsiveness, and emotional engagement. See if you can summarize the pattern that takes over your relationship by filling in the blanks in the following statements. Then edit them into a paragraph that best fits you and your relationship. Share it with your partner.

When _____

_____ **, I do not feel safely con-**

nected to you.

Fill in the cue that starts up the music of disconnection, e.g., *when you say you are too tired for sex and we have not made love for a few weeks, when we fight about my parenting, when we don't seem to speak for days.* No big, general, abstract statements or disguised blaming is allowed here, so you can't say things like *when you are just being difficult as usual.* That is cheating. Be concrete and specific.

I tend to _____. I move this way in our dance to try to cope with difficult feelings and find a way to change our dance. (Choose an action word, a verb, e.g., *complain, nag, zone out, ignore you, run, move away.*)

What I then say to myself about our relationship is _____. (Summarize the most catastrophic conclusion you can imagine, e.g., *"You do not care about us," "I am not important to you," "I can never please you."*)

My understanding of the circular dance that makes it harder and harder for us to safely connect is that when I move in the way I described above, you seem to_____ _____. (Choose an action word, a verb, e.g., *shut down, push me to respond.*)

The more I _____, the more you _____. We are then both trapped in pain and isolation. (Insert verbs that describe your own and your partner's moves in the dance.)

Maybe we can warn each other when this dance begins. We can call it _____. Seeing this dance is our first step out of the circle of disconnection.

Once you can identify these negative cycles and recognize that they trap both of you, you are ready to learn how to step out of them. The next conversation explores more deeply the strong emotions, particularly the attachment fears, that keep these negative dances going.

Conversation 2: Finding the Raw Spots

We all are vulnerable in love; it goes with the territory. We are more emotionally naked with those we love and so sometimes, inevitably, we hurt each other with careless words or actions. While these occasions sting, the pain is often superficial and fleeting. But almost all of us have at least one additional exquisite sensitivity — a raw spot on our emotional skin — that is tender to the touch, easily rubbed, and deeply painful. When this raw spot gets abraded, it can bleed all over our relationship. We lose our emotional balance and plunge into Demon Dialogues.

What exactly is a raw spot? I define it as a hypersensitivity formed by moments in a person's past or current relationships when an attachment need has been repeatedly neglected, ignored, or dismissed, resulting in a person's feeling what I call the "2 Ds"—*emotionally deprived* or *deserted*. The 2 Ds are universal potential raw spots for lovers.

These sensitivities frequently arise from wounding relationships with significant people in our past, especially parents, who give us our basic template for loving relationships; siblings and other members of our families; and, of course, past and present lovers. For example, recently when my husband John's eyelids began drooping while I was speaking to him, I hit the ceiling, enraged. He was tired and drowsy, but it sent me back to the days when an ex-partner would fall instantly asleep every time I tried to start a serious conversation. Dozing off was a not-so-subtle form of withdrawing, disconnecting from the relationship. This experience made me hypervigilant—sudden sleepiness signals emotional abandonment to me.

Francois, one of my clients, is highly sensitive to any hint that his wife, Nicole, might not desire him or may be developing an interest in another man. In his painful first marriage, his wife was openly unfaithful to him many times. Now he goes into total blinding panic when Nicole smiles at his accomplished friend at a party or when she is not home when he expects her to be there.

Linda complains that she really hurts when her husband, Jonathan, "holds back from telling me I look nice or that I have done a good job. It is like being instantly flooded with hurt, and then I get resentful and critical" of him. Linda traces her sensitivity back to her mom. "She refused to ever compliment me or praise me for anything and always told me that I looked unattractive," she tells her husband. "She once said that she thought that if you praised people, they would stop striving. I hungered for that recognition from her and resented her for withholding it. And now, I guess, I long for that from you. So when I am all dressed up and I ask you how I look, and you just seem to dismiss me, it hurts. You know I need that praise, but you refuse me. At least that is how it feels. I just can't see straight, it stings so much."

People can have several raw spots, although usually one is paramount in terms of putting the spin in a couple's negative cycle. Steve feels a double whammy when his wife, Mary, says she would like to have sex more often. This could be taken as a very positive request. But for Steve, her declaration is a guided missile that demolishes his sexual confidence; his amygdala, the fear center in his brain, screams "incoming," and he hits the floor. Steve reacts to Mary by shutting down and shutting her out. "It's like I am suddenly back in my first marriage, hearing that I am this big disappointment and getting real anxious about performing in general, but especially in bed." An echo from his childhood also inflames this raw spot. Steve was the smallest kid in his class, and his dad constantly asked him in front of his brothers, "Am I talking to Steve or Stephanie?" That experience left him feeling that he was not "male enough for any woman."

But raw spots are not always a reminder of past wounds; they can crop up in a current relationship, even a generally happy one, if we feel especially emotionally deprived or deserted. Raw spots can occur during big transitions or crises—such as having a child, becoming ill, or suffering the loss of a job—when the need for support from our partner is particularly intense, but it doesn't come. They can also develop when a partner seems chronically indifferent, producing an overwhelming sense of hurt that then infuses even small issues. The failure of our loved one to respond scrapes our emotional skin raw.

Jeff and Milly had a great relationship until Jeff's best friend got promoted to the job that Jeff had worked so hard for and Jeff fell into a depression. Instead of offering comfort and reassurance, an anxious Milly hounded him to "just snap out of it."

They had found their way through this crisis and back to being close, but the experience left Jeff hypersensitive to his wife's reaction to any expressions of distress on his part. His sudden, seemingly irrational flashes of anger whenever he thinks Milly is unsupportive soon have her withdrawing into defensive silence and feeling like she is failing as a wife. You can predict what happens next. They get into their Demon Dialogue.

Helen was devastated when she found herself being blamed by a therapist for her adolescent son's drinking problem. During an assessment session, Sam, Helen's generally loving husband, echoed the therapist's viewpoint. Later, when Helen expressed her hurt, Sam got caught up in justifying his opinion, and a series of painful arguments ensued. Helen then decided to put her "foolish" hurt aside and concentrate on the good things in her marriage, and she believed that she had done this.

But suppressing significant emotions is hard to do and often ends up being toxic to relationships. Helen's hurt begins to leak out. She pesters Sam for his opinion of her every action, and Sam, unsure of what to say, says less and less. Suddenly they are fighting about everything. Sam accuses Helen of becoming more and more like her "paranoid" mother. Helen feels more and more lost and alone.

Jeff's and Helen's raw spots are being rubbed, but they don't see it. Surprisingly, many of us miss the same thing. Indeed, we don't even recognize that we *have* raw spots. We are only aware of our secondary reaction to the irritation—defensively numbing out and shutting down, or reactively lashing out in anger. Withdrawal and rage are the hallmarks of Demon Dialogues, and they mask the emotions that are central to vulnerability: sadness, shame, and, most of all, fear.

If you find yourself continually stuck in a Demon Dialogue with your lover, you can bet it is being sparked by attempts to deal with the pain of a sore spot, or more likely, sore spots in both of you. And unfortunately, your raw spots almost inevitably rub against each other. Chafe one in your lover and his or her reaction often irritates one in you.

Consider Jessie and Mike, who have done nothing but fight since Jessie's twelve-year-old daughter moved in with them. Jessie says, "Suddenly, like overnight, Mike changed from this warm tender guy to this tyrant. He gives orders, makes all these rules for my kid. He is screaming most of the time he's home. He looks just like all the abusive men in my family. I just can't bear someone yelling and giving orders. No one protected me, but I can protect my kid."

Mike flips between sad protests about how much he loves his wife, even though she refuses to speak to him for days on end, and loud indignant rants about how he never wanted to become a parent to her impossible, disrespectful child. He goes up in flames when he speaks of how he had pampered Jessie for years and then found that he "doesn't exist when this kid is around." Mike recalls falling ill with shingles but Jessie, he says, was too preoccupied with her daughter's issues to comfort him. Smacking each other's raw spots has trapped them in the Protest Polka.

Tom and Brenda's raw spots sent them into a different Demon Dialogue, Freeze and Flee. Brenda is obsessed with their new baby. Tom's attempts to draw some attention his way irritate Brenda, and one night she blows up. She's tired of his demands, she says, and calls him "oversexed" and "pathetic." Tom is stricken. Although he's a dishy-looking guy, he is quite shy and insecure with women. He's always needed to feel desired by Brenda.

He retaliates: "Fine, fine. Obviously you are not in love with me anymore, and all your stuff with me in the last years has been a sham. I don't need hugs from you. I don't need to be with you.

I'm going out dancing, and you can just take care of the baby." He leaves signs around the house indicating that he's flirting with a woman in his ballroom dance group. Brenda grew up feeling like the plain girl and has always wondered why attractive and successful Tom chose her. Terrified, she withdraws more into the baby. Tom and Brenda barely speak. Constantly protecting their raw spots completely sabotages the loving responsiveness they both long for.

Stopping these destructive dynamics depends not only on identifying and curbing the Demon Dialogues (Conversation 1) but also on finding and soothing our raw spots and helping our lover to do the same. People who have grown up in the haven of secure, loving relationships will have an easier time healing these scrapes. Their raw spots are few and not so deep. And once they understand what underlies their negative interactions with their loved one, they are more able to step out of them quickly and soothe the hurts.

For others, though, who have been traumatized or badly neglected by those they have loved or depended on, the process is longer and more arduous. Their raw spots are so large and so tender that accessing their fears and trusting in a partner's support are huge challenges. Kal, an abuse survivor and army veteran, says, "I am just one big raw spot. I crave soothing, but lots of times if my lady really touches me, I can't tell if it's a caress or another cut."

Still, we are not prisoners of the past. We can change for the better. Recent research by psychologist Joanne Davila at Stony Brook University in New York, as well as others, confirms what I see in my sessions: that we can heal even deep vulnerabilities with the help of a loving spouse. We can "earn" a basic sense of secure connection with the aid of a responsive partner who helps us deal with painful feelings. Love really does transform us. And as God is the ultimate source of love, turning to our faith can also help us deal with raw spots in a way that leads to positive connection. Reaching for God and finding reassurance in our relationship with Him offers us a path to feeling valued and special that soothes our vulnerability. When William is triggered by his wife's apparent dismissal of his special efforts to please her, and this reminds him of the pain he felt when his parents withheld their approval from him, he turns to God in a moment of prayer. He draws strength from his faith as he is reminded how special he is in God's eyes.

RECOGNIZING WHEN A RAW SPOT IS RUBBED

There are two signs that tell you when your raw spot or your partner's has been hit. First, there is a sudden radical shift in the emotional tone of the conversation. You and your love were joking just a moment ago, but now one of you is upset or enraged, or, conversely, aloof or chilly. You are thrown off balance. It's as if the game changed and no one told you. The hurt partner is sending out new signals and the other tries to make sense of the change. As Ted tells me, "We are in the car having this ordinary chat, and suddenly there is ice on the inside of the car. Like she is looking away from me out the window, her mouth in this taut line, and she is all glum as if she wishes I didn't exist. Now where did that come from?"

Second, the reaction to a perceived offense often seems way out of proportion. Marla says, "We usually make love on Friday nights. So I was waiting for Pierre, but then I got all caught up in a call from my sister, who was upset. It was about a fifteen-minute call, I guess. Pierre came downstairs and went ballistic. We got into the usual fight. He is just being unreasonable when he does that." No, it's just that Marla doesn't yet understand the logic of love and Pierre can't quite explain his rawness to himself or his wife. He tells her, "My head says, 'What are you getting all upset about? Just cool it.' But I am already on the ceiling."

These signs are all about primal attachment needs and fears suddenly coming online. They are all about our deepest and most powerful emotions suddenly taking over. To really understand our raw spots, we need to take a closer look at the deeper emotions that are key to this sensitivity and unpack them in a way that helps us deal with them. If we don't do this, we will speed right past them into a defensive response, usually anger or numbing, that gives our partner completely the wrong message. In insecure relationships, we disguise our vulnerabilities so our partner never really sees us.

Let's break down what happens when a raw spot gets rubbed.

1. An attachment cue grabs our attention and turns on our attachment system, our longings and fears. An attachment cue is a trigger that plugs you in emotionally. It can be a look, a phrase, a change in the emotional tone of an interaction with your partner. Attachment cues can be positive or negative, bringing up good or bad feelings. An attachment cue that irritates a raw spot sets off an "uh, oh" alarm. "Something strange, bad, or painful is approaching," says your brain. Your alarm might go off when you hear a "critical" tone in your lover's voice or when your partner turns away just as you ask for a hug. Marie tells her husband, Eric, "I know you are trying to be caring. And you are right. You do talk to me about my problems. And it's fine, until you say, 'Look' in that tone, like I am a stupid little kid who doesn't know anything. That is like a needle in my skin. I get that you are exasperated with me. You think I am stupid. And that hurts." This is news to Eric; he thought they were arguing because she didn't like any of his ideas.

2. Our body responds. People say, "My stomach churns and I hear my voice go shrill," or "I go cold and still." Sometimes the

only way we can know how we feel is to listen to our body. Strong emotion mobilizes the body. It puts it in survival mode with lightning speed. Each emotion has a specific physiological signature. When we are afraid, blood flow increases to the legs; when we are angry, blood flow increases to the hands.

3. Our intellect, sitting behind our forehead in the brain's prefrontal cortex, is a little slow. Now it catches up with our emotional brain, our amygdala, and goes looking for what all this means. This is when we check our initial perception and decide what the attachment cue is telling us about the safety of our bond. Carrie's catastrophic conclusions roll out here on cue. She says, "When it seems like we're getting ready to make love and you say you are tired, I get really upset. It's like you have no desire for me. That I am just like one of your buddies. I'm just not special to you." Her husband, Derek, says, "Can't I just be tired?" Carrie answers, "Not when you have been flirting with me all night and setting up all kinds of expectations. Then if they are not going to work out, I need a little help dealing with that. I don't want to just get stuck in being angry."

4. We get set to move in a particular way, toward, away from, or against our lover. This readiness to act is wired into every emotion. Anger tells us to approach and fight. Shame tells us to withdraw and hide. Fear tells us to flee or freeze, or in real extremes to turn and attack back. Sadness primes us to grieve and let go. Hannah says about her fights with her husband, "I just want to run. I need to get away. I see his angry face and I'm gone. He says I dismiss him, but I hear his anger and my feet are moving. I just can't stay and listen."

All this happens in a nanosecond. Differing Christian views on his origins theory aside, look at what Charles Darwin had to say about the power of emotion and its role in the struggle for survival.

Darwin wanted to see how much control he had over his emotions. He used to stand at the glass in the London Zoo where a giant adder was housed and try again and again not to leap back as the adder struck out at him. He never succeeded. His body always reacted in fear even when his conscious mind told him he was quite safe.

The relational version of this might be that in the middle of an open tender moment, I suddenly hear my partner make a critical comment. I feel my body freeze up. The registering of hurt and instant withdrawal probably took less than two-hundredths of a second (this is about the time scientists estimate it takes to register the emotion on another's face). The tender moment is lost. Emotions tell us what matters. They orient and direct us, like an internal compass.

PLAY AND PRACTICE

IDENTIFYING YOUR RAW SPOTS

Can you pinpoint a time in your current relationship when you got suddenly thrown off balance, when a small response or lack of response suddenly seemed to change your sense of safety with your lover, or when you got totally caught up in reacting in a way that you knew would tie you into a Demon Dialogue? Maybe you are aware of a moment when you found yourself reacting very angrily or numbing out. Let's go beneath that surface reaction to the deeper emotions and unpack this incident.

- What was happening in the relationship?
- What was the negative attachment cue, the trigger that created a sense of emotional disconnection, for you?

- What was your general feeling in the split second before you reacted and got mad or went numb?
- What did your partner specifically do or say that sparked this response?

For example, Anne, a young medical student who has only been with Patrick, a lawyer, for a few months, says, "It was last Thursday evening. We got really stuck. The bad feelings went on for days. It started when I was telling Patrick about my school assignments. How I was struggling. I just ended up totally freaking out. I got into that reactive anger thing that is my part of our cycle. Let's see. I remember his voice starting to go up into that distant lecture thing he does. And then he said that he couldn't help me if I was just going to get all obsessed and silly about it. That voice says danger for me. It turns a disagreement into some kind of crisis."

- As you think of a moment when your own raw spot is rubbed, what happens to your body? You might feel spacey, detached, hot, breathless, tight in the chest, very small, empty, shaky, tearful, cold, on fire. Does this body awareness help you give the experience a name?

Anne says, "I just get all agitated. I react like a cat having a hissy fit. Patrick would say I just get mad. That is what he sees. But deep down, that agitated feeling is more like shaky, like scared."

- What does your brain decide about the meaning of all this? What do you say to yourself when this happens?

Anne says, "In my head, I say to myself, 'He is judging me.' So

I kind of get mad with him. But that's not quite it. It's more like 'He's not with me here. I have to do this all on my own.' My need for support doesn't matter. That is scary."

- What do you do then? How do you move into action?

Anne says, "Oh, I yelled and shouted and told him he was a creep for not helping and that he could get lost. I didn't need his help anyway. Then I stewed silently for a few days. Feels like I am drinking poison when I do that. It's like I try to bypass my deeper feelings. And I decide that you can't trust anyone anyhow. People won't be there for you."

- See if you can tie all these elements together by filling in the blanks below:

In this incident, the trigger for my raw feeling was _____. **On the surface, I probably showed** _____. **But deep down, I just felt** _____. (Pick one of the basic negative emotions, e.g., *sadness, anger, shame, fear.*)

"The trigger is Patrick's tone," Anne says. "It's a judgment I hear. Dismissal. I probably just showed anger to him, but deep down I felt scared and alone. I longed for his reassurance, that it was okay to be worried about school, to be unsure and to ask for his support. The main message I got about our relationship was that I couldn't go to him and expect caring."

- In this situation, what is your understanding of your raw spot?

Anne says, "I just can't handle it when I let myself need him and tell him I need help and then he seems to refuse me. He even tells me I shouldn't want or need that. Inside I just feel scared."

- See if you can identify other moments when this raw spot gets rubbed.
- Is the raw spot you have described the only one for you in this relationship, or are there others? People can have more than one raw spot, but usually there is one main attachment cue that occurs in different situations.

FINDING THE SOURCE OF YOUR RAW SPOTS

- Think about your history. Did your raw spot arise in your relationship with your parents or your siblings, in another romantic relationship, even in your relationship with your peers as you grew up? Or is it a sensitivity that was born in your current relationship? Another way of thinking about this is to ask yourself, when you feel pain from your raw spot, are there ghosts standing behind your lover? Either way, can you pinpoint the hurtful response from a person in your past and see this as the beginning of the vulnerability?

Anne says, "My mom always told me that I'd never amount to much and that my sister was the only one who was going somewhere. I was on my own in that house. My dreams were irrelevant. When I met Patrick he seemed to believe in me. For the first time, I felt safe. But now when I perceive him as critical and dismissive when I need support, it brings up that old feeling of not being cared for. All that hurt comes alive in me again."

- Do you think your partner sees this raw vulnerability in you? Or does he just see the reactive surface feeling or the action response?

Anne says, "Oh no! I don't let him see that hurt place. That never occurs to me. He just sees me go berserk and gets ticked off."

- Can you guess at one of your partner's raw spots? Do you know exactly what you do to irritate it?

SHARING WITH YOUR PARTNER

We are naturally reluctant to confront our vulnerabilities. We live in a society that says we're supposed to be strong, to be *in*vulnerable. Our inclination is to ignore or deny our frailty. Rather than face her sadness and longings, Carey holds on to her anger. "Otherwise I guess I'd turn into this weak, sniveling little needy person," she observes. We fear, too, getting stuck in our own pain. Partners tell me, "If I let myself cry, maybe I won't be able to stop. Suppose I lose control and cry forever?" Or, "If I let myself feel these things, I will only be even more hurt. The hurt will take over and be unbearable."

We are perhaps even more reluctant to confess frailty to a lover. It will make us less attractive, we think. We recognize, too, that admitting vulnerability seems to put a powerful weapon in the hands of the person who can hurt us the most. Maybe our partner will take advantage of us. Our instinct is then to protect ourselves.

When we are the loved one, we are sometimes loath to acknowledge signs of distress in a partner, even when the signals are obvious. We are unsure what to do or feel, especially if we have no template for how to respond effectively. Some of us have never seen secure bonding in action. Or we don't want to acknowledge or get caught up in our lover's or, by implication, our own vulnerability. It always fascinates me that when a child cries we prioritize this signal. We respond. Our children don't threaten us, and we accept that they are vulnerable and need us. We see them in an attachment frame. But we have been taught not to see adults this way.

The truth is, we will never create a really strong, secure connection if we do not allow our partners to know us fully or if our lovers are unwilling to know us. My client David, a high-powered executive, understands. He says, "Well, in my head, I guess I can see that always staying away from these big emotions, from my sadness and fears, kind of twists things. If I am hunkered down, avoiding every sign of upset from someone and listening for negative stuff so I can run, it does kind of limit how we connect."

We want and need our lovers to respond to our hurt. But they can't do that if we don't show it. To love well requires courage — and trust. If you harbor real and substantial doubts about your lover's good intentions (for example, if you physically fear your partner), then of course it is best not to confide, and you probably should find a therapist or even reconsider being in the relationship.

When you're ready to share your vulnerability, start slow. There's no need to bare your soul. Often the way to begin is to talk about the act of sharing. "It's hard for me to share this..." is a great opening. It is easier then to go on to reveal a little of what you are sensitive about. Once you feel comfortable, you can talk more openly about the sources of the hurt.

This should open the door to your partner reciprocating and

revealing his or her raw spots and their origins. Such disclosures are often met with amazement. In my sessions with distressed couples, the first time one partner really owns and voices vulnerability, the other usually responds with shocked disbelief. The mate has only seen his or her lover's surface emotional responses, the ones that cloak and hide the deeper vulnerabilities.

Of course, simply recognizing and revealing our vulnerabilities won't make them disappear. They've become built-in alarms, signaling that our emotional connection with key loved ones is in danger, and they can't be easily turned off. This probably reflects how important attachment is to us; the data in a primary survival code aren't removed easily.

The key emotion here is fear, fear of the loss of connection. And our nervous system, as Joseph LeDoux at the Center for Neural Science at New York University points out, favors sustaining links between fear alarms and the amygdala, the part of the brain that maintains a record of emotional events. The entire system is designed to add on information, not to allow for easy removal. If we are to avoid danger, it's better to err on the side of false positives than false negatives. These links can be weakened, however, as you'll learn in the next chapter.

But even just talking about one's deepest fears and longings with a partner lifts an enormous burden. I ask David, "Do you feel more hurt or scared when you let yourself connect with those difficult feelings and talk about this stuff?" He laughs. He looks surprised. "No," he says, "funny, that. Once I got that there was nothing wrong with me, that these feelings are wired in, it wasn't so hard. In fact, it kind of helps to walk in there to that scary place and tie those feelings down. Once they make sense, it kind of takes the bite out of them." As I look at him, he literally seems more balanced, more present in his own skin, than when he was busy dodging his fears and his lady's "scary" messages. This reminds me of something my tango teacher, Francis, tells me: "When you are balanced on your feet, tuned in to yourself, then you can listen to me and move with me. Then we can move together."

Vincent and Jane found that out, too. Vincent moves away and goes silent when things get difficult with Jane. "What can I say?" Vincent tells me. "I don't know how I feel. I don't know what happens when she starts to go on about how our relationship isn't that happy. Jane wants to 'talk it out.' How can I talk about what I don't know? So I blank out, keep quiet, and let her talk. But she just gets more and more upset." We know that when our safe haven with a lover is threatened we get overwhelmed by a helpless sadness, shame about feelings of inadequacy or failure, and desperate fears of rejection, loss, and abandonment. The basic music here is panic.

As we discussed earlier, our attachment alarm system gets switched on by a sense of deprivation: we cannot gain emotional access to our loved one and so are deprived of needed attention, care, and soothing—the soothing that Harry Harlow called "contact comfort." The second switch is a sense of desertion. This sense may emerge from feeling emotionally abandoned ("There is no answer when I call, no response. I am in need and alone") or rejected ("I feel unwanted or criticized. I am not valued. I never come first"). Our brain responds to deprivation and desertion with intimations of helplessness.

Vincent has not been able to grasp and voice these emotions and ask for Jane's help in allaying them, so they have become reactive "hot" raw spots that signal instant peril and call up his protective distancing.

If Vincent goes through and unpacks the elements of his raw spot emotions, what happens? He begins to focus in on what happens for him just before the habitual "blank out" response that

Jane dreads so much. What is the specific *cue* for this "blank out"? Once he slows down and thinks a little, Vincent is able to tell me, "It's her face, I think. I see those brows come together. I see frustration, and I know I am a dead man. And if I tune in to how I feel in my *body* as I talk about this, I feel jittery, like there are butterflies in my stomach, like I'm failing a test in school. When I think about what *meaning* this has, it's that we are doomed. It's hopeless. Whatever it is that she wants, I obviously don't have it."

Jane says, "And all that adds up to feeling what exactly?" Vincent calmly tells her, "Well, *anxious* is a good word." And I notice that his face relaxes here. Even when the news isn't good, it feels good to be able to order your inner world. Then he continues, "So if the next question is how does this feeling *move* me, make me *act,* that is easy. I just do nothing. There is no way forward that won't make things worse. I just stay really still and wait for Jane's frustration to go away."

So now Vincent can describe the raw spot that gets touched in him and how it sparks off his inability to respond to his partner. He feels sad, anxious, and hopeless and tries to stay still with the faint hope that the problem will go away. He tells me that his emotions are "unknown territory" for him, so it's new for him to tune in to them. I compliment him on his courage and openness and I chat with him about the fact that his shut-down strategy works just fine in many situations. But in love relationships, it simply alarms his partner and writes the next part of the story with a negative slant. We talk about where this raw spot comes from. He remembers that he was very confident with Jane at the beginning of their love and was able to sometimes express his feelings. But through the years, they have grown apart. Their distance was exacerbated when Jane suffered a back injury that left her in such pain that she could not bear to be touched. Vincent then began to feel less confident and more and more wary of negative cues coming from Jane.

Jane responds to Vincent, "Well, until now I never saw your anxiety. Not for a minute. I just see someone who disappears on me, and then we go off into that demon thing. It's frustrating to talk to a blank, you know." But she is also able to tell Vincent that she is beginning to understand how it's hard for Vincent to put his emotional world together when Jane gets so mad so fast. Jane is then able to talk about her own raw spot and how she feels that Vincent has "deserted" her for the excitement of his acting career. When Vincent tells his partner, "I may be a big shot on the set but I still get totally freaked-out by your angry messages," he is dealing with his vulnerability in a whole new way. He is more present, more accessible.

Generally in love, sharing even negative emotions, provided they don't get out of hand, is more useful than emotional absence. Lack of response just fires up the primal panic of the other partner. As Jane tells Vincent, "I get so I just want to strike out at you to prove that you can't just turn me off." Vincent and Jane are now on the elevator going down into each other's emotional worlds. Changing the level of the conversation clarifies our own emotional responses and sends clearer messages about attachment needs to our partner. Then we offer our partner the best chance to lovingly respond to us.

Let's take some snapshots of Jane recognizing her raw spot and how Vincent helps her in the process. Vincent asks about the cue that triggers Jane's frustration. Jane considers, then says, "I am just waiting for it to happen now. Watching for you to 'forget' about our plans to spend time together." But then Jane gets sidetracked into all kinds of details about how this "habit" of Vincent's started. So Vincent suggests that Jane try to focus more on how she knows when this is happening. What is the cue and Jane's first take that something is wrong?

As Jane's eyes close for a moment, I hear the emotional down elevator begin to ding. "It's like Vincent looks distracted. He doesn't focus on me at all," Jane says, tearing up. If we quietly stay with our emotions, they often just develop, like a fuzzy image gradually getting clearer. Jane continues, "So I get this lump in my throat. I feel sad, I guess. My brain says, 'There he goes again. Off to be by himself with his book. And here I am, by myself.' We have this lovely life, lots of things. But I'm all by myself in it."

Vincent, who in previous sessions reacted by talking about how much he had given Jane and how Jane should be more independent anyway, is now listening attentively. I validate Jane's loneliness and her longing for loving contact with Vincent. Jane continues to listen to her feelings, reaching for the message in her emotions. Her voice goes quiet now and she murmurs, "I guess I decide then that Vincent doesn't need me. He is always there but just out of reach."

Now Jane's voice is even softer, and she turns more toward Vincent. "If I don't get mad, I feel a little shaky. I feel shaky and sad right now. And I don't want to look at you. I am thinking that you must just be put off by this. Your work is your real love. I try to accept that, but all this fear and sadness just turns into bitterness." She passes her hand over her face, and suddenly there is a defiant anger where just a moment before I saw sadness and vulnerability. "I don't want to be here. Maybe we'd be happier apart."

Oops! A flip into anger. It's hard to stay with our more profound feelings. But Vincent is brilliant. He sees that Jane is struggling and helps her out. "So under the frustration, you are telling me that you are shaky and sad. You want to know that it is not all work with me. Okay. I'm not good at talking about needs. I'm just learning now. But I really do need you to stop with the 'happier apart' bit. I'd just as soon be miserable *with* you, if that's okay?" Jane collapses in laughter.

They are on their way. They are learning to deal with raw spots in a way that brings them close.

PLAY AND PRACTICE

See if you can each think of a time when you shared a sense of vulnerability or a hurt feeling with your partner, and they responded in a way that helped you feel close. What was it that your partner did that really made a difference?

Now see if you can agree on a typical recent interaction where you both felt disconnected and ended up stuck for a while in a Demon Dialogue. In this situation, who turned up the emotional heat or tried to turn it down and avoid strong emotions? Come up with a phrase to describe how you usually deal with more vulnerable feelings in difficult interactions and share this with your partner. Some examples: I turn to stone, go icy, get into battle mode, run and hide.

If you habitually deal with your partner in this way, it is probably because it seemed like the only viable option for you in past love relationships. How did this way of dealing with emotion work to keep the most important relationships in your life intact? For example, did your approach help to get a loved one's attention or make him or her less obviously rejecting or unresponsive?

In the recent interaction with your partner, did you stay with surface reactive feelings or were you eventually able to explore and share deeper feelings? Share with your partner on a scale of 1 to 10 how hard it was for you to talk about your more vulnerable emotions. How is it to talk about them right now? Is there any way that your partner can help you share more of these feelings? Don't forget: we are all turkeys in the same emotional soup, trying to make sense of our emotional lives as they unfold, doing the best we can, and making mistakes.

When you think of this interaction where you got stuck as a couple, can you each identify the cue that had you lose your emotional balance and spin into raw insecurity? Try to report this to your partner as a fact. No blaming allowed here. Anne says, "It was that I was weeping and you were just silent." Patrick replies, "I saw your face. The hurt on your face. I felt so bad inside. I don't know what to do at those times."

There are only so many colors to the hurt that comes up in raw spots. See if you can use the words and phrases below to describe to your partner the softer feelings that came up in your recent interaction. If it is too hard to speak them, you can circle them on this page and show them to your partner.

In this incident, if I listen to my most vulnerable feelings, I felt: lonely, dismissed and unimportant, frustrated and helpless, on guard and uncomfortable, scared, hurt, hopeless, helpless, intimidated, threatened, panicked, rejected, like I don't matter, ignored, inadequate, shut out and alone, confused and lost, embarrassed, ashamed, blank, afraid, shocked, sad, forlorn, disappointed, isolated, let down, numb, humiliated, overwhelmed, small or insignificant, unwanted, vulnerable, worried.

Can you share this feeling with your partner? If this is too hard to do right now, can you instead share the worst catastrophic result of this kind of sharing that you can imagine? Can you tell your partner:

When I think of sharing my softest feelings with you here, it is hard to do. My worst fantasy is that what will happen is

_____.

Can you ask your partner how he or she feels when you share

this way? How does he or she help you feel safe enough to share? What impact do you both feel this kind of sharing has on the relationship?

Can you create together a new version of that difficult interaction you began this exercise with? Can you each, in turn, describe the basic way you moved in that dance (e.g., "I shut down and avoid"), and name the surface feelings that were obvious both of you (e.g., "I felt uncomfortable and on edge, like I wanted to get away. I just felt ticked off")?

I moved in the dance by _____ **and I felt**

_____ **.**

Now we can go a little deeper. Try to add the specific attachment cue that sparked the powerful emotions you circled in the list above. Perhaps it was something you thought you heard in your partner's voice. Then add the feelings that you picked from the list above to this description.

When I heard/saw _____ **, I just felt**

_____ **.**

Try to stay with simple, concrete language. Big, ambiguous words or labels can scramble this kind of conversation. If you get stuck, just share that with each other and try to go back to the last place that was clear and start again.

Now we can put all these elements together.

When we get stuck in our cycle and I _____

_____ *(use an action word, e.g.,* **push***),* **I feel** *(surface* *emotion).* **The emotional trigger for my sense of disconnection**

is when I see/sense/hear _____

(the attachment cue). **On a deeper level, I am feeling**

_____.

What did each of you just learn about the other person's raw spots? You rub these raw spots simply because you love each other.

In any interaction, even if both of you are paying attention, you cannot be tuned in all the time. Signals get missed, and there will be moments when attachment vulnerability takes center stage. The secret is to recognize and deal with raw spots in ways that don't get you into negative patterns. In the next chapter you will learn more about how to work with these attachment feelings to de-escalate the destructive patterns we fall into.

Conversation 3: Revisiting a Rocky Moment

"It's fixing mistakes that matters—even just the willingness to try again."

—*Deborah Blum*, Love at Goon Park

"A gentle answer turns away wrath, but a harsh word stirs up anger."

—*Proverbs 15:1*

Auntie Doris, a very large lady with peroxided hair and whiskers on her chin, was pouring rum over a huge Christmas pudding. She was also arguing with my almost inebriated uncle Sid. She turned to him and said, "We is getting into a doozy here. One of them dead-end doozy fights we does. You are half-drunk and I sure don't feel like no shiny Christmas fairy. Are we going to fight it out? I'll swing like always and you duck if you can. Both feel bad then. Do we need to do it? Or can we just start over?" Uncle Sid nodded solemnly, softly muttered, "No doozy, no ducking," and then, "Lovely pudding, Doris." He patted my aunt on the backside as he tottered into the other room.

I recall this little drama vividly because I knew that Uncle Sid was going to be Santa Claus that night and any "doozy" probably meant that I was going to be out of luck for presents. My Christmas was saved by a compliment and a pat. But now, all these years later, I see their interaction in another, less self-centered way. In a moment of conflict and disconnection, Uncle Sid and Aunt Doris were able to recognize a negative pattern, declare a cease-fire, and reestablish a warmer connection.

It was probably pretty easy for Doris and Sid to cut short their fight and change direction because, on most days, their relationship was a safe haven of loving responsiveness. We know that people who feel secure with their partner find it easier to do this. They can stand back and reflect on the process between them, and they can also own their part in that process. For distressed lovers, this is much harder to do. They are caught up in the emotional chaos at the surface of the relationship, in seeing each other as threats, as the enemy.

To reconnect, lovers have to be able to de-escalate the conflict and actively create a basic emotional safety. They need to be able to work *in concert* to curtail their negative dialogues and defuse their fundamental insecurities. They may not be as close as they crave to be, but they can now step on each other's toes and then turn and do damage control. They can have their differences and not careen helplessly into Demon Dialogues. They can rub each other's raw spots and not slide into anxious demands or numbing withdrawal. They can deal better with the disorienting ambiguity that their loved one, who is the solution to fear, can also suddenly become a source of fear. In short, they can hold on to their emotional balance a lot more often and a lot more easily. This creates a platform for repairing rifts in their relationship and creating a truly loving connection.

In this conversation, you'll see how to take charge of moments of emotional disconnection, or mis-attunements, as attachment theorists call them, and tip them away from dangerous escalation and toward safety and security. To learn how to do this, I have couples revisit rocky moments in their relationship and, applying what they have learned in Conversations 1 and 2 about the way they communicate and their attachment fears, figure out how to smooth the ground. In my practice, we replay turbulent big-bang arguments as well as quieter continual disconnections. I slow down the action, asking partners questions ("What just happened here?"), guiding them to key moments when insecurities spiraled, and showing them how they could have cut their conflict short and moved in a different and more positive direction.

When Claire and Peter fight they don't mess around. They qualify for the Oscar in marital spats. This time it starts with Claire pointing out that Peter could have done more to help her during her bout with hepatitis. "You just went on like nothing unusual was happening," she says. "When I suggested you do some chores, you were nasty and irritable. I don't know why I should put up with that."

"Put up with!" exclaims Peter. "Oh, you don't put up with anything as far as I can see. You make sure I suffer for every little error. Of course, it doesn't count that I was working like mad on a big project. I am just one big disappointment to you! You make that perfectly clear. You weren't so sick when you turned around and gave me a lecture on the proper care of bathrooms." He moves his chair as if he is about to leave.

Claire throws back her head and yells with frustration, "Little errors! Like the fact that you then frosted me out, wouldn't talk to me for two days. Is that what you mean? A creep is what you are." Peter, his face turned to the wall, comments dryly, "Yeah, well, this 'creep' doesn't feel like talking to the taskmaster." Expert demolition of love relationship is now in progress.

SEVEN TRANSFORMING CONVERSATIONS

DE-ESCALATING DISCONNECTION

Now let's replay this little drama and see how they can create a new kind of dance. Here are the steps that can set them on the path to greater harmony:

1. Stopping the Game

In their argument, Claire and Peter were totally ensnared in attack and defend: who is right, who is wrong; who is victim, who is villain. They are antagonists, using the pronouns *I* and *you* almost exclusively. "I am entitled to caring here," Claire belligerently declares. "And if you can't step up and do that, then I can do without you." The victory is a little hollow though, since this isn't what she wants. Peter quietly responds, "Can we stop this? Aren't we both defeated in this spiral?" He has changed the pronoun to *we*. Claire sighs. She changes her perspective and her tone. "Yes," she says thoughtfully. "This is the place we always go to. We get trapped here. We both want to prove our point, so we do that till we end up totally exhausted."

2. Claiming Your Own Moves

Claire complained that Peter tuned her out, that he didn't try to hear her point when things got hot between them. They name their moves together. Claire reflects, "It started with me complaining and getting very angry and you, what did you do?" "I got into defending myself, attacking back," he replies. Claire continues, "And then I lost it and accused more, really I was objecting to your withdrawing from me." Peter, calmer now, risks a quip. "You missed a bit. Then you threatened, remember? The bit about how you could do without me?"

Claire smiles. Together they come up with a short summary of their moves: Claire loses it while Peter plays impervious; Claire gets louder and threatens; Peter sees her as impossible and tries to escape. Peter laughs and says, "The impervious rock and the bossy broad. What a conversation. Well, I can see that talking to a rock must be frustrating." Claire follows his lead and acknowledges that her angry, critical tone probably triggers his defensiveness and contributes to his moving away after this kind of fight. They both agree that it is hard to be honest.

3. Claiming Your Own Feelings

Claire is now able to talk about her own feelings rather than, as she puts it, "focusing on Peter and disguising them in a big fat blame." She shares, "There is anger here. Part of me wants to tell you, 'All right, if I am so hard to live with, I'll show you. You can't get to me.' But I feel pretty shaken up inside. Do you know what I mean?" Peter murmurs, "Oh yes, I know the feeling." Clear admissions like these of the roiling surface emotions, of anger and confusion, are the beginning of being accessible to your lover. Sometimes it helps to make these admissions by using the language of "parts." This seems to help us acknowledge aspects of ourselves that we don't feel great about and also helps us express ambiguous feelings. Peter might say, "Yeah, part of me is numb. It's my automatic response when we get stuck like this. But I guess part of me is shaken up, too."

4. Owning How You Shape Your Partner's Feelings

We need to recognize how our usual ways of dealing with our emotions pull our partner off balance and turn on deeper attachment fears. If we are connected, my feelings naturally will affect yours. But seeing the impact we have on our loved ones can be very difficult in the moment when we are caught up in our own emotions, especially if fear is narrowing the lens. In the fight, things happen so fast and Claire is so upset that she really does not see how her critical tone and the phrase "put up with" hit Peter on a raw spot and trigger his defensiveness. In fact, she states that his behavior is all just about his personal flaws. He is a creep!

In the moment, Peter does not see how his statement about not wanting to talk to the "taskmaster" leads Claire to escalate into threats about how she can do without him. To really take control of Demon Dialogues and soothe raw spots, both partners have to own how they pull the other into negative spirals and actively create their own distress. Now Peter can do it. He says, "In these fights, I defend and then stop talking. That's when my shutting down gets you all freaked out, isn't it? You start to feel like I am not here with you. I do shut down. I don't know what else to do. I just want to stop hearing about how you are so angry with me."

5. Asking About Your Partner's Deeper Emotions

During the fight and the period of alienation that usually follows the fight, Peter and Claire are way too busy to tune in to each other's deeper emotions and recognize that they are touching each other's raw spots. But when they can look at the big picture and slow down a little, they can begin to be curious about the other's softer, underlying emotions, rather than just listening to their own hurts and fears and assuming the worst about their lover.

Now Peter turns to his wife and says, "I get into thinking that you are just out to put me down. But in these situations, you are not just mad, are you? Under all that noise and raging you are hurting, aren't you? I get that now. I know your sensitive spot is about being left and abandoned. I don't want you to hurt. I guess

I used to just see you as the righteous principal busy proving how useless I was as a spouse." When Claire asks Peter about the softer feelings that came up for him in this fight, he is able to look inside and pinpoint how the phrase "put up with" ignited all his fears of failure.

And Claire, remembering their raw spot conversations, adds, "So it's like whatever you do, I am going to be disappointed. And that feels so bad, you just want to give up and run." Peter agrees.

Of course, it really helps here if partners have been able to be very open about their raw spots in previous conversations, but assuming you have a big impact on your partner and being actively curious about his or her vulnerabilities helps too.

6. Sharing Your Own Deeper, Softer Emotions

Although voicing your deepest emotions, sometimes sadness and shame, but most often attachment fears, may be the most difficult step for you, it is also the most rewarding. It lets your partner see what's really at stake with you when you argue. So often we miss the attachment needs and fears that lie hidden in recurring battles about everyday issues. Unpacking moments of disconnection like this helps Claire explore her own feelings and risk sharing them with Peter. Claire takes a deep breath and says to Peter, "I am hurting but it's hard to tell you that. I have this sense of dread. I can feel it like a lump in my throat. If I stopped coming to you, trying to get your attention, you might just watch us drift off into more and more separateness. You might just watch our relationship fade out, go off the screen. And that is scary." Peter listens and nods. He tells her, "It helps me when you risk telling me that. I feel like I know you in a different way when you say things like that. Then you are more like me somehow. It's easier to feel close. And it makes me want to reassure you. I may zone out sometimes but I wouldn't let you drift away from me."

7. Standing Together

Taking the above steps forges a renewed and true partnership between lovers. Now a couple has common ground and common cause. They no longer see each other as adversaries, but as allies. They can take control of escalating negative conversations that feed their insecurities and face those insecurities together. Peter tells his wife, "I like it when we can stop and turn down the volume. I like it when we both agree that this conversation is too hard, that it is out of hand and scaring both of us. It feels very powerful for us to agree that we are not going to just get stuck the way we usually do. Even if we are not quite sure where we go next, this is a lot better. We don't have to get caught in that stuck place all the time."

All this doesn't mean that Peter and Claire feel really tuned in to and connected with each other in a secure bond. But it does mean that they know how to stop a rift before it widens into an unbridgeable abyss. They are aware of two crucial elements of de-escalation: first, that how a partner responds at a key moment of conflict and disconnection can be deeply painful and threatening to the other; and second, that a partner's negative reactions can be desperate attempts to deal with attachment fears.

Couples won't always be able to apply this knowledge and the specific steps of de-escalation every time they disconnect. It takes practice, going over an unsettling past encounter again and again until it makes coherent sense and, unlike the original event, can draw a possible supportive response from the other partner. Once couples have mastered this, they can begin to integrate these steps into the everyday rhythm of their relationship. When they argue or feel distanced from each other, they can take a step back and ask, "What's happening here?"

Even with practice, couples won't always be able to do this;

the heat may be too high at certain times. Normally, when my husband misses my signaling for connection, I can step back and reflect on our interaction. I am still balanced and can choose how to respond. But sometimes, I become so raw and vulnerable that the universe instantly narrows down into what feels like a life-and-death struggle. I react harshly to create some sense of control, to limit my helplessness. All my husband sees is my hostility. When I'm calmer, I search him out. "Hmm, can we just go back and do that again?" I ask. Then we press the mental rewind button and replay the incident.

By doing this sort of thing over and over, couples develop a fine sense of when they're stepping onto faulty territory. They feel the ground shaking sooner, and they are able to escape it faster. They develop confidence in their ability to take charge of moments of disconnection and so shape their most precious relationship. It will take a while, though, before most couples develop the abbreviated, almost shorthand, de-escalation language of Auntie Doris and Uncle Sid.

RECOGNIZING YOUR IMPACT ON YOUR PARTNER

Kerrie and Sal, an upwardly mobile, cool-looking couple who have been married for twenty years, provide a detailed example of the ins and outs of the de-escalation process. The only thing they agree on is that the last four years have been awful. They're continually getting into a negative spiral over the fact that Kerrie, busy with a new career after years of being a stay-at-home mom, is coming to bed much later than Sal. They have tried negotiating about this but deals get made and broken.

They have been sniping at each other for about ten minutes in my office. I ask if this sniping is the usual way they relate to each other. Kerrie, a tall, elegant woman dressed all in red, including her Italian leather briefcase, told me incisively, "No. Usually I just stay real calm. I prefer politeness. And I go off into my head when he does his aggressive thing. But just recently I have felt more and more cornered, so I just come out swinging to get him to back off for a while." I suggest that the mutual attack cycle I was seeing was then maybe a minor deviation from a pattern of Kerrie holding back emotionally and Sal trying to get some sense of control and engage his wife more. They agree.

Sal, an articulate corporate lawyer with a touch of gray at his temples, launches into a diatribe about how deprived he is in this marriage. He is offered no affection, attention, or sex. He is not listened to. He quotes the Bible to Kerrie, reminding her that a wife is supposed to honor her husband and respect him. Sal is mad, and he is entitled to be mad. Kerrie raises her eyes to heaven, crosses her legs, and begins to wave her red-high-heel-clad foot up and down. I point out how the pattern is occurring right here. He is getting mad and demanding attention. She is giving "You can't get to me" signals.

Kerrie breaks the tension here, openly laughing as she recognizes her own strategy. Sal then offers a few insights into how Kerrie's upbringing has damaged her ability to be empathetic and some advice about how she can address that, particularly about how she can be true to her role as a supportive Christian wife. Kerrie of course hears only that she is the problem and must work to fix her deficiencies. The tension returns.

We talk a little about attachment and love and how our primal programming dictates that when Sal feels disconnected, he will aggressively reach for Kerrie, and she, seeing only his anger, will defensively withdraw to try to calm herself and the relationship. This basic "It's not your inadequacies, it's how we are wired" message seems to help a lot.

This couple's pattern of "You will listen/You can't make me" has been in place throughout their marriage but became more powerful and toxic once Kerrie started her successful career as a real estate broker. Each began to fit their fights, rifts, and every-day hurts into the pattern. In an intellectual sense they understand that this pattern now runs their relationship and that they both end up being, as Sal puts it, "victims of the emotional spin cycle."

But it is clear that Kerrie sees Sal through a narrow prism of distrust. She does not really understand the impact her distancing has on him in the here and now and how it pulls him into their cycle. She doesn't truly see how she unwittingly shapes his response to her.

At one point she turns to him and asks sharply, "So why is it that you get so pushy then? Okay, so there is this wired-in need for contact and I can be kind of cool, that is my style. But I have been a pretty good wife to you. Don't you think so?" Sal nods solemnly, staring at the floor. "But like this morning, you just launched into this thing about how busy I am, how I didn't come to bed till late last night. This is a real issue with us. It comes up all the time. If I don't go to bed with you or come later than you want, you go ballistic. There is something I don't get here. It's like nothing matters except what you want in that moment, even if we have had time together during the day. And you even start beating me over the head with the Scriptures and how I am not doing my duty as a Christian wife!"

Sal starts into an elaborate set of points about how he is not really so demanding. Kerrie is off in some other world before he finishes his first rational sentence.

We need to change the level of dialogue here and get a little more emotional engagement. I ask him if he remembers how he feels, waiting for Kerrie to come to bed. He takes a moment and then retorts, "Oh, it's great waiting for your wife all the time, wondering if and when she is going to deign to turn up!" At first glance, he looks like just what he is, a man used to being in charge and having people jump to please him. But underneath the reactive anger, I hear the doubt about her "turning up" to be with him.

I ask, "What is happening to you right now as you speak about this? You sound angry, but there is a bitterness here behind the sarcasm. What does it feel like to be waiting for her, feeling that she does not care how long you wait or may not come at all?" I have pushed the down elevator button. After a long silence, he answers.

"It is bitter," Sal admits. "That's the word. So I turn it into straight anger. But what does it feel like to be waiting?" And suddenly his face crumples. "It's agonizing, that is what it is." He covers his eyes with his hand. "And I can't handle feeling that way."

Kerrie moves her head back in surprise. She furrows her brow in disbelief. In a soft voice, I ask Sal to help me understand the word *agonizing*. As he starts to speak, all traces of Sal, the terror of the courtroom, fade away. "It seems to me that I am always on the edge of Kerrie's life," he says. "I don't feel important to her at all. She fits me in the cracks in her busy schedule. We used to always be close before going to sleep. But now when she doesn't come to bed for hours, I just end up feeling pushed aside. If I try and talk about it, I just get dismissed. Lying in bed by myself, I go into feeling so unimportant. I don't know what happened here. It wasn't always like this. It feels like I am all by myself here."

I pick up on the words *by myself* and *pushed aside* and his sense of loss. I remember listening to him talk in the first session about his lonely childhood, mostly spent at expensive boarding schools, while his diplomat parents traveled the world. I remember him telling me that Kerrie is the only person he has ever felt close to or trusted and that finding her had opened a whole new world for

144

him. As I reflect these thoughts and his own words back to him, I legitimize his pain. Then I ask how it feels right now to talk about these difficult feelings of being pushed aside. He continues, "It feels sad and kind of hopeless."

I ask, "Is it like some part of you says that you have lost your place with her? You aren't sure how important you are to Kerrie anymore?" "Yes." Sal's voice is very quiet. "I don't know what to do, so I get mad and make lots of noise. That's what I did last night." I comment, "You are trying to get Kerrie's attention. But you feel hopeless. It is scary for most of us when we are unsure of our connection, when we cannot get the person we love to respond to us." "I don't want to feel this way," Sal adds. "But you are right. It is scary. And it's sad. Like last night, I lay there in the dark and my mind said, 'She is busy. She can take her time.' And here I am, I feel like some kind of pathetic fool." As he says this, his eyes fill with tears.

And this time when I look at Kerrie, her eyes are wide open. She has leaned forward toward her husband. I ask her how she is reacting to the things her husband is sharing. "I am really confused here," she says, and turning to Sal, she asks, "Are you serious? You are. You get mad at me because you don't feel important to me! You feel alone? I have never ever seen that in you. I have never imagined..." Her voice trails off for a few seconds. "I just see this belligerent man out to get me."

We talk about how strange it is for her to hear about how her being less accessible affects him and that he now lives in a world where he misses her and is scared that he has lost his place with her. "I really understand that you would see me that way," Sal goes on. "I do try to stay away from these feelings. It's easier to just get angry or sarcastic, so that is what you see."

Kerrie looks like she is struggling here. Her husband is not the man she thought he was. I cannot resist pointing out that Sal's anger pushes Kerrie away and as she distances they both step into a spiral of insecurity and isolation.

"I really didn't know you felt that way," says Kerrie. "I didn't know that my staying apart, trying to avoid all the angry exchanges...I never knew you were waiting for me and feeling so hurt. I didn't know how painful that was for you. That it mattered to you so much that I come to bed. When we fight it sounds like it is all about how you want more sex." Now her face and her voice have softened. Then in an amazed whisper she says, "I didn't know I mattered that much to you. I just thought you wanted to be in control."

I asked her if she could see that her distancing to avoid Sal's anger switched on his attachment fears, touched him on a raw spot, and triggered his anger, pulling him into the spiral of distress.

"Yes, I see that," she acknowledges. "I guess that is why he can't just decide to stop being so angry, even when we have discussed it and how I don't like it. I guess I'm hearing how my staying distant and busy sparks all those feelings in him. And then his anger is too much for me and I run away more. And then we are stuck." She turns to Sal. "But I...I never knew you were waiting alone in the dark for me. I never got that I had that impact on you. I just didn't see that. That you might be feeling alone in the dark."

Kerrie and Sal are really beginning to see the power they have over each other on an emotional attachment level. They can begin to grasp how each of them triggers the other's fears and keeps their Protest Polka going. He protests her distance. She protests his aggressive ways of trying to connect with her. Sal and Kerrie start to see, in a concrete way, how they hook each other into their negative patterns.

RECOGNIZING HOW FEAR
DRIVES YOUR PARTNER

In a different session, Kerrie and Sal are revisiting another rocky moment, this time when Kerrie had asked Sal for his opinion about the dress she was planning on wearing to a family wedding where she felt very much like an outsider. Kerrie had been angling for support from him, but he missed the cue. Instead he became vaguely critical, implying that she already knew he disliked this dress and that his opinion, or what he found attractive, didn't matter anyway. This had rapidly escalated into an argument about the quality of their sex life. Enter the old dance of Kerrie shutting down and avoiding a more and more irate Sal. But this time, knowing their cycle, they replayed the argument and picked up insights about how their mutual attachment fears keep them desperate and distant.

"Well, you did ask me about your dress," Sal says. " 'Does it work?' you asked. I gave my opinion, that's all." Kerrie turns her face to the window. She struggles to keep from crying. When I ask her what is happening, she turns and lunges at Sal. "Yes, I asked you. And you know it is a big issue for me, how I look in that group. I don't feel safe there. You could have just said something supportive. But no. I get snarky comments about how I am not interested in pleasing you. I asked, didn't I? I wanted *support,* not a whole bunch of criticism. What do you want from me? I can't do anything right here. This is one of these moments when I just want out of here, like 'Beam me up, Scotty!' And in the end it's always all about the fact that you want more sex." She turns her whole body away from him and stares pointedly at the opposite wall.

"You are right," he answers in an intense clipped voice. "You did ask. But since when did my opinion really make a difference here? You will wear what you want. What I want is irrelevant. And yes, it doesn't help that you are so cold with me in bed. But that is just part of all this. It's not just that I want more sex."

I invite Sal and Kerrie to pause here and press replay. What would a movie camera have seen in the last few minutes? I knew they could do this. I had seen them exit from their cycle this way only the week before. Sal smiles and leans back in his chair. Then he paints a picture of how they get stuck. "Yeah, okay. Here comes the push–step back thing again. I guess this isn't really about the dress, is it? And it's not even about sex."

I love that he says this. He understands that they are missing the point—the attachment feelings and needs that drive their drama. He sees the negative spiral as it is happening. Now he needs to take a step out of his critical stance. He turns to Kerrie. "I am getting kind of pushy here, I guess. I think I am still smarting from last night. If you remember, I suggested that we cuddle a little in the study. But you were tired." He pauses, looks down. "That happens a lot."

Sal has just changed the level of the conversation in a powerful way. He turns his attention to his own reality and invites her in. Now I wait to see how Kerrie will react. Will she stay distant and unavailable? Will she take this opportunity to smack him with a comment like, "Oh, so *you* are smarting. Well, listen up, buddy..."? Or will she respond to his attempt to escape their usual loop of anxious pursuit and injured withdrawal?

Kerrie takes a deep breath and lets it out. She speaks softly. "Right. This is about you reaching for me and me being tired. So then you get all hurt and bitter and now this is all about how I don't really value your opinion and didn't come to snuggle."

She puts the attachment story together, the plot behind the drama of the moment, identifying the emotional issue in their struggle. She continues, "I did want your advice about the dress, but you got stuck in all this anger, is that it? Hey, we have been here a thousand times before. We have gone over this. Why can't we just stop this?"

I can't resist pointing out that they are doing just that right now. They are seeing the bigger pattern rather than narrowing in on and reacting to the other's negative moves. Kerrie now takes another step toward creating more safety. She leans toward Sal. "Well, I guess I am still learning about your raw spots. I can see that you might have felt that I was cold last night. I was just so exhausted. I kind of chickened out of trying to explain that to you. I knew you wanted to be close. Maybe I was scared we would get into this stuff. So I just zoned out."

"Was it one of those times we have talked about," Sal asks, "when you think that nothing but a two-hour hot lovemaking session will please me? One of those times when you get that feeling of pressure, that you just can't meet my demands?"

This response just amazes me. Once they have slowed down their Demon Dialogue, the space opens up for curiosity, for reaching for the other's reality. Sal isn't just trying to sort out his own feelings; he is putting himself in her shoes and embracing her feelings.

Kerrie is obviously touched by this, and I notice that she reaches down and takes off her red high heels, her "snippy shoes," as she called them. Those shoes announce to the world that she is strong and to be reckoned with. She moves her chair closer. "Yup, I did feel that pressure. And I guess I did just zone out. But we know now that that kind of moment is really loaded for you, yes? Then you go for me and I withdraw more. That is how it usually goes."

There is a new music in the room. Each partner is looking down at their dance and naming their steps in it. But more than this, they are seeing exactly how they pull each other in. But do they really see the impact and how this cycle traps them both in isolation and fear? I comment, "And that is so hard for both of you. You both end up so alone."

"Yes," says Sal, "then I go into that sad and scary place, I guess. That is kind of what I was trying to say in my angry comments. 'Why was she asking my opinion, like what I say matters to her anyway?' Once that feeling comes up..." He goes still and silent.

"That is when you get afraid, unsure of how important you are to Kerrie," I point out. "And that is the way it is for all of us. That fear is just part of loving. But it's hard to sit with and recognize, easier to just move into mad." Kerrie is now totally focused on her husband, speaking in a quiet, matter-of-fact voice. "So that fear just kind of drives you into that dark place..." "Yes," Sal answers, "and I just flip into trying to deal with it, fix it. I just get mad."

"And then, Sal, your anger just turns on Kerrie's own fears," I note. "Right," Kerrie agrees. "That's where I go into my funk about how I cannot ever please this man. I am just not enough. The silly thing is that I like cuddling on the couch. I like our lovemaking. We both get triggered and get done in by this silly dance."

I point out that they have just caught the demon in the dialogue and wrestled it to the ground. They have dealt with their fears in a different way, a way that soothes their anxieties, rather than puts them through the roof. But Sal has one more very important thing to say. He seems to have grown bigger in his chair, as if he suddenly finds himself on more solid ground. "We are starting to get a handle on this. If we can see where we get stuck and if we can do something about these raw places and how they are triggered, why, we might even be able to be" — he pauses and searches for the right words—"well...more together even," he finishes and smiles. Kerrie laughs and reaches for his hand.

What did we just see Sal and Kerrie do here in these last two conversations?

- They have started to go beyond just doing the steps in their negative dance and to see the pattern it is creating as it occurs and begins to take over their relationship.
- They are acknowledging their own steps in this dance.
- They have begun to see how these steps trigger each other into the primal program of attachment needs and fears.
- They are starting to grasp the incredible impact they have on each other.
- They are understanding, voicing, and sharing the hurt of rejection and fears.

All this means that they have the ability to de-escalate conflicts. But more than that, every time they do this, they are creating a platform of safety on which they can stand to manage the deep emotions that are part of love.

Now that you see how de-escalation works, it's time for you to make it work for your relationship.

PLAY AND PRACTICE

1. With your partner, pick a brief, unsettling (but not really difficult) incident from your relationship, one that happened in the past two or three weeks, and write down a simple description of what happened as seen by a fly on the wall. Hopefully you can both agree on this description. Now write out in a plain sequence the moves you made in that incident. How did your moves link

up with and pull out the moves your partner made? Compare notes and come up with a joint version you can agree on. Keep it simple and descriptive.

2. Add in the feelings you both had and how each of you helped to create this emotional response in your partner. Share your responses and agree on a joint version. Now ask about the deeper, softer feelings that might have been happening there for your partner. Be curious. Being curious gives you valuable information. If your partner has a hard time accessing his or her softer feelings, see if you can guess using your sense of your partner's raw spots as a guide. Confirm or revise with your partner what his or her deeper feelings were.

3. Using the information above, see if you can together describe or write out what you might have said to each other at the end of this incident, if you had been able to stand together and complete it in a way that left you both feeling safe. What would that have been like for you? How would you have felt about each other, your relationship?

4. Try the previous three practice questions with a difficult, unresolved incident. If you get stuck, just acknowledge that a certain part of the exercise is hard for you. If your partner finds the exercise hard, ask if there is any way you can help him or her right at this moment. Sometimes a little comfort is all people need to be able to stay with this task.

5. If you knew that you could take moments of conflict or disconnection and defuse or review them in this way, what impact would this have on your relationship in general? Share this with your partner.

With what you've learned in the first three conversations, you now have the ability to de-escalate conflicts. That is a great deal. But to really have a strong, loving, healthy relationship, you must be able not just to curtail negative patterns that generate attachment insecurities, to see and accept each other's attachment protests, but also to create powerful positive conversations that foster being accessible, responsive, and engaged with each other. You'll do just that in the following conversations.

Conversation 4: Hold Me Tight — Engaging and Connecting

"When someone loves you, the way they say your name is different. You just know that your name is safe in their mouth."

—Billy, age four, defining love,
as reported on the Internet

"Oh, love me—and right now!—hold me tight! Just the way you promised. Now comfort me so I can live, really live; your revelation is the tune I dance to."

—Psalm 119:76–77

There is one image of love that Hollywood has right. That is the moment when two people gaze deeply into each other's eyes, move slowly into each other's arms, and begin dancing together in perfect synchrony. We know instantly that these two people matter to each other, that they are connected.

These moments on-screen almost invariably signal that a couple is in the intoxicating early days of a romance. Rarely are they used to illustrate a more mature stage of love. And that's where

Hollywood gets it wrong. For such moments of intense responsiveness and engagement are vital throughout a relationship. Indeed, they are the hallmarks of happy, secure couples.

Almost all of us are naturally and spontaneously tuned in to our partner when we are falling in love. We are hyperaware of each other and exquisitely sensitive to our partner's every action and word, every expression of feeling. But with time, many of us become less attentive, more complacent, and even jaded with our partner. Our emotional antennas get jammed, or maybe our partner's signals get weaker.

To build and sustain a secure bond, we need to be able to tune in to our loved one as strongly as we did before. How do we do this? By deliberately creating moments of engagement and connection. In this conversation, you'll take the first step toward doing that, and subsequent conversations will show you how to actively further a sense of closeness so you'll be able to deliberately create your own truly significant bonding moments that go way beyond any image Hollywood offers.

The Hold Me Tight conversation builds on the sense of safety you and your partner have started to produce as a result of Conversations 1, 2, and 3, which taught you how to halt or contain *negative* patterns of interacting with your partner as well as to mark and name at least one of the deeper feelings that come up in negative cycles and moments of disconnection. Effectively seeking connection and responding supportively is hard without a basic platform of safety. In this conversation, you'll learn how to generate *positive* patterns of reaching for and responding to your loved one. In effect, you'll be learning how to speak the language of attachment.

Think of it this way: If Conversations 1, 2, and 3 are a little like going for a walk in the park together, then Conversation 4 is like dancing the tango. It's a new level of emotional engagement.

All of the previous conversations are preparation for this one, and all the upcoming dialogues hinge upon a couple's ability to create this one. A Hold Me Tight conversation is the ultimate bridge spanning the space between two solitudes.

Stepping aside from our usual ways of protecting ourselves and acknowledging our deepest needs can be hard, even painful. The reason for taking the risk is simple. If we don't learn to let our partner really see our attachment needs in an open, authentic way, the chances of getting these needs met are minuscule. We have to send the signal loud and clear for our partner to get the message.

If we have generally found others to be safe havens and have a secure bond with our partner, then it is easier for us to keep our emotional balance when we feel vulnerable, connect with our deepest feelings, and voice the attachment longing that is always part of us. If we are feeling unsure of our relationship, it is harder to trust our longings and risk being vulnerable. In that situation, some of us try to stay in control of our emotions at all costs, to hide them, and instead demand what we need. Others deny that the emotions and needs even exist. But they are there. As the perceptive but murderous villain of the movie *In the Cut* murmurs to Meg Ryan, the heroine who avoids closeness with others, "You want it so much, it hurts."

Conversation 4 has two parts. The first—What Am I Most Afraid Of?—requires further exploring and elaborating on the deeper feelings you tapped into in the previous conversations. In those dialogues, you were taking the elevator down into your emotions. To discover your attachment priorities, you must now go all the way to the ground floor.

The second part—What Do I Need Most from You?—is crucial, the tipping-point encounter in EFT. It involves being able to openly and coherently speak your needs in a way that invites your partner into a new dialogue marked by accessibility, responsiveness, and engagement, an A.R.E. conversation.

There is a sense in which Christian partners may have an advantage in this conversation. Prayer is a place where we learn to open our hearts and risk showing our deepest vulnerabilities to the one we love: God. From our most fragile places, we then turn to God, show Him our hearts and our longings. As He draws near to us, we are comforted by this connection and held in His love. For Christian partners, reaching from a place of doubt and vulnerability is a well-worn and valued path to connection with God. This is the same path that can lead us to secure connection with our life mate. Timothy Keller, in his recent book *Prayer: Experiencing Awe and Intimacy with God,* reminds us that when we pray, at best we seek not only to get more blessings from Him, but also a way to get more of God Himself and to draw closer to Him. Our ability to reach for God in a heartfelt way is a model for how to open up to and reach for our partner.

A COUPLE IN TROUBLE

Charlie and Kyoko are a young immigrant couple who come from an Asian culture where the husband is very much the head of the household and emotional expression is frowned upon. Kyoko had been placed on antidepressant medication by her doctor when she became "hysterical" after being refused entry to a university graduate program. Charlie tried to help her by offering advice. But it consisted largely of telling her how unsuited she was to any of her career choices. Needless to say, that didn't help. This is where they are when they come to see me.

Charlie and Kyoko easily identify their Demon Dialogue: he stays emotionally removed and delivers logical lectures full of shoulds, while she dissolves into angry tirades and teary hopelessness. After a few sessions, they can touch on their raw spots, although it is still hard for them to really explore their sensitivities. Kyoko, small, exotic, and speaking very fast in her lilting English, confides that her childhood was full of rigid rules and that she was shunned by her family until she complied with these rules.

I frame it that Kyoko is now allergic to being told how she "should" be and feels punished when Charlie is distant. She tries to explain to Charlie. "It is like I am already on the floor, feeling small, and you come in to take charge. You tell me, 'Yes, you should feel small, now do this and do that.' So I fight you. Your advice just puts me down. I get hurt and angry. Then you give me more rules about not being angry. And I am alone. With no comfort." She allows that her husband is "incredible" in many ways. He is responsible and conscientious, and she respects him very much. But their fights and his physical and emotional distancing are "driving me crazy. I think you call it nuts. I only get more depressed."

Charlie, a physics whiz, has a very hard time taking this in at first. His idea of love has been to protect his wife from her own "upset" and to "guide her" in this new North American world. As to his own emotions, he admits at one point that his heart is "shattered" by Kyoko's angry "explosions." But mostly he minimizes his hurt and focuses on his wife's "problems."

Charlie slowly moves from criticizing Kyoko's reactions ("Kyoko has a psychological problem; she is like the weather") into discussing his own reactions ("I do protect myself. I can't deal with her unreasonable outbursts. We never spoke like that at home. That kind of talking is foreign to me") and finally into exploring his own emotions and motives ("I get overwhelmed here. So I give her advice, formulas to stop her being so angry").

Kyoko becomes clearer on how she "pushes" to get her point across and stop Charlie from moving away from her. She acknowledges her hurt at Charlie's censure, and goes on to reveal that she feels "discarded" since Charlie has pulled away from making love or any physical contact. The words *overwhelmed* and *discarded* seem to echo around my office. By the end of the hour, Charlie concludes, "I guess my advice and my logic wind up hurting Kyoko, and make her feel small. Trying to push her feelings aside just makes everything worse." Kyoko, in turn, says she now sees how Charlie's detachment and logic are a cover for his discomfort with her "upset."

They move on to a Revisiting a Rocky Moment conversation. The moment occurred when Charlie had been away visiting a friend and Kyoko, feeling lonely, had called him. Although he had heard the emotion in her voice, Charlie cut her off, saying he was busy and had to hang up. But when they replay that moment, they are able to hash out what happened. Kyoko discloses how she had been thinking about their relationship problems and had this sudden urge to call to get some reassurance. Charlie explains how, once he heard the emotional intensity in her voice, he had become "anxious" and had simply run away from the explosion that he feared was coming. Kyoko then concedes that she does indeed get "crazy upset" when Charlie distances and that she can see how this might confuse and overwhelm him. They both feel good that they can now share how they sometimes "lose their way" in their marriage and get stuck in complaining about each other.

It is time now for Charlie and Kyoko to move into Conversation 4 and risk acknowledging their deeper needs.

WHAT AM I MOST AFRAID OF?

This part of the conversation is aimed at gaining greater emotional clarity. I ask Charlie how Kyoko can help him get the safe, loving feeling they had once experienced back into their relationship. "Well,

I wouldn't get anxious and lecture her, if she would just quit exploding," he replies. I then invite him to talk about himself and his feelings. He tells me that he is not sure where to begin. This world of feelings is "foreign" to him. But he does now see, and he gives me a big smile here, that maybe there is a "logic" to being able to listen to feelings and share them. He turns to Kyoko and tells her that he does see her as more predictable, as "safer," now that he understands that she feels pushed away and punished by his advice giving. But he is not sure how to really get into his own *deeper* feelings here.

I ask him how he identified his feelings in the previous conversations. Where did he start? He is a very clever man, and he tells me what we therapists often take years to learn. He says, "Oh, I look first at what blocks me, what makes it hard to focus on feelings. I look at that moment when I stay away from my feelings and go off into my head sorting for formulas." I agree, and Kyoko helpfully joins in, telling him, "It must be like me learning English. If feelings are a foreign language for you, it's hard to feel comfortable. We try to stay away from what is strange. Strange is scary." Charlie laughs and replies to his wife, "Yes. I go away from feelings because they are strange. I don't feel in control. It is easier to make up an improvement program for you."

He turns to me and makes a second point. "In our best conversations, it helped to take what you call 'handles' and mull them over." Handles are descriptive images, words, and phrases that open the door into your innermost feelings and vulnerabilities, your emotional reality. Kyoko and I remind Charlie of some of the handles he has used to describe his reactions to Kyoko: *a shattered heart, overwhelmed, anxious, freaking, and fleeing.* Charlie nods his head but looks doubtful. "It's hard for me to slow down and stay with those handles," he whispers. "Even just to let myself explore. To listen for the cues that spark my feelings and thoughts. I don't know where this will go. I trust thinking more. But maybe it's not enough here." I nod and ask him what handle holds his attention right now. He says quietly, "Oh, that is obvious. I go off in my head when I cannot stand the disquietude, the foreboding."

Kyoko and I both lean back a little. "What does *disquietude*, this big abstract term, have to do with anything?" I wonder aloud. Then Kyoko chimes in. She has learned from previous conversations to unpack big abstract words like this so that they don't hijack the conversation. She leans forward and asks, "Charlie, is it like you stay away from your emotions and from mine because of big anxieties?" Charlie stares at the floor and nods slowly.

He sighs. "I just want to keep everything under control, so I guess there are big anxieties. I do get overwhelmed when Kyoko gets so upset with me, and then I start to feel lost. I don't know what to do." At this point, I want to go to the root of a partner's fears, so I ask, "And what is the biggest catastrophe that could happen here, Charlie? What are you most afraid of?" But I don't need to ask. Charlie goes there by himself.

"The word *shattered* keeps coming up in my head," he says. "If I stay and listen to Kyoko's upset, I will be shattered. I will lose control. The explosion will kill us." Charlie has said a lot here. We need to mine this moment a little. So I try to take it piece by piece, and help Charlie expand on it. It's always best to start with identifying the emotion.

I ask, "So, Charlie, the basic emotion I hear in this is fear. Is that right?" He nods solemnly. "I feel it right here," he says, and pats his chest. So I continue, "But what does this fear tell you? What are the terrible ifs here? Maybe if you don't stay totally cool, she will go even more out of control? Maybe, you will hear that she wants something that you don't know how to give her? If you stay open and hear that your wife hurts, then you haven't been the perfect husband you should be? Then you might lose her completely?"

Charlie nods vigorously. "Yes, all of it. All of it. I have tried so hard. But what I know how to do doesn't work. The more I try to get her to be reasonable, the worse it gets. So I feel helpless. Really helpless. I am good at everything I do. I follow the rules. But now..." He spreads his hands in a gesture of defeat.

Don't we all want the one or two infallible rules for how to love and be loved? But love is improvisation. And Charlie cuts off his best guide, his and his lady's emotions.

I ask him, "Listening now to this sense of fear and helplessness, what is the main threat, the most frightening message? Can you tell Kyoko?" He sits bolt upright and shouts out, "I don't know how to do this. I can't figure it out." He turns more toward Kyoko and continues, "I don't know how to deal with it when you're not happy with me. And you can explode anytime. I never feel sure of myself with you. And I need that. I feel very sad. We came across the world together. If I don't have you..." He weeps. Kyoko weeps with him.

What has happened here? Charlie has moved into and laid out the deeper emotions that speak to his need for a safe emotional connection with his wife. He is shaping a coherent attachment message out of his emotional turmoil. As I look at him, he is actually smiling at me. He does not seem helpless or overwhelmed. I ask him, "How are you doing, Charlie, having said all this?" "So strange," he replies. "It feels good now, to be able to say these things. I did not shatter. Kyoko is still here, and I feel stronger somehow." When we examine and make sense, or as I put it, "order and distill" our experience, no matter how painful the process, there is a sense of relief and empowerment.

This is a new, more accessible Charlie. How Kyoko responds at this point is critical. Too often in unhappy relationships, when one person takes a risk and opens up, the other partner doesn't see or is afraid to trust the revelation. I have heard partners dismiss their lover's new steps toward them with everything from "That's ridiculous" to some version of "So let's see you prove it." Then they spin back into their Demon Dialogue.

The truth is, no one takes the risk of being rebuffed by disclosing, like Charlie has, unless the other person really matters. And sometimes disclosing partners have to be willing to hang in there and keep repeating their message until their loved one gets used to seeing them in a new way. Couples stuck in a Demon Dialogue can also get moving again by doubling back through Conversations 1, 2, and 3.

Happily for Charlie and Kyoko, she responds in a supportive way to his overture. "I understand much more now how you go into that cold rational place and end up giving me instructions," she says. "I never knew I mattered enough to you to hurt you that much. I respect you for doing this kind of sharing. It makes me feel closer to you." Charlie simply grins at her and gives his chair a twirl or two.

The ability to attend to our partner's deeper disclosures is the beginning of mutual responsiveness and engagement. The word *attend* comes from the Latin *ad tendere,* which means to reach toward. Kyoko has reached toward Charlie.

Now it's Kyoko's turn to unpack her emotions and see if Charlie can attend to her. She goes back to the rocky moment, and tells Charlie, "When you came home, I told you I was upset and you said, 'Now don't get all crazy on me,' that if my outbursts didn't stop you might need to leave. This was the bottom for me. I cannot always be calm and logical." Charlie looks uncomfortable and mutters "Sorry" under his breath. He admits that he doesn't really understand her hurt at these times.

Kyoko hits the emotional elevator button and goes down a

few more floors. She begins, "I feel so very sad, we cannot seem to come together anymore." Charlie nods his head and responds, "But you should not be, because we are working on our relationship." He catches himself, shakes his head, and continues, "I think I will try to learn about your hurt. What was the worst moment, the worst feeling for you?" This was a very good question, and by asking it, Charlie helped Kyoko get to the heart of the matter.

But Kyoko cannot answer. She sits silently, and large tears roll down her face. Charlie pats her knee. "I only say you are crazy because I get scared of the bad feelings between us," he whispers. Kyoko tells him, "The worst moments were when you put the phone down, and later when you said you would leave. I was so 'unreasonable,' you said."

Charlie, now very worried, says, "I don't know how to make this better. What shall I do?" he asks, turning to me. "To make it better, Kyoko needs to feel that you are here with her," I reply. "To let her know you care about her pain." He opens his eyes wide in disbelief. She continues, "If I am sad or scared or upset with you, you just turn off. You don't comfort me. And now you don't make love or hold me either. Just when I need you, you go off in your disapproval. You turn away and discard me. I am not the wife you want."

It is hard to listen to Kyoko's outpouring of rejection and abandonment. No wonder she sometimes loses her balance and gets stuck in angry protests or in depression. But here she is clear and precise. "It kills me when you pass over me, turn to your rules. I have never been more alone." Now she looks up directly at him. "Charlie, you are not there for me, with me. So I panic. Do you hear me?"

He reaches for her hands and holds them in his. He nods again and again. "Yes, yes, yes." Very quietly, Charlie tells her,

"This is sad, to hear this. I am sad." And he is. His emotional presence is as tangible as the chair he sits on. Kyoko has turned her clear awareness of her deeper emotions into a clear attachment signal to her lover. She has distilled her deepest pain, the primal code of loss and panic that sounds when our loved one is not there for us, and he has heard her.

Both partners have connected with their own emotional realities and opened up to each other.

PLAY AND PRACTICE

Charlie does a number of things that make a real difference in how he connects with and shares his deeper emotions. See if you can recall or go back and find examples of the following:

- Charlie starts to examine the present moment and how hard it is to connect with his feelings. What's blocking him from saying how he feels?
- Charlie identifies some handles from previous conversations and holds the images, phrases, or feelings up to the light. When he looks at them closely, he can see that they are really descriptions of fear, shame, or sadness and loss.
- Charlie identifies Terrible Ifs, the worst things that might happen if he acknowledges his partner's feelings. Listing catastrophic consequences uncovers his worst core fears: that he'll be helpless and alone. This is a key part of Conversation 4.
- Charlie reveals his fears to his wife and reflects on what it is like to share these deep feelings with her.

Now look at Kyoko's revelations and try to answer these questions:

- What was the worst moment for Kyoko?
- What is the catastrophic conclusion she comes to?
- Name four things that Charlie does when Kyoko is sad and scared that heighten her attachment fears. Kyoko describes them in simple action words.
- What are Kyoko's two core emotions?

Go back to a rocky moment in your current relationship and find your own handles and write them down. Ask your partner to do the same. Then sit with your partner. Which one of you is the more withdrawn? This partner begins the conversation. This is because it is harder for more actively protesting partners, who are usually more tuned in to their hurts and fears, to begin reaching out without some sign of engagement from their more reserved lover. If you are the more reserved partner, follow in Charlie's steps and tune in to your core fears, share them, and say what it feels like to reveal them.

If you are the listening partner, respond by saying what it was like to hear the disclosures. Was it easy or hard to understand the message? If it was hard, at what point did it become difficult to listen? What feeling came up then? Examine the feelings together.

Now the listening partner repeats the disclosure process.

This conversation will be especially beneficial for distressed couples, but it is also valuable to those in secure relationships. We all have attachment fears, even if they have no edge or urgency at the moment.

Above all, keep in mind that this is a sensitive conversation; you are both exposing your deepest vulnerability. You each must respect the risk the other is taking. Remember, the two of you are taking this step because you are special to each other and are trying to create a very special kind of bond between you.

WHAT DO I NEED MOST FROM YOU?

Being able to declare our core attachment fears naturally leads to a recognition of our primary attachment needs. Fear and longing are two sides of the same coin.

The second part of Conversation 4 involves directly stating the attachment needs that *right now* only your partner can satisfy.

This conversation can be smooth and easy or it can be fraught with doubt. It is one thing to acknowledge and accept your own emotional reality, but another to open it up to your partner. This is a great leap for those of us who have had little experience of real safety with others. So why do it? Because we long for connection, and remaining defended and isolated is a sad and empty way to live. The author Anaïs Nin expresses the idea beautifully: "And the day came when the risk to remain tight in the bud was more painful than the risk it took to blossom."

Rosemary, a client, puts it another way. In Canada, we play hockey. Sometimes we even think of life as a hockey game! Rosemary, an avid player, turns to her partner, Andre, and tells him, "I am wearing this face mask. And I have to drop it if I want you to understand what I need and ask you for what I want. Some part of me says that opening up like that is just asking to be smashed in the face like I was in that hockey game last month. Keeping the mask up is not because I don't love you or that you are a bad partner. It's because I always play defense. To turn and ask, that is a whole new position. That is scary. But if I'm honest, I'm empty behind the mask. Can't win the game that way either."

Let's return to Charlie and Kyoko and see how they wend their way through this crucial part of Conversation 4. I prompt Charlie, "What do you need from Kyoko right now to feel more, as you put it, 'safe and sure'? What do you long for, Charlie? Can you tell Kyoko exactly what you need from her?" He considers for a moment, then turns toward her and begins. "I need to know that when I am not the perfect husband and get confused, do not know what to do, you still want to be with me. Maybe that you want me even if you are upset. Even if I get overwhelmed and make mistakes, hurt your feelings. I need to know you will not leave me. When you are depressed or very mad, it seems like you have already gone. Yes, this is right. I have said it right." And then, as if suddenly realizing the risk he has taken, he turns away and nervously rubs his knees. He says quietly, "This is very hard for me to ask. I have never asked anyone for such a thing."

The obvious emotion on Charlie's face moves Kyoko. She responds softly but firmly, "Charlie, I am here with you. That is all I want, to be with you. I do not need a perfect husband. If we can talk like this, we can be close again. That is all I have ever wanted." Charlie looks relieved and a little dazed. He giggles and says, "Oh, now that is good, that is very reasonable indeed." She giggles with him.

When it is Kyoko's turn to state her needs, she starts by discussing how she now knows that her desire for reassurance and comfort is "proper, even natural." This helps her think about what she needs from Charlie. But then she veers off course. Looking at the ceiling, she says, "I think I want him to ..." I stop her, and ask her to listen to her deepest feelings, turn her chair toward Charlie, and look at and speak directly to him.

Kyoko turns to Charlie and takes a deep breath. "I want you to accept that I am more emotional than you and that this is okay. It is not a flaw in me. There is nothing wrong with me that I do not find comfort in reasons and shoulds. I want you to stay with me and come close, to show me you care when I don't feel strong. I want you to touch me and hold me and tell me I matter to you. I just want you to be with me. That is all I need."

Charlie looks completely stunned. He says, "You mean you just want me to come close?" Kyoko asks him, "What is it like to hear me say these things?" He shakes his head. "It is like I have been working so hard to keep us on this one track that I have not seen the simple easy way just off to the side here." Then he smiles softly. "This feels good. It is better. I can do this. I can do this with you."

Both Charlie and Kyoko are now tuned in to their core needs and can give coherent signals about these needs to their partner. They can do what securely attached partners can do. By knowing and trusting their own emotions and reaching past their fears, they are stronger, individually and together. When couples can do this, they can more easily repair conflicts and rifts and shape a nurturing, loving connection.

Charlie and Kyoko have not only become accessible, responsive, and engaged with each other, they have also expanded their sense of who they are individually. Kyoko is more assertive, and Charlie is more flexible. Now that they know how to invite each other into an A.R.E. conversation, they can help each other grow on a personal level.

Let's take a look at key moments in the Hold Me Tight conversations of three other couples. These pairs have more troubled personal histories and a more fragile sense of emotional safety than do Charlie and Kyoko. Yet they, too, are able to make this call from the heart.

Diane and David have fought for their relationship for thirty-five years, through the fog of fear, deprivation, and depression left over from their histories of abuse and violation by those they needed the most. At the beginning of our sessions, Diane told David, "I have to leave. I can't be badgered every time you get scared. Going to my room for days on end doesn't work anymore. I can't live behind this wall." Now, in the Hold Me Tight conversation, she says to David, "I love you. I do want to be close but I cannot be pushed into closeness. I want to feel safe with you. I want you to give me the room to move, to hear when I tell you I am getting overwhelmed. You trying to move my feet in tune with yours doesn't work. After all these years, I want you to believe that I won't let you go, us go. When we dance together, it's lovely. I want you to help me feel safe with you and then to ask, to reach for me. Then I can turn to you and we can dance."

When it is David's turn to talk about his needs, rather than channeling his attachment anxiety into hostile comments about Diane, he talks about his fear of loss and the other side of this fear, his longing for connection. He has a coherent message, one that takes his wife into account and that clearly reflects his deepest emotions and needs. This is "secure talk." There is no flipping into reactive anger or avoiding by intellectualizing. He can now reach for his wife.

"I don't know how to say this," he begins. "It's like when I was in the military and I was jumping out of planes. Except here there is no parachute! I am a fearful person, Diane. I have learned to watch for danger all the time. I guess it's so hard for me to not go straight into take-charge mode. But now I know how my taking charge has made it hard for you and pushed you away." He is silent for a few moments, then continues. "So some part of me is always afraid that you can't really love me. I am always pushing for that acknowledgment, that I matter to you. I am always wanting that reassurance. Wanting to know that I am loved, even with all my problems, my temper. But it is so hard for me to ask. I am in free fall here! I need that certainty. And it is so hard for me to ask. Can you love me, even with all my problems?"

Diane's face shows that she sees his pain and fear, and she leans toward him and says very slowly and deliberately, "I love you, David. I have loved you since I was sixteen. I wouldn't know how to stop now. When you talk like this, I want to hold you forever."

Huge smiles erupt on both their faces.

Phillipe and Tabitha are very different from David and Diane. They both had unhappy first marriages and are heavily invested in their very successful, high-profile careers. The crisis in their five-year relationship is that each time they talk about a deeper commitment, Phillipe changes his mind. They are both highly intellectual, accomplished people who tend to withdraw whenever any tension arises. Phillipe pulls his expensive fedora hat down over his eyes and retreats into his religion and platonic friendships with other women, while Tabitha shops for more elegant suits and artwork or immerses herself in a frenzy of work projects. Both are a little surprised that they cannot seem to walk away from each other, and Tabitha has finally given Phillipe an ultimatum. Commit, or the relationship is over.

Phillipe's initial position is captured by his statement, "I do not believe in needing people. I decided long ago that this was just foolishness. I have many friends and I am best on my own. I have never known how to do all this lovey-dovey nonsense." Now he tells Tabitha, "I understand that every time we get really close, when commitment comes up, some part of me goes into panic and slams the door. I think I decided a very long time ago never again to put all my eggs in one basket. Never to give anyone that power to hurt me, to crush me again. It is very hard for me to admit that I want your caring, to place myself in your hands. Even now, as I say that, there is an ocean of weeping waiting for me here. I need to know that you will not ever just turn away and shut me out. I can see myself as a small boy being told to go away when my mother became ill. In a sense, that little boy is the one who tells me to run when I begin to feel this need for you. I want to let you come close. Can you help me learn to trust? Can you tell me that you will not turn away no matter what?"

Tabitha is able to do just that and to keep doing that as this couple move into deeper connection. When it's her turn to engage in an A.R.E. conversation, she is able to say, "On some level, I know that you get pulled away from me by your fear. But I have to know that I am important enough to you that you will fight that fear. I cannot deal with all this uncertainty. It hurts too much. I want you to invest in us, in our connection. I love you, and I think you can trust me. But I need that stability, a place that I can count on with you. It's hard for me to say this. I get afraid that I am not good enough, perfect enough to make this kind of claim on you. I get caught in how it is maybe my fault that you are still afraid and that maybe I want too much. I think in the past this has stopped me drawing this line. Do I really deserve this? Am I entitled? Well, whether I am or not, I want your commitment that you will let me matter to you! I can't risk any more without that safe place. It is too scary, too painful. I want you to risk and open up to me. I won't let you down."

Phillipe, visibly moved by her words, replies in a soft voice, "Yes. I think you want to be with me. And you do deserve for me to take this risk. I have been caught up in my own fear, too afraid to really open up. But I cannot lose you. So I am investing, and it's scary and I'm here."

Once Phillipe is able to give her this reassurance in an engaged, loving way, this relationship opens out into a secure base for both of them.

Brett and Monica are a missionary couple on furlough from

West Africa. Married twenty-three years, they have come to seek therapy because of their terrible conflicts about whether to return to Africa to continue their mission. Monica wishes to remain in the United States, saying that she feels alone and depressed on mission. Brett states that he is doing God's work, which requires sacrifice and struggle from both of them. Monica goes silent and whispers that he will have to go back to Africa alone. Brett then angrily berates her, reminding her that she signed up for this life when they married, that if she leaves him, then his ministry is over, his purpose in life is at an end, and they have broken their word to God — just because of her emotional problems.

This couple cannot move out of this cycle of quiet protest and silence followed by dismissal and coercive blaming. Brett declares, "You cannot say these things to me. God called you too. You are turning your back on God here, not just on me. You need to expect less of me and turn to prayer when you are unhappy. God is the only one who can meet these needs." Monica finds her voice and retorts, "I do indeed turn to God, but I don't believe He wants me to feel so alone here, in this empty marriage. Doesn't God's law tell you to be a tender, loving partner? You care more about the people you serve than you do about me. You listen to their pain instead of criticizing them." Each person brings his or her faith into the fight to try to convince the other of his or her point of view. They end up simply threatening each other.

Gradually, Brett and Monica are able to use Conversations 1, 2, and 3 to create a secure base and open up. The key sharing moments in their Hold Me Tight conversation unfolded like this:

When Monica touches and shares her fears and needs, she tells Brett, "When I hear that there is no room for me and my pain to matter in this relationship, I feel discarded, unimportant to you, and hopeless. I have lost you as a partner. I turn away because this sears me like a flame. God made me to long for closeness with you, not just to numbly take on His mission like a burden to prove I am a good wife. I am so lonely for you. I need you to see my hurt, to hold me, to let me in so we can share our life calling together and find joy in it." Hearing this, Brett is able to tune in to his softer emotions and he tells his wife, "I berate you and quote Scripture at you because I am terrified. I cannot lose you and I hear that I have failed as a husband. I do not know how to turn to you. It's easier to focus on my ministry, where I know what to do. I cannot lose you. I want to be there for you. My calling is to find love with you, then I can be strong and serve my God. I need your reassurance and support. I need you to help me learn to be more loving in my life, not just my ministry. I need you to trust in me again. I will be there with an open heart."

At this point, instead of using the language of their faith against each other, this couple allows its principles to help them repair their bond and find their emotional and spiritual balance. Brett reminds me that Scripture honors the sharing of our vulnerable places and the courage it takes to reach for others. This is at the core of love and loving. The story of the woman who washes Jesus's feet in the Pharisee's house (Luke 7:36–48) provides an excellent example. The woman is a "sinner" who finds Jesus and washes His feet with her tears. In Hebrew and Middle Eastern cultures, women and men would be given a small alabaster bottle in which they would collect the tears they shed at moments of pain, helplessness, and joy, together with perfume to preserve these tears. They would then carry the bottle with them all their life and it would be buried with them. This woman risks crossing the boundaries of propriety and entering the Pharisee's house, falls at Jesus's feet, weeping, and pours all her tears from her bottle onto His feet. She trustingly lays every moment of her heartfelt experience at His feet. She then dries His feet with her hair. The

Pharisee judges her as a sinner and judges Christ for acknowledging her. Christ replies that He sees love in her actions and that He respects her. He responds to her vulnerability and the enormous courage it took for her to reach for Him.

THE NEUROSCIENCE OF HARMONY

My research shows that every time a couple has a Hold Me Tight conversation, a moment of deep emotional connection occurs. Physicists speak of "resonance," a sympathetic vibration between two elements that allows them to suddenly synchronize signals and act in a new harmony. It is the same vibration that I hear in the climaxes of a Bach sonata when one hundred musical tones come together. Every cell in my body responds, making me and the music one. When I observe similar moments between mother and child, between lovers, between people who reach for and find a deep connection, my response is always the same: I feel a sudden joy.

That sense of connection is expressed not just in our feelings, but also in our very cells. As partners respond to each other with empathy, I know from recent research that specific nerve cells, called mirror neurons, in the prefrontal cortex of their brains are buzzing. These neurons appear to be one of the basic mechanisms that allow us to actually feel what someone else is experiencing. This is a different level of understanding than grasping someone's experience through our intellect. When we watch a person act, these brain cells fire off just as though we were performing the action ourselves. Mirror neurons are part of our general "wired to connect" heritage, and they prime us for love and loving.

Neuroscientists discovered mirror neurons by accident in 1992 when a researcher who was mapping a monkey's brain and eating an ice cream cone noticed that the monkey's brain lit up as if *he* were eating the cone! The neurons allow us to read intentions and emotions, to bring another inside us. Neuroscientists, borrowing from physics, now speak of reverberating states of empathic resonance. This sounds very abstract. What it means for lovers is that there is a tangible power in actually looking at each other. It helps us be emotionally present and pick up on our partner's nonverbal cues. This creates a level of engagement and empathy that is lost in a less direct conversation. Mirror neurons allow us to see emotion expressed by another and feel this emotion within our own body. It is scientific validation for the attachment concept that authentic connection is about "feeling felt." It is no accident that when Michelangelo painted the Sistine Chapel showing the moment when God reaches to touch Adam's outstretched hand and thereby create mankind, the intensity of the gaze between Adam and God is palpable. The artist has captured the moment when God tunes the human nervous system and shapes Adam for connection with Him.

At the beginning of their sessions, Charlie and Kyoko did not resonate. They hardly looked at each other, and they seemed to speak a different language. During their Hold Me Tight conversation, however, as the corners of Charlie's mouth turned down and his eyelids drooped, Kyoko's eyelids also began to droop. As he laughed, she smiled. His emotional song became a duet. This kind of responsiveness seems to be at the core of empathic emotion, where we literally feel for and with another and therefore naturally act more lovingly.

This is surely the same kind of engagement of mind, body, and emotion that happy lovers feel when they make love or that a mother and baby feel when they gaze, touch, and coo. They are moving in emotional synchrony, without conscious thought or spoken word. There is calmness and joy.

176

Mirror neurons aren't the entire explanation. A substantial number of recent studies add to our understanding of the neurochemical basis of attachment. This research shows that in moments of responsive emotional engagement, our brains are flooded with oxytocin. Dubbed the "cuddle hormone," oxytocin, which is produced only by mammals, is associated with states of contented bliss. It seems to create a cascade of pleasure, comfort, and calm.

Researchers discovered the power of oxytocin when they compared the mating habits of two different kinds of prairie voles. In one species, males and females are monogamous, rear their young together, and form lifelong bonds; in the other, males and females take the one-night-stand approach and leave offspring to fend for themselves. The faithful rodents, it turns out, produce oxytocin; their promiscuous cousins do not. However, when scientists gave monogamous voles a chemical that counteracts oxytocin, these little animals had sex but didn't bond with their partners. And when researchers gave the same rodents extra oxytocin, they bonded tightly, whether they mated or not.

In humans, oxytocin is released when we are in proximity to or physical contact with an attachment figure, especially during moments of heightened emotion, such as orgasm and breast-feeding. Kerstin Uvnäs Moberg, a Swedish neuroendocrinologist, discovered that merely thinking about loved ones can trigger a rush of oxytocin. Oxytocin also reduces the release of stress hormones like cortisol.

Preliminary studies indicate that giving humans oxytocin increases the tendency to trust and interact with others. These findings help explain my observation that once distressed partners learn to hold each other tight, they continue reaching out to each other, trying to create these transforming and satisfying moments again and again. I believe that A.R.E. interactions turn on this neurochemical love potion. Oxytocin seems to be nature's way of promoting the attachments God created us to feel.

PLAY AND PRACTICE

Read over the description of Charlie and Kyoko taking the leap into secure connection again.

On your own, focus on a past secure relationship with a lover, a parent, or a close friend. Imagine that person is in front of you now. What would you tell him or her is your deepest attachment need? How do you think he or she would have answered?

Now consider a past relationship where you did not feel securely connected. What was it that you really needed from this person? Try to express this in two simple sentences. How would he or she have replied?

Now move on to your relationship with your current partner. Think about what you most need in order to feel secure and loved. Write it down. Then begin this conversation for real with your partner.

Here is a list of some of the phrases partners use in this conversation. If it helps you, you can simply check the one that most fits for you and show it to your partner.

I need to feel, to sense that:

- I am special to you and that you really value our relationship. I need that reassurance that I am number one with you and that nothing is more important to you than us.
- I am wanted by you, as a partner and a lover, that making me happy is important to you.
- I am loved and accepted, with my failings and imperfections. I can't be perfect for you.
- I am needed. You want me close.
- I am safe because you care about my feelings, hurts, and needs.

- I can count on you to be there for me, to not leave me alone when I need you the most.
- I will be heard and respected. Please don't dismiss me or leap into thinking the worst of me. Give me a chance to learn how to be with you.
- I can count on you to hear me and to put everything else aside.
- I can ask you to hold me and to understand that just asking is very hard for me.

If this is too hard to do, take a smaller step and talk about how difficult it is to explicitly formulate and state your needs. Tell your partner if there is some way he or she can help you with this. This dialogue contains the key emotional drama of our lives, so sometimes we need to edge up to it slowly.

If you are the partner who is listening and you find yourself unsure as to how to respond or too anxious to respond, just share this. Being present is the secret here, rather than responding in any set way. Confirming that you have heard your partner's message, that you appreciate that he or she is sharing with you, and that you want to be responsive is a positive first step. Then you can explore how you might begin to meet your lover's needs.

With your partner, discuss which of the other couples' stories in this chapter—David and Diane's, Phillipe and Tabitha's, or Brett and Monica's—resonated most with you.

After the two of you have had your own Hold Me Tight conversation, write down the key statements each of you made. The female partner will probably find this task easier. Women have been shown in many studies to retain stronger and more vivid memories of emotional events than do men. This appears to be a reflection of physiological differences in the brain, not a sign of the level of involvement in the relationship. If necessary, the women can assist the men a little here.

The key statements will help the two of you further clarify your internal and external dramas and guide you in future Hold Me Tight conversations.

The Hold Me Tight conversation is a positive bonding event. It offers an antidote to moments of disengagement and negative cycles and enables you to face the world together as a team. But more than this, each time you can create these moments of emotional resonance, the bond between you grows stronger. The power of these conversations to connect and transform our relationships is clear. Such exchanges have an impact on all other aspects of relationships, as you'll see in the following conversations.

Conversation 5: Forgiving Injuries

"Everyone says that forgiveness is a lovely idea,
until they have something to forgive."

— C. S. Lewis

"Be kind and compassionate to one another, forgiving
each other, just as in Christ God forgave you."

— Ephesians 4:32

Conrad and his wife, Helen, are deep into the Hold Me Tight conversation, and the air is buzzing with emotional resonance. "Let me hold you," Conrad entreats. "Tell me what you need." Helen turns to him and smiles as if ready to respond to his request. But suddenly her face goes blank. She stares at the floor. And then in a detached voice, she says, "And I was there, I was sitting on the stairs, and I said to you, 'The doctor thinks I probably have it. Breast cancer. I've been waiting all my life, knowing it was coming. My mother died of it. My grandmother, too. And now it's come for me.'"

Her voice changes; she sounds bewildered. "And you brushed

past me as I sat there"—she touches her shoulder, as if still feeling the touch—"and you said, 'Get yourself together. There's no point in freaking out and getting all upset when you are not sure. Just calm down, and we can discuss what to do later.' You went upstairs to your office and closed the door. You didn't come down for the longest time. You left me sitting alone. You left me dying on the stairs."

Then her voice changes again. In a cheery businesslike tone, she tells me that she and Conrad have made great progress in therapy and no longer have the terrible fights that brought them in to see me. In fact, things are so much better that there probably isn't much more to discuss. Conrad is confused and puzzled by what has just happened. The stairway conversation occurred more than three years ago, and the doctor's suspicions were wrong—Helen did *not* have breast cancer. Eager not to stir up trouble, he quickly agrees with his wife's assessment that therapy is going fine and there is nothing to discuss.

SMALL EVENTS, BIG FALLOUT

I have seen this sort of abrupt disconnect occur before. Couples are making steady progress, tender feelings are flowing, and then...wham! One partner brings up an event, sometimes an apparently minor one, and it's as if all the oxygen has been sucked from the room. All at once, warm hope is exchanged for chill despair.

How can one small incident have this kind of overwhelming power? Well, clearly it's not a minor incident. To one partner at least, it is a *grievous* event.

Over the decades of research and therapy, I've discovered that certain incidents do more than just touch our raw spots or "hurt our feelings." They injure us so deeply that they overturn our world. They are relationship traumas. In the dictionary a trauma is defined as a wound that plunges us into fear and helplessness, that challenges all our assumptions of predictability and control.

Traumatic wounds are especially severe, observes Judith Herman, professor of psychiatry at Harvard Medical School, when they involve a "violation of human connection." Indeed, there is no greater trauma than to be wounded by the very people we count on to support and protect us.

Helen and Conrad have come face-to-face with a relationship trauma. Even though the stairway encounter was three years back, it has remained very much alive, nixing any possibility of Helen reaching for her husband. In fact, since the incident, Helen has been irritable and wary with Conrad, swinging from vividly recalling the incident, to numbing out and avoiding closeness. Hypervigilance, flashbacks, and avoidance are the established indicators of traumatic stress. When Helen did try to discuss her feelings, Conrad minimized the incident, leaving her even more upset. So now, when Conrad asks Helen to risk with him, to put herself in his hands, she instantly remembers the time when she was totally vulnerable with him. An alarm sounds, and she refuses to go there again. I call this the "Never Again" moment. No wonder the Hold Me Tight conversation hits a dead end.

Lack of an emotionally supportive response by a loved one at a moment of threat can color a whole relationship, observe attachment researchers Jeff Simpson of the University of Minnesota and Steven Rholes of Texas A&M University. It can eclipse hundreds of smaller positive events and, in one swipe, demolish the security of a love relationship. The power of such incidents lies in the searing negative answer they offer to the eternal questions "Are you there for me when I am most in need? Do you care about my pain?"

There isn't much room for compromise or ambiguity when we feel this kind of urgent need for our loved one's support. The test is pass or fail. These moments can shatter all our positive assumptions about love itself and our loved one's dependability, beginning the fall into relationship distress or further fraying an already fragile bond. Until these incidents are confronted and resolved, true accessibility and emotional engagement are out of the question.

When I and my colleagues first started watching tapes of Hold Me Tight conversations, we thought that wounds that bleed the life out of a relationship were always betrayals. Except *betrayal* didn't seem to fit exactly when we listened to injured partners probe their pain. "There have been lots of hurts and hard times in our relationship," Francine explains to Joseph, who has had an affair with a colleague. "I can accept that you felt neglected after the twins were born and that you were sexually frustrated when you met this woman. I can even understand how your relationship with her kind of just unfolded, pulling you in. It's not the affair itself that is the big problem for me. What I can't get past is how you told me about it. I think about it all the time. You saw how devastated I was. I was literally on the floor. And when I was most down, what did you do? You blamed me for your affair. You listed all my bad qualities and went on and on discussing possibilities for how your life might take shape without me. It was as if I wasn't even there. You didn't take me into account at all. That is the piece I keep going back to. If you had ever loved me at all, then how could you do that?"

Plainly, Francine is distressed by more than Joseph's infidelity and disloyalty. I've come to see that although wounded partners often do feel betrayed, they primarily feel *abandoned* by their mate. Their cries are usually some version of "How could you leave me in that life-and-death moment?" Partners typically suffer relationship trauma at times of intense emotional stress when attachment needs are naturally high, including the birth or miscarriage of a child, the death of a parent, the sudden loss of a job, the diagnosis and treatment of a serious illness.

The mates who inflict these injuries are not being malicious or purposely insensitive. Indeed, they usually have the best of intentions. Most simply do not know how to tune in to their loved one's attachment needs and offer the comfort of their emotional presence. Some, too, are absorbed by attempts to contain their own anxiety. As Sam sadly tells his wife, "When I saw all that blood, I just freaked out. I didn't even think of losing the baby. I thought you were going to die. I was going to lose you. I went into problem-solving mode. I left you alone in the back of the taxi and sat in front with the driver, giving him directions to the hospital. I didn't understand what you needed from me."

Partners often try to handle relationship injuries by ignoring or burying them. That is a big mistake. Everyday hurts are easily dismissed and raw spots can fade away (if we stop rubbing them in Demon Dialogues), but unresolved traumas do not heal. The helplessness and fear they engender are almost indelible; they set off our survival instincts. It's wiser, in survival terms, to be wary and discover there is no real danger than to be trusting and find out the danger is real. This wariness will limit an injured partner's ability to risk deeper emotional engagement. And the traumas fester. The more Helen demands an apology from Conrad for leaving her on the stairs, the more Conrad offers dismissing rationalizations. That only confirms her sense of isolation and feeds her anger.

Sometimes partners do succeed in compartmentalizing traumas, but this results in a cool and distant relationship. And the barricade works only for a while. Injured feelings break out at some point when attachment needs come to the fore. Larry, a high-powered executive, had neglected his wife, Susan, for years. Since retiring, he had been trying to "court" Susan. They had improved their relationship, but in the Hold Me Tight conversation, when Larry reached for his wife's comfort, she exploded. She told him that after his actions "in the kitchen on Morris Street," she had resolved to never again let him close enough to hurt her.

Larry does not have any idea what Susan is talking about, but he knows that they have not lived on Morris Street for seventeen years! Susan hasn't forgotten what happened on one hot afternoon. She had been depressed, physically ill from a car accident, and overwhelmed with caring for their three small children. Larry had come home to find her weeping on the kitchen floor. Although normally a very reserved woman, she had begged him to hold her. He had told her to pull herself together and had gone off to make phone calls. Susan tells Larry, "That afternoon, lying there, I came to the end of weeping. I went cold. I told myself I would never make the mistake of expecting that kind of caring from you again. I would rely on my sisters. And all these years, you never even noticed! And now, suddenly, you need me and want me to open up?"

The only way out of these attachment injuries is to confront them and heal them together. Preferably immediately. This was brought home to me when my then eight-year-old son came down with acute appendicitis at a summer lake party my husband, John, and I were hosting. I dashed off to the nearest hospital with instructions to John to shut down the party and follow us. The small local hospital could not operate, and we had to make a long and anxious trip into town. By the time we got there, things looked bad. A surgeon hurried in to look at my son and announced that he had to operate "now." I called my husband again, and he was still at the lake! Two hours later, as I was watching my son being wheeled into intensive care, my husband came waltzing breezily down the corridor. I ignited. He was horrified that I had been so scared and felt so alone. He tolerated my anger and distress, explained why he was late, and reassured me. Still, I needed to be very sure that he understood my hurt. We went over the incident quite a few times in the following weeks before this injury was fully healed.

For Conrad and Helen, the healing process begins in my office when he reveals that after he left her on the stairs, he had wept for an hour. He had thought that allowing his own fear and impotence to show would be letting her down.

The first goal for partners is *forgiveness.* Just as with love, forgiveness has only recently become a topic of study by social scientists. Most scholars speak of forgiveness as a moral decision. Letting go of resentment and absolving a person's bad conduct are the right and good things to do. But this decision alone will not restore faith in the injuring person and the relationship. What partners need is a special type of healing conversation that fosters not just forgiveness but the willingness to trust again. Renewed trust is the ultimate goal.

About five years ago, I began mapping out the steps in the dance of forgiveness and reconciliation. Together with my students and colleagues, I watched tapes of counseling sessions and saw how some couples hit the "Never Again" moment and got stuck, and others worked through the injury. We learned that couples had to be able to manage Conversations 1, 2, and 3 and create a basic safety in their relationship before they could engage in a Forgiving Injuries conversation.

A recent research project has further sharpened our understanding of relationship traumas. We've learned that they are not always obvious, that what's important is not the events themselves, but the vulnerabilities they arouse. For some partners at certain times, a flirtation may prove more wounding than an affair. We've also found that couples can suffer multiple traumas, and that the greater the number, the harder it is to renew trust. The overriding lesson is you have to take your partner's hurt seriously and hang in and ask questions until the meaning of an incident becomes clear, even if to you the event seems trivial or the hurt exaggerated.

Mary and Ralph have identified their Demon Dialogues and can talk about their raw spots and replay rocky moments, but Mary is balking at starting the Hold Me Tight conversation. Instead, she keeps harping on the photos of Ralph and very scantily clad secretaries at an office party that he left in his desk drawer at home, which he knows she regularly tidies. Ralph apologizes, admits that the party got a little out of hand and that the photos are inappropriate, but he is adamant that no hanky-panky went on. He doesn't really understand why she's so hurt. He keeps trying to tune in to Mary's story and finally picks up on the fact that Mary keeps repeating the phrase "Right then, after 'that' time." "What's so important about the timing of all this?" he asks.

Mary bursts into tears. "How can you ask that? Do you not remember? It was after those terrible discussions where you told me that I just was too inhibited for you. You demanded that I go out and get some silky underwear and read some of those sex books. I grew up in such a strict home. I told you that I was just too shy to do this. But you insisted. You told me that unless I did this, we weren't going to make it as a couple. So I went and did it, for us. I did it all, but I was so ashamed, so mortified. And you didn't seem to really notice. You never even said you were pleased! Not once. But you looked really pleased posing in those photos, and those girls looked like they were having fun. They weren't shy like me. I turned myself inside out to be like those girls in the photos, and it didn't matter. And the very last thing was that you knew I cleaned out your desk, and you never even thought how I would feel if I found the photos! I was just invisible to you!" Ralph now tunes in to his wife's pain. He reaches out to hold her hand and comfort her. He whispers tenderly, "I am so sorry. I see how I hurt you now."

Both Mary and Ralph showed courage and determination here in sifting through an event until its import became evident. Sometimes we don't know what is so painful to us in a particular event until we can really explore it with our partner. And sometimes it is very hard to just come out and show the core of our hurt to the one who hurt us. But the pain always makes sense if we relate it to our attachment needs and fears.

SIX STEPS TO FORGIVENESS

This chapter's opening quote from Ephesians shows the centrality of forgiveness in the Christian faith. But how do we "put feet to" this verse in the Forgiving Injuries conversation?

1. The hurt partner needs to speak his or her pain as openly and simply as possible. This is not always easy to do. It means resisting making a case against your partner, and staying focused on describing the pain, the specific situation in which it occurred, and how it affects your sense of safety with your partner. When it is hard to capture the essence of an injury, we try to help people plug into the emotions that arose by asking the following questions:

- At a moment of urgent need, did I feel deprived of comfort?
- Did I feel deserted and alone?
- Did I feel devalued by my partner when I desperately needed validation that I and my feelings were important?
- Did my partner suddenly appear to be a source of danger to me rather than the haven of safety that I needed?

This speaks directly to the traumatic nature of attachment injuries.

Sorting through the emotional soup to find the essence of your hurt can be difficult. And it's just as hard for the "guilty" partner to hang in and try to hear the other's anguish. Having already explored your Demon Dialogues and your individual raw spots should help each of you tune in when the other is sharing, even if what's being said triggers your anxiety. Once the two of you are able to understand the underlying attachment hurts, needs, and fears that are being played out, you can slow down and help each other work through them.

After months of recriminations, Vera is finally able to tell Ted, "Never mind those times when it was hard for you to come with me to the chemotherapy. I know that this cancer thing sends you back to being twelve years old and watching your mom, the only person who ever cared for you, die of cancer. The image that just stops my breath is the day when I came home and cried and cried. I told you that I couldn't go on anymore. And you said nothing. You did nothing. But then my sister came over, remember? And she got all upset and burst into tears, and you leapt up out of your chair to comfort her. You held her, you whispered to her." Vera bursts into breathless sobs, then continues, "You did it, but not with me. Your comfort, your touch, wasn't for me. That night, I told myself I'd rather die alone than ask you for that kind of caring again. But that pain is still here, and I am still all alone with it." Ted stares at Vera, suddenly comprehending her grief and rage. This is a terrible message, but at least it makes sense. Vera has pinpointed the wound. Ted has seen it. Now the healing can begin.

2. The injuring partner stays emotionally present and acknowledges the wounded partner's pain and his or her part in it. Until injured partners see that this pain has been truly recognized, they

will not be able to let it go. They will call again and again to their partner, preoccupied with protesting and demanding. This makes perfect sense if we understand attachment. If you do not see how you have hurt me, how can I depend on you or feel safe with you?

In past discussions of the trauma, the injuring partner may have retreated into shame and self-blame. It helps to remember that in love, mistakes are inevitable. We all sometimes miss our loved ones' calls for closeness. We all find ourselves distracted. We all get stuck in our own fear or anger and fail to catch loved ones as they fall. There is no perfect soul mate, no flawless lover. We are all stumbling around, treading on each other's toes as we are learning to love.

Perhaps a partner has never before tuned in to attachment messages and only now really begins to understand the pain he or she has caused. It is important to remember that, even though the incident happened in the past, an injuring partner can change how it affects the future. Helping the wounded lover understand the injuring partner's response helps to restore predictability. And staying emotionally present allows the hurt partner to deal with pain in a different way.

Ted says, "Now I'm getting it. The last few times we talked about this, I was able to tell you how your cancer made me freeze like a 'deer in the headlights.' It was like a replay of when my mom was sick. But you are right. That day you watched me just up and give your sister the support you were starving for..." Vera nods and weeps, and he sees this and his voice softens. "That was unbearable for you." She nods again. "That was worse even than my freezing up. I did not and still do not really offer comfort to you, even when I see you hurting. How come I don't do that? I guess it's the way I see you. You are so strong, stronger than I am, for sure. I know it's really stupid, but I think it was easier to reach for your sister right then just because every time I looked at you, all I saw was my own loss and helplessness. Because you are so important to me." Vera considers this for a moment and then lifts her mouth into a tentative smile.

3. Partners start reversing the "Never Again" dictum. I think of it as couples revising their script. Vera moves out from behind her protective wall and shares with Ted the depth of her loneliness, grief, and despair. She tells him, "The day after this incident, I decided that all this was too hard for you. I wasn't sure if you really cared if I made it through. So the battle with the cancer was suddenly pointless. I thought of just giving up." As she speaks, she watches Ted's face. He looks hurt too. He tells her, "I don't want you to feel this way, and I can't bear that you thought of giving up. Giving up because I couldn't comfort you. That's terrible."

4. Injuring partners now take ownership of how they inflicted this injury on their lover and express regret and remorse. This cannot take the form of an impersonal or defensive apology. Saying "Look, I'm sorry, okay?" in a cool tone doesn't signify regret, only dismissal of the partner's pain. If we want to be believed here, we have to listen to and engage with our lover's pain as expressed in step 3. We have to show that our lover's pain has an impact on us. When Ted turns to Vera and speaks, you can hear sadness and remorse in his voice and see it on his face. He tells her, "I really let you down, didn't I? I wasn't there for you. I am so sorry, Vera. I got all overwhelmed and left you to stare down your enemy by yourself. It's hard for me to admit this. I don't want to see myself as the kind of person, the kind of husband, who would let you down like this. But I did it. You had a right to get angry. I never saw my support as that important. But I know now that I hurt you very badly. I wasn't sure what to do, so I dithered and did nothing. I want to try to make this better. If you will let me."

Vera is obviously very moved by Ted's apology. What does he do that is so effective here? First, his manner makes it clear that he feels and cares about Vera's pain. Second, he explicitly tells her that her hurt and her anger are legitimate. Third, he owns up to exactly what he did that was so hurtful. Fourth, he expresses shame. He tells his wife that he too feels dismayed and disappointed by his behavior. Fifth, he reassures her that he will now be there to help her heal.

Now that is one stellar apology! It took me three tries to get just half of what Ted included into an apology to my daughter after I had badly hurt her feelings. *Ted's apology is not just a statement of contrition, it is an invitation to reconnect.*

5. A Hold Me Tight conversation can now take place, centering on the attachment injury. Injured partners identify what they need right now to bring closure to the trauma. They then directly ask for these needs to be met, that is, for their lovers to respond differently from the way they did in the original incident. This shapes a new sense of emotional connection that acts as an antidote to the terrifying isolation and separateness the incident precipitated. "I needed your comfort and support then. I needed your touch. I need it now!" Vera declares to Ted. "Those feelings of being scared and helpless are still with me. When I think about the cancer coming back, or even when I feel the distance between us, I need to have your reassurance." Ted responds, "I want you to feel that you can count on me and I will be there. I will do whatever I have to do. I am not always good at plugging into people's feelings, but I am learning. I don't want you to feel alone and scared." This is now a healing A.R.E. conversation.

6. The couple now creates a new story that captures the injuring event, how it happened, eroded trust and connection, and shaped Demon Dialogues. Most important, the story describes

how they together confronted the trauma and began to heal it. This is like weaving all the threads together into a new tapestry. Now, as a team, they can discuss how to help each other learn from and continue to heal this injury and prevent further injuries. Continuing to heal might involve setting out rituals that reassure the hurt partner. For example, after an affair, a couple might agree that any contact with the old lover will be immediately disclosed to the wounded partner, or that the injuring partner will call during the day with his or her whereabouts. Ted tells his wife at one point in this conversation, "The crazy thing is that it was easier for me to comfort your sister just because she isn't as important to me as you are! I am not worried about messing up and making mistakes with her. I understand why, once this had happened, you would naturally not come to me at other times, like when you got scared about cancer coming back. I see how we got more and more emotionally distant. I know how much courage it must have taken to bring all this up again with me. And I didn't help you when you tried this before, did I? You were trying to send out a distress flare, and I saw you as burning the house down. It feels good to me when we can share like this and not get stuck in all the hurt around this." Vera, in her turn, tells Ted, "I liked when you suggested that I help you out by waving a flag signaling 'It's a Hold Me Tight time, Ted.' It feels like you are really thinking about how to tune in and make sure this doesn't happen again."

Ted and Vera moved smoothly through these steps. But other couples may have more trouble. If Demon Dialogues are chronic and trust and safety have dropped to low levels, the Forgiving Injuries conversation may have to be repeated several times. So, too, if there are multiple traumatic events. Even in such cases, however, one injury usually stands out. And when that one is healed, the others topple like a house of cards.

On the other hand, certain events, most notably affairs, also complicate the process of forgiveness. There are so many points of distress. But here, too, there is usually one moment that encapsulates the injury. Remember Francine and Joseph? It was the way he told her about his unfaithfulness that broke her apart. That affair was brief. Affairs that go on for a long time are much thornier. Intentional long-term deception undermines our sense of our partner as familiar and able to be known. As a result, we cannot define our own reality and be sure of what is "true." As we tell our children, "It is best not to trust strangers. You never know what they will do."

Injuries may be forgiven, but they never disappear. Instead, in the best outcome, they become integrated into couples' attachment stories as demonstrations of renewal and connection.

PLAY AND PRACTICE

1. The first step in healing an attachment injury is to recognize and articulate it. Think of a time, an incident, in the past when you were very hurt by someone important to you, but not your partner. The trauma may be one described above or a hurt of less significance. What was the main cue for that hurt? Was it a remark, a specific action, or a lack of action on the part of the other? In the incident above, Vera says the worst moment was when she realized that Ted could offer comfort to others during this stressful time, but not to her. In your own incident, what alarming conclusion did you come to about this important person in your life? For example, did you decide that he or she just didn't care, that you weren't important and might be abandoned? What were you longing for when you were wounded? If this is hard to articulate, see if you can figure out what would have been the

ideal response to you. What protective moves did you find your-self taking? For example, did you change the subject and walk out of the room? Or did you become aggressive and demand an explanation?

Ask yourself: Did I feel deprived of support? Did my pain or fear get dismissed? Did I feel deserted? Did I feel devalued? Did I suddenly see this person as a source of danger, as taking advan-tage of me, betraying me?

Once you have a sense of this past hurt, see if you can share it with your partner. Marc tells his wife, Amy, about how her first response to the news that he had dropped out of the degree pro-gram for engineering to apply to seminary had really hurt him. "I remember the whole thing," says Marc. "You and I were in the kitchen. I almost whispered it, I was so scared of saying it. Your face was like stone. You said, 'I guess how you live your life is up to you. But this isn't what I signed up for; it's not what we agreed on. This isn't what all that education was for.' I felt like I'd been punched in the chest. I think I felt all those Ds, but for sure I felt 'devalued.' I left. That was what happened. I just kept my wall up. I guess I was longing for you to accept me and support me. In fact, I didn't let you close enough to really hurt me for a long time."

2. Reflect on how easy or how difficult it is for you to apolo-gize, even in small things. Rate yourself from 1 to 10 on this abil-ity. Ten means that you readily acknowledge that you have blind spots and make mistakes. Can you remember a time when you voiced your regrets in any of the following ways:

- The four-second "where is the exit" apology: "Yes, well, sorry 'bout that. What shall we have for dinner?"
- The minimizing responsibility apology: "Well, maybe I did that, but..."

- The forced apology: "I guess I am supposed to say..."
- The instrumental apology: "Nothing is going to work till I say this, so..."

These are token apologies that can sometimes work for very small hurts, but generally in the kind of injuries we are talking about, they only increase the wounded person's pain.

3. Can you think of a time when you hurt a loved one? A time when they might have felt deprived of your support or comfort, even deserted by you? Where you might even have seemed dangerous or rejecting to them?

Can you imagine sincerely acknowledging this to them? What might you say? What might be hard for you in acknowledging the injury? Partners often use the following simple statements when they talk about having hurt their loved one:

- "I pulled away. I let you down."
- "I didn't see your pain and how you needed me. I was too lost, afraid, angry, preoccupied. I just shut down."
- "I didn't know what to do. I got all caught up in feeling stupid and worrying about doing the wrong thing."

Think of the five elements in Ted's apology to Vera. He says he cares about her pain; he tells her that her hurt is warranted; he owns up to his hurtful actions; he expresses shame for his behavior; and he reassures her that he will help her to heal. Which one of Ted's actions would be the hardest for you to pull off?

How do you think your acknowledgment might make the injured party feel? How might it help them?

4. Now turn to dealing with a specific injury in your current relationship. You can do this on your own or while your partner listens and tries to understand. If this sharing seems difficult,

start with a relatively small recent hurt. Then if you wish, you can do the exercise again with a more significant hurt. Try to make it as specific as possible. Big, vague hurts are difficult to address. Perhaps you went through a difficult period when there were lots of hurt feelings. Was there one moment when that hurt crystallized? What was the trigger for the pain? What was the primary feeling? What decision did you make about the relationship, and what moves did you make to protect yourself?

"It was that time when I was just starting all those new courses and was so unsure of myself," Mary tells Jim. "One evening after supper, I gathered up my courage and asked you what you thought about all my struggles and what I had done so far. I really hoped that you'd say that you recognized how far I'd come and tell me that you believed in me. But you didn't seem to hear me, and I felt dismissed somehow. I didn't show you how sad I felt. How much I needed your encouragement. So I decided to just create my dream on my own. I keep that whole part of my life separate now, separate from us."

5. See if you can now tell your partner what you hoped for in that hurtful incident, and how it felt to not get that response. You might also share what it feels like right now to take the risk and express what you longed for. As you do this, try to avoid indicting your partner for causing you pain. That will only sabotage the conversation. As the listening partner, try to hear your lover's vulnerability and share what this evokes in you. Usually, when we really listen to someone we love express a need for us, we respond with caring.

6. If you are the partner who has hurt your loved one, see if you can help your partner understand why you responded the way you did at the moment of injury. You may have to dig deep and "discover" for yourself how this response evolved. Think of this as a step in making your actions more predictable for your partner. See if you can help your partner feel safe enough to reveal his or

her vulnerable feelings to you so that you will have a complete picture of what the incident meant in terms of attachment needs.

7. As the partner who did the hurting, can you now recognize your partner's experience, own how you inflicted pain, and, the big A word, apologize? This is hard to do. It takes courage to admit that we are disappointed in our own behavior; it is humbling to confess that we have been insensitive or uncaring. Perhaps we can only apologize when we allow ourselves to be moved by our loved ones' hurts and fears. If we can do this with sincerity, we are giving our loved ones a great gift.

8. As the injured partner, can you accept the apology? If you can, it puts the two of you on a new footing. Trust can begin to grow again. You can comfortably seek reassurance when echoes of this injury occur in the future, knowing that your partner will try to respond sensitively. And your apologizing partner can now offer the love that went astray in the original event.

9. Finally, sum up this conversation with your partner in a short story about the painful event, the impact it had on your relationship, and how you both recovered and intend to ensure that it doesn't happen again.

If you can't imagine doing this Play and Practice, you can experiment by simply sharing with your partner how strange or difficult a forgiving conversation seems to you. Another way to begin is to agree on an injury that needs healing and write out in a few sentences how the conversation might sound if it followed the steps outlined above. Then share this with each other.

Understanding attachment injuries and knowing that you can find and offer forgiveness if you need to gives you incredible power to create a resilient, lasting bond. There is no injury-proof relationship. But you can dance together with more verve and panache if you know you can recover when you step on each other's toes.

Conversation 6: Bonding Through Sex and Touch

"We waste time looking for the perfect lover, instead of creating the perfect love."

— *Tom Robbins*

"Let her be as the loving hind and pleasant roe; let her breasts satisfy thee at all times; and be thou ravished always with her love."

— *Proverbs 5:19 (KJV)*

Passion comes easily in the early days of a marriage. Almost every word, glance, and touch vibrates with lust. It's nature's way of drawing us together. But after the first captivating rush of desire, what's the place of sex in a relationship? Besides pulling us in, can sex also help to keep us together, to build a lasting relationship? Emphatically, yes. In fact, good sex is a potent bonding experience. The passion of infatuation is just the hors d'oeuvre. Loving sex in a long-term relationship is the entrée.

But we don't typically think of sex in this way. We've been conditioned by our culture and a myriad of relationship gurus to regard passion as more of a passing sensation, less as a durable force. We are told that the sexual fires that burned so brightly at the start of love inevitably burn down, just as our relationships, once filled with excitement, inexorably turn into prosaic friendships.

Moreover, we've been taught to see sex as an end in itself. Slaking desire, preferably with a big orgasm, is the goal. We emphasize the mechanics of sex, the positions, techniques, and toys that can heighten our physical bliss. Sex is all about immediate physical satisfaction, we are told. All this buzz in our culture often crowds out the Christian message—that sex is sacred and an inherent part of the bond between husband and wife. It is meant for mutual satisfaction and to celebrate this unique bond; the Song of Solomon is a beautiful example of this kind of celebration.

Here again we see the parallel between bonding science and spiritual wisdom. In fact, this science tells us that secure bonding and fully satisfying sexuality go hand in hand; they cue off and enhance each other. Emotional connection creates great sex, and great sex creates deeper emotional connection. When partners are emotionally accessible, responsive, and engaged, sex becomes intimate play, a safe adventure. Secure partners feel free and confident to surrender to sensation in each other's arms, explore and fulfill their sexual needs, and share their deepest joys, longings, and vulnerabilities. Then, lovemaking is truly making love.

Just how important is satisfying sex in sustaining a love relationship? Good sex, it turns out, is integral though not paramount to happy relationships. Sex educators Barry and Emily McCarthy of American University in Washington, D.C., have surveyed the research in this area. Contented spouses, they conclude, attribute only 15 to 20 percent of their happiness to a pleasing sex life, but unhappy mates ascribe 50 to 70 percent of their distress to sexual problems. Satisfied partners see sex as just one of many sources of pleasure and intimacy, while despondent partners home in on sex and often view it as the chief source of trouble.

Why is sex such a huge issue for dissatisfied partners? Because typically it's the first thing affected when a relationship falters. It's not the true problem, though. Think of sexual distress as the relationship version of the "canary in the mine." What's really happening is that a couple is losing connection; the partners don't feel emotionally safe with each other. That in turn leads to slackening desire and less satisfying sex, which leads to less sex and more hurt feelings, which leads to still looser emotional connection, and around it goes. In shorthand: no safe bond, no sex; no sex, no bond.

It's easy to understand. As Harry Harlow noted in his book *Learning to Love,* humans are set apart from other animals by affectionate face-to-face sex during which "the most vulnerable surfaces of the body are openly exposed in compromising positions." We simply are not wired to be wary or afraid and turned on at the same time.

The safety of our emotional connection defines our relationship in bed as well as out. Depending on how comfortable we are with closeness and how safe we feel about needing our loved one, we will have different goals in bed. I call these three kinds of sex Sealed-Off Sex, Solace Sex, and Synchrony Sex.

SEALED-OFF SEX

In Sealed-Off Sex, the goal is to reduce sexual tension, achieve orgasm, and feel good about our sexual prowess. It happens with those who have never learned to trust and don't want to open up, or who are feeling unsafe with their partners. The focus is on sensation and performance. The bond with the other person is secondary. This kind of impersonal sex is toxic in a love relationship. The partner feels used and objectified rather than valued as a person.

As her spouse, Kyle, listens, Marie tells me, "I am a blow-up Barbie for him. Our sex is so empty. It takes me to the end of alone." "I guess it can be like that," Kyle agrees. "But we used to be closer in bed. Since all the fighting started, I have given up on us. I stop feeling, and sex becomes mechanical. Then I see you as 'the woman.' It's safer that way. At least I know how to do sex. Closeness is harder. If I see you as 'Marie' and think of all our problems, I just get upset. So, I focus on the sex thing. It makes me feel better, at least for a moment or so."

Kyle shuts down emotionally because he doesn't know how to do "closeness." But others, especially if they've felt betrayed by past lovers, stay emotionally aloof by habit or by choice. They prefer sex in which arousal and orgasm are ends in themselves. They are more likely to have sexual encounters that are short, often lasting no longer than a night. And they hold back from any actions that could invite emotional engagement, such as reciprocal touching and kissing, according to research by psychologist Jeff Simpson of the University of Minnesota and his colleagues. Indeed, the porn star Ron Jeremy advocates partner swapping to alleviate sexual boredom, but his rule is "absolutely no cuddling." Emotional connection, the door to real eroticism, is kept shut. However, without doubt, the poster boy for performance-oriented sex is James Bond. In five decades, he's run through a host of women who are virtually always potential enemies and not to be trusted. Only once has he been in love, simultaneously emotionally and sexually involved. (Bond marries the woman and, conveniently, she is killed off on their wedding day.)

Sealed-Off Sex seems to be practiced mostly by men. This may be due to the hormone testosterone, which fires up sexual drive, or it may be pure cultural conditioning. Men are taught early on that displaying too much emotion is wimpy. Not knowing where to draw the line, they often avoid emotion altogether. Sealed-Off Sex might also be the result of men's sexual wiring. Who was it who said, "Men are like microwaves, but women are slow cookers"? A man can move through arousal to orgasm in seconds with minimal communication. A woman takes longer to become aroused, and it is harder for her to stay focused on simple sensation. She needs her partner to coordinate movements and responses with her. She needs communication and connection for good sex.

For both men and women, emotional disengagement closes off the richer dimension of sexuality. Young people who stay emotionally distant have more sexual partners, but they don't enjoy sex as much as those who are comfortable getting close to others, finds Omri Gillath, a psychologist at the University of Kansas. In this kind of sex, there is excitement, but the passion is short-lived. The experience is one-dimensional, impersonal, and so continual novelty, in the form of new partners or new techniques, is necessary if the turn-on is to continue. More and more sensation is the name of the game.

For some Christian partners, impersonal sex may be especially seductive since it has the allure of the forbidden. And so pornography is a problem in many Christian communities. As a Catholic priest is reported to have said, the trouble with pornography is not what it shows but what it leaves out. It leaves out human connection. Ironically, the evidence is that a steady diet of porn often shuts the door on arousal and passion with one's real-life lover. As I suggest in my book *Love Sense*, true passion occurs when the longing for connection comes together with emotional attunement and erotic play. This kind of passion can be reignited again and again as a couple experiences moments of renewed and deeper connection over time.

SOLACE SEX

Solace Sex occurs when we are seeking reassurance that we are valued and desired; the sex act is just a tagalong. The goal is to alleviate our attachment fears. There is more emotional involvement than in Sealed-Off Sex, but the main emotion directing the sexual dance is anxiety. Gillath's research demonstrates that the more anxious we are about depending on others, the more we tend to prefer cuddling and affection to intercourse. Mandy tells me, "Sex with Frank is okay. But to be truthful, it's the cuddling I really want. And the reassurance. It's like sex is a test, and if he desires me, then I feel safe. Of course, if he ever isn't horny, then I take it real personally and get scared." When sex is an antianxiety pill, it cannot be truly erotic.

Solace Sex can help keep a relationship stable for a while, but it can also feed into raw spots and negative cycles. When anything goes wrong in the mutual desire department, there is instant hurt and negativity. If this kind of sex is the norm in a relationship, partners can get caught in obsessively trying to perform to please or in being so demanding that it turns off sexual desire. When physical intimacy becomes all about tamping down attachment fears, it can drive lovers apart.

So Cory tells his wife, Amanda, "Well, what is wrong with lots of lovemaking? I bet lots of people make love every morning and every night. And lots of women have two or three orgasms each time." Amanda looks at me, and our faces register instant exhaustion and dismay. Cory sees this and turns away. He looks sad and defeated. "Yes, well. It's not really about the sex in the end, is it?" he says. "The only time I am really sure you love me, the only time I feel really safe with you, is when I have you in my arms or when we are making love and I am really turning you on and you are responding to me with your body. Then I know you love me and want me. When I think about it, I know that these demands for sex are too much. The more I push you into it, the less you like it. Truth is, I am so obsessed with losing you. Since our breakup last year, I am just scared all the time, so making love is like my security blanket." Amanda moves her chair closer and puts her arms around him. Cory rests in her arms for a little while and then says, in a voice full of wonder, "Hey, you're holding me! You don't think less of me, saying that?" Amanda kisses him on the cheek. When Cory realizes that he can reach out for intimate touch and the comfort of being held, Cory and Amanda's relationship changes for the better and so does their sex life.

Solace Sex often happens when partners are battling Demon Dialogues, and regular safe, comforting touch—the most basic bonding connection—is missing. "Sex used to be a place we could really come together," laments Alec, whose ten-year marriage to Nan is falling apart. "But now she never wants to make love. I just feel rejected all the time. Sometimes I get enraged. Every time I think of how she doesn't seem to care about making love with me, it hurts. She says I am too pushy, and she sleeps in the spare room. In fact, never mind sex, we don't even touch each other anymore."

When partners tell me that they cannot be considerate of and watch out for each other with everyday acts of caring, I worry. When they tell me that they are not making love, I am concerned. But when they tell me that they do not touch, I know they are really in trouble.

The approximately eighteen square feet of skin we carry as adults is the largest sense organ we have. Tender caressing and stroking of our skin and the emotions these actions evoke are, for most of us, the royal route into love relationships. Touch brings together two fundamental drives, sex and our need to be held and recognized by a special other. As the late anthropologist Ashley Montagu noted in his book *Touching*, skin-to-skin contact is the language of sex *and* the language of attachment. Touch arouses, and it also soothes and comforts.

We have a vital need from our earliest moments to the end of our days for touch, observes Tiffany Field, a developmental psychologist at the University of Massachusetts, who argues that North Americans are among the world's least tactile people and suffer from "touch hunger." In children, a lack of touch, of holding and caressing, seems to slow the growth of the brain and the development of emotional intelligence, that is, the ability to organize emotions.

Males may be particularly vulnerable to touch hunger. Field points out that right from birth, boys are held for shorter periods and caressed less often than are girls. As adults, men seem to be less responsive to tender touch than are women, but in the men I see, they crave it just as much as do the women. Men do not ask to be held, either because of cultural conditioning (real men don't hug) or lack of skill (they don't know how to ask). I think of this whenever my female clients complain that men are obsessed with sex. I would be, too, I say, if sex were the only place apart from the football field where I ever got touched or held.

"I just want Marjorie to reach for me and touch me," Terry maintains. "I want to know she wants me to come close. I want to feel desired, wanted. And not just in a sexual way. It is more than that." "No, you just want bang-bang and an orgasm," Marjorie disagrees. "Maybe that is all I have known how to ask for," he retorts. We cannot funnel all of our attachment needs for physical and emotional connection into the bedroom. When we try, our sex life disintegrates under the weight of those needs.

The best recipe for good sex is a secure relationship where a couple can connect through A.R.E. conversations and tender touch. Even sex therapists concur that the essential building block of a healthy sexual relationship is "non-demand pleasuring." For this reason, I often suggest to couples that they abstain from making love for a few weeks. With intercourse temporarily forbidden, neither partner gets anxious or disappointed, and they can both concentrate instead on exploring all the sensations of touching. Getting used to asking for tender touch deepens a couple's bond, and knowing each other's bodies more intimately, what moves and pleases each other, becomes a precious part of a couple's "only for you, only with you" connection.

SYNCHRONY SEX

Synchrony Sex is when emotional openness and responsiveness, tender touch, and erotic exploration all come together. This is the way sex is supposed to be. This is the sex that fulfills, satisfies, and connects. When partners have a secure emotional connection, physical intimacy can retain all of its initial ardor and creativity and then some. Lovers can be tender and playful one moment, fiery and erotic another. They can focus on achieving orgasms in one interlude and in the next on gently journeying to the place poet Leonard Cohen calls "a thousand kisses deep."

I used the word *synchrony* first in Conversation 4 to describe partners' emotional harmony. I expand it here to include physical harmony as well. Psychiatrist Dan Stern of Cornell Medical School also uses the word when he observes that secure lovers are attuned to each other, sensing each other's inner state and intention and responding to each other's shifting states of arousal, in the same way that an empathic mother is attuned to her baby. The infant opens his eyes and squeals with delight; the mother coos back, pitching her voice to his excited squeal. The lover turns his head and sighs; the beloved smiles and strokes his flank following the rhythm of the sigh. This synchrony gives a "tacit sense of deep rapport" and is the essence of connection—emotional, physical, and sexual. Emotional safety shapes physical synchrony, and physical synchrony shapes emotional safety.

Responsiveness outside the bedroom carries on into it. Connected partners can reveal their sexual vulnerabilities and desires without fear of being rejected. We are all afraid that we are somehow not "enough" in bed. "Look at me," says Carrie. "I'm just a mess of freckles. Do you ever see a model with freckles all over her? I hate them. And when I think about it, I just want to put the lights out." Her husband, Andy, smiles. "Now that would be a shame," he says softly. "I like your freckles. They're part of you. I want to be with you. I don't want a model woman. I like polka dots, they turn me on. Just like you say you think bald men like me are the sexiest. You do think that, right?" Carrie smiles and agrees.

Secure, loving partners can relax, let go, and immerse themselves in the pleasure of lovemaking. They can talk openly, without getting embarrassed or offended, about what turns them off or on. Psychologists Deborah Davis of the University of Nevada and Cindy Hazan of Cornell University find in their studies that securely attached partners can more openly express their needs and preferences and are more willing to experiment sexually with their lovers. In the movies, lovers never have to talk about what to do in bed. It just happens. But trying to make love without feeling safe enough to really talk is like bringing a 747 in to land without a guidebook or help from the control tower.

Secure partners can soothe and comfort each other and pull together to overcome unavoidable problems that are never shown in the movies but are part of everybody's everyday sex. Frank, who now sometimes has erectile difficulties, which he shamefacedly describes as "Charlie deciding to take a nap," is recounting a recent lovemaking "date" with his wife that had all the earmarks of a disaster. "Sylvie said something about my weight at the beginning and I got ready to pout," says Frank, "but then she realized what had happened and hugged me back to feeling okay. Then at a crucial moment, our eighteen-year-old came home early and Charlie went for, well, I'd have to say a snooze on me. Sylvie reminded me of the book we had read that said that in a forty-minute lovemaking session many men lose their erection for a moment or two, but that if they don't panic, it comes back. We found a way to laugh about it all and stay close." Sylvie is now giggling uncontrollably. "Finally," Frank continues, "when everything was back on track, I got a bit rambunctious and knocked the candle over. So then the curtain started to smoke!" He cracks a huge grin at his wife and quips, "Hot date, eh, sugar?" Picking up the story, Sylvie recounts how they decided to give up on making love and make hot chocolate instead. "But then"—she giggles again—"Frank said something sexy and we made love after all." She throws her arms up and tilts her head to one side in a Marilyn Monroe–like pose.

These kinds of stories thrill me. They demonstrate that we can still have spontaneous, passionate, and joyful sexual encounters and make startling discoveries about our partners decades into a relationship. They show that we can connect and reconnect, fall in love again and again, and that eroticism is essentially play and the ability to "let go" and surrender to sensation. For both of these, we need emotional safety.

In a secure relationship, excitement comes not from trying to resurrect the novel moments of infatuated passion, but from the risk involved in staying open in the moment-to-moment, here-and-now experience of physical and emotional connection. With this openness comes the sense that lovemaking with your partner is always a new adventure. "Practice and emotional presence make perfect" is the best guide for erotic and satisfying sex, I tell couples, not seeking endless novelty to combat "boredom." No wonder a recent survey on sex in America by Edward Laumann of the University of Chicago shows that married partners who have spent years together and built up emotional security have more frequent and more satisfying sex than unmarried folks.

When experts suggest that only fresh relationships flying the flags of conquest and infatuation can offer exciting sex, I think of an older, long-married couple I know and how they dance the Argentine tango. They are completely present to and engaged with each other. Their moves are achingly deliberate, totally playful, and stunningly erotic. They are so attuned and responsive to each other that even though the dance is fluid, improvised in the moment, they never miss a step or a turn. They move as one, with grace and flair.

RESOLVING SEXUAL PROBLEMS

The most common sexual problems reported in North America are low sexual desire in women and premature ejaculation or lax erections in men. This does not surprise me. Most distressed couples are caught in Demon Dialogues. Women typically feel alone and disconnected. They either push for Solace Sex or shut down sexually. Men become insecure. They move into Sealed-Off Sex or experience sexual difficulties. Most often when a couple can create secure connection, their sex life improves automatically or through their concerted effort. The shared pleasure and intimacy of renewed sex, as well as the flood of oxytocin at orgasm, in turn enhance their relationship.

Once she is feeling more secure, Ellen is finally able to confide in Henry that she cannot orgasm with him. For years, she has been faking it. Henry is not offended or threatened by this. He is comforting and supportive. He also hits the library and reassures Ellen with the information that roughly 70 percent of women cannot orgasm from intercourse alone. Together they come up with three erotic strategies for the "Orgasms for Ellen" project.

Let's take a close look at how connection and bonding entwine in one relationship. Passion is not a constant. Desire naturally waxes and wanes, with events, with the seasons, with health, with a thousand reasons. These fluctuations, however, hit a nerve in most of us and, unless we can talk about them openly, can easily spark or heighten relationship problems. Many partners can tolerate infrequent intercourse, but they cannot tolerate feeling that their partners do not desire them. Dealing with such feelings is a challenge most partners have to face, even relatively secure ones. And so too for Laura and Bill.

They've come to see me soon after Laura has recovered from a depression triggered by losing her job. Her doctor, who knows that a healthy relationship is the best protection against relapse, picked up that she had some issues with her husband and sent them to me for a marital "checkup." Laura lays out her concerns. "We love each other very much," she says. "But, well, Bill was always horny. He was always touching me. And I liked that. If I didn't want to make love, I could say 'No' and he'd accept it. We'd still cuddle and play and feel close. But now, in the last few years, he just doesn't come on to me. When we do make love, it's great, but if I don't initiate it, it doesn't happen. This hurts so much. We have been together for about twenty years. Is it that I am older now and not sexy enough for him? I am finding that I just go to bed later, when he is asleep. To avoid all that. But we are getting pretty distant here." Bill responds, "I just don't have the same drive I used to. These days work also completely drains me—you know that. But I like making love, and you are one sexy lady. I don't see the problem here. Well, except that you are feeling bad, of course."

This is one of those times when being able to have an A.R.E. conversation really matters. The question is, can Laura stay with her hurt and reach out to Bill, and can he hear her protest and respond? "Like you were saying," Laura tells me, "when we fight we can get caught in a kind of 'I push and Bill goes moody' thing, but we can talk and make up. And I think we have a good marriage. But it's hard for us to talk about sex. We have tried, and it gets a little better for a while, but then it is the same as before." Since they had already been able to look at negative spirals in their relationship and create more responsiveness between them, I suggest that we talk in the same kind of way about their sex life.

I ask what their sexual expectations are. Bill says he would like to make love every two weeks or so. Laura says she'd prefer every ten days. We all laugh. The problem suddenly seems to have shrunk. But then we focus a little more. Bill says that the only problem he sees is that Laura seems to be irritable and a little distant. "If I ask her to come and cuddle at night, she often doesn't come, and I miss that," he offers. "In fact, if I think about it, I miss it a lot." Laura starts to tear up. "I just don't want to cuddle and then get into that place where I start to think you might show some interest in lovemaking and be disappointed. And I guess I have been too scared to even talk about that. You just ask me if I am sexually frustrated and then when I say, 'Not really,' the conversation ends." I see Laura's anticipatory anxiety and her move into avoidance to protect herself. We agree that this inability to talk about the changes in their sexual life is beginning to come between and hurt them.

I ask them to expand on their hurt. Laura struggles for a while and then is able to distill what is so painful for her. "Some of it is a fear that you don't see me as a woman anymore. I am just the wife. More wrinkles and a little pudgier than before. It's scary that I am maybe not sexy anymore, not desirable to you. You hug me like I hug a friend. You don't seem to pay me that kind of keen attention anymore. It used to make me feel so good. And so close."

Bill is really listening, and he helps his wife out by asking, "Is that the heart of it? You feel rejected, that I don't think you're sexy anymore?" Laura sighs and weeps and nods her head. "Well, then when we do make love, I feel tense somehow. I do feel desired. For a moment. I know you are overworked and very tired, but I get that you can take sex or leave it. It's not important. Sometimes I think that if I don't come on to you, then that part of our life will just fade out. And you will let it go. I get mad now, thinking that. So I say to myself, 'Fine, I won't start it. He can just get lost.' But then I have this hurt." She touches her heart. Bill reaches out and takes her hand.

I ask her, "Is that it, Laura? Hurt is usually about sadness and anger and fear. You feel that sex with you is not that important to Bill. Is that it? Is there more?" She nods, then continues. "If I don't go and reach out to you and suggest making love, I am stuck with all these feelings. If I do…" Her voice trails off, and she purses her lips tight. "This is so hard to say. It shouldn't be so hard. We have a good marriage, and I am a strong person. But it is terrifying for me to come to you. It's like diving off a cliff. I never had to do that before. And when you smile sweetly and say that you are tired and turn to sleep, I just die inside. I pretend that it is no big deal, but it really costs me to ask you." Bill murmurs, "I never knew that."

"What do all these feelings tell you about what you need from Bill?" I ask Laura. She tells him, "I guess I need your reassurance that you really value our lovemaking. That you are still invested in it. That you still desire me. I need us to maybe put times aside that I can count on, so that being with me that way comes first sometimes. I need you to show me — the way you used to — that you are still my man." Bill responds eagerly. In a rush, he tells her that he has been so burned-out that he is "sleepwalking" most of the time. That he loves her and thinks of her with desire during his day. "But I never understood that suggesting lovemaking was so hard for you. I am so sorry," he says. "I worry that if I come on to you and then am too tired, my erection won't work so well, so I back off unless I'm sure." They both begin to laugh and recount a few times when this happened and they simply ended up holding each other with a little erotic touching and lots of feelings of closeness.

This conversation was all that Bill and Laura needed to move their sex life back into a secure zone of play and connection. But it also acted as a wake-up call. I suggested that they come up with a sensual scenario to follow when intercourse wasn't in the cards. Bill helped Laura do this, and he began to suggest making love more often. He was also more careful to reassure Laura that when she did suggest sex, he appreciated her taking this risk. He in turn told her explicitly that he needed to know that she wanted him, that he did not want her to avoid closeness or sex with him. He reiterated that he loved and desired her.

Bill and Laura also began to pay more attention to their love-making. Every room needs a little cleaning and redecorating from time to time, and that includes the bedroom. They reported that their sex life had improved, and so had their relationship.

As I told Bill and Laura in their last session, sexual technique is just the frill, not the real thrill! They had the best sex manual of all, the ability to create closeness, tune in to each other, and move in emotional synchrony.

PLAY AND PRACTICE

On Your Own

Was there a comment or a statement in this chapter that started you thinking about your own sex life? What feeling did it bring up in you? Write it down. What does this feeling, whether it is a body sensation or a clear emotion like anger, tell you about your own sexual life?

In bed with your partner, do you generally feel emotionally safe and connected? What helps you feel this way? When you do not feel this way, how could your partner help you?

What is your usual sexual style — Sealed-Off, Solace, or Synchrony Sex? In any relationship all three will probably occur sometimes. But if you habitually move into Sealed-Off or Solace Sex, then this tells you something about your sense of safety in your relationship.

What are your four most important expectations in bed? Think carefully about your answers. Sometimes they are not what we think of first. Partners have told me that their most important expectation after sex was to be held tenderly and caressed gently, but they'd never expressed that desire to their lovers.

Do you feel that you do enough touching and holding in your relationship in general? A single stroke can express connection, comfort, and desire. When would you like to be touched and held more?

If you wrote out a "Brief Guide for the Lover of _____" and inserted your name, what would you put in it? Basic directions might include answers to the following: What helps you begin to open up emotionally and physically to sex? What turns you on the most before and during lovemaking? How long do you expect pleasuring or foreplay and intercourse to last? What is your preferred position? Do you enjoy fast or slow lovemaking? What is the most stirring way for your lover to move you into, stimulate you into, deepest engagement in lovemaking? Can you ask for this?

What makes sex most satisfying for you? (This may not be orgasm, or even intercourse.) When do you feel most unsure or uncomfortable during sex? When do you feel closest to your partner?

If you can share the above with your lover, great. If not, maybe you can begin a conversation about how hard it is to share this kind of information.

WITH YOUR PARTNER

Can you agree on what percentage of the time you expect sex to be really stellar? Remember that in surveys couples report that at least 15 to 20 percent of sexual encounters are basically failures, at least for one partner. What do you want to be able to do as a couple when sex isn't working for you physically? What do you do when sex isn't working for you emotionally? How can your partner help you here? You can even think of yourself as characters in a movie if this helps you talk it through.

Play the Perfect Game. It starts with,

If I were perfect in bed, I could, I would _____

_____, and then you would feel more

_____.

See if you can share at least four of your responses. Then tell each other one way in which the other is sexually perfect for you in bed and out of bed.

Can you each think of a time in your relationship when sex was really satisfying? Share the story of this event with your lover in as much detail as possible. Tell each other what you have learned from listening to these stories.

Think of all the ways sex can show up in your relationship. Can it be simply fun, a way of getting close, a straight physical release, a comforting way to deal with stress or upset, a route into romance and escape from the world, an erotic adventure, a place of tender connection, a burst of passion? Do you feel safe experiencing all of these with your lover? What might be a risk that you would like to take in bed? Can you tell each other the risk, and explain how the other might respond if things went badly or if things went well?

We used to think that thrilling, erotic sex and a safe, secure relationship were contradictory. Now we know that secure relationships are a supple springboard for the most arousing adventurous encounters. And in turn, keeping your physical relationship open, responsive, and engaged helps keep your emotional connection strong. The next and final conversation further explores how to keep your love vibrantly alive.

Conversation 7: Keeping Your Love Alive

D o you guys see the incredible changes you have made in your relationship?" I ask one of my most delightful couples at the end of a very positive session. Inez, loud, red-haired, and always full of passion, replies, "Yes, but can we keep it, this feeling? My sister, she's mean. She tells me, 'You think you have found this love again with Fernando. But marriage is just about habit. It has a "best before" date like milk. In six months, you will be back to all the old nonsense. You can't keep a hold on love. That is just the way it is.' I feel afraid when she tells me that. Maybe we will slip back into all that fighting and loneliness."

The session ends there, but as I write up my notes I find I have two voices in my head. One offers a quote from the Greek philosopher Heraclitus: "All things flow, nothing abides." This has to be true of love, I muse. Just consider the high relapse rates from couple therapy. Maybe Inez's sister is just being realistic. But then the other voice pipes up with a quote from the eleventh-century Chinese poet Su Tung-p'o: "Year after year, I recall that moonlit night we spent alone together among the hills of stunted pine." Perhaps moments of deep attachment are powerful enough to hold lovers together year after year. I think of our research showing that couples hold on to the satisfaction and happiness they create in EFT sessions, even through hugely stressful lives.

Then I know the answer to Inez's question. In the next session, I tell her, "Everything moves and changes, but for love relationships there is no 'way it is' anymore. We are finally learning how to 'make' and 'keep' love. And it is up to you and Fernando now to decide the way it will be in your relationship. Probably, if you don't actively care for your relationship, the gains you have fought for will fade. But love is like a language. If you speak it, it flows more and more easily. If you don't, then you start to lose it."

A.R.E. conversations are the language of love. They shore up the safe haven that is your relationship and nurture your ability to be flexible, to explore, and to keep your love alive and growing. Conversation 7 is a road map for taking your love into the future. The steps entail:

• Recapping and reflecting on the danger points in your relationship where you slide into insecurity and get stuck in Demon Dialogues. This will allow you to figure out detours and shortcuts that lead you back into safe connection.

• Celebrating the positive moments, big and small. We are made for connection, and as Psalm 118:24 suggests, we should rejoice in the gifts given to us. The psalmist says, "This is the day the Lord hath made; we will rejoice and be glad in it" (KJV). This involves, first, reflecting on the moments in your daily lives that foster openness and responsiveness and reinforce your understanding of the positive impact you have on each other; and second, articulating the turning points in your recent relationship history when your love intensified.

• Planning rituals around the moments of separation and reunion in your daily lives to mark recognition of your bond, support, and responsiveness. These rituals are a way of holding your relationship safe in a distracting and chaotic world. The word *ritual* comes from Sanskrit and signifies "visible order," shaping actions or gestures that reflect the deeper nature of the cosmos. One of the great strengths of believers is that they know how to create rituals to celebrate the more profound spiritual elements in life, including their relationships.

• Helping each other identify the attachment issues in recurring differences and arguments and deciding together how to defuse these issues up front to deliberately create emotional safety and trust. This will allow you to resolve problems without letting hot attachment issues get in the way. I call this the Safety First strategy. Once emotional safety is established, one partner can bring up a problem in softer, less aggressive ways, and the other partner can stay emotionally engaged in the discussion, even if he or she does not agree with the view that is being presented.

• Creating a Resilient Relationship Story. This story describes how the two of you have built and are continuing to build a loving bond. It tells how you get stuck in conflict and distance and how you have learned to repair rifts, reconnect, and forgive hurts. It is a story about falling in love again and again.

• Creating a Future Love Story. This story outlines what you want your bond to look like five or ten years down the road and how you would like your partner's help in making the vision a reality. The Bible reminds us that marriage is not just a social arrangement but a spiritual exercise, a journey toward greater communion with God and others. For a Christian couple, shaping a Future Love Story sets them on the path to endless growth.

Conversation 7 is built on the understanding that love is a continual process of seeking and losing emotional connection, and reaching out to find it again. The bond of love is a living thing. If we don't attend to it, it naturally begins to wither. In a world that is moving ever faster and requiring us to juggle more and more tasks, it is a challenge to be present in the moment and to tend to our own and our partner's need for connection. This final conversation asks you to be deliberate and mindful about your love.

Let's see how this works in action.

DANGER-POINT DETOURS

Small moments of danger are easy for Inez and Fernando to identify. They had been doing the Protest Polka for years, a polka made wilder by Fernando's excessive drinking and Inez's flamboyant threats and vengeful flirting. Now, in this conversation, Inez can tell Fernando, "When you go still and turn away from me, that still freaks me out. I want to be able to tell you then, 'Hey, Fernando, please can you stay with me here?' Do you think you could hear that? That would really help me. I don't think my anxiety would get away from me then." Fernando in turn tells Inez that what he wants is for her to simply say she is mad at him and state exactly what has upset her, rather than immediately throw out ultimatums. Both agree that these detours could help each of them keep their emotional balance and stay out of negative spirals.

Another couple, Christine and Darren, had nearly divorced over his infidelity. "I think we are recovering from the affair," she tells him. "But I want you to know that right now, even the slightest suggestion that we may not be having enough sex makes me want to run and hide. Just for a second, the fear that you will always want more than I can give just leaps out at me. It doesn't take over anymore, but I still feel sick to my stomach at that moment." Darren responds, "I understand. When I made that kind of remark the other night, it was my clumsy way of trying to tell you that I desire you. How can I help here?" Christine, obviously relieved, murmurs, "Maybe just tell me right off the bat that the sex we have is good and that you are happy to be with me." He smiles and replies, "I can do that."

CELEBRATING MOMENTS OF CONNECTION

Mostly we don't tell our partners the specific small ways that they touch us with a spontaneous word or gesture and create a sense of belonging. Fernando, with a little embarrassment, confesses that when Inez, after all they had been through, introduced him to a colleague by saying "And this is my dear one, my husband," he melted inside. It made him feel that he was "precious" to her. He thinks of it every day.

No one forgets the turning points when love suddenly comes into sharper focus. These A.R.E. moments stay with us. And it's important to share them. Kay tells Don, "A key moment for me in healing our rift was that night when, even after forty-five years of being married to me, you told me how much it means to you that I hold your hand. You always reach out your hand, and I guess sometimes I take it and sometimes I don't. When you told me how important it was for you that I take your hand, how for you that means that we are together, that we can do anything, I was touched. I suddenly saw you as someone who needed me, rather than this big dominating man who liked making up rules."

In a session with another couple, we are discussing how Lawrence's depression has devastated his life. "I don't think I would have made it without you," he tells his wife, Nancy. "Even though I was so withdrawn, you kept being there for me. That day when I went for that job interview and they gave the job to that other guy, and I came home feeling like the biggest failure in the world, do you remember what you said?" Nancy shakes her head. "You kissed me and said, 'You're my guy. No matter what. We'll make it through. I love you, mister.' I'll always remember that. And it still helps me when things get rough and I doubt myself."

Even when partners are caught in Demon Dialogues, one of them can make a leap of empathy that just takes my breath away. I encourage them to hold on to that moment like a light in the dark as they struggle to renew their relationship. Maxine, who is usually angry at Rick for his "silences," suddenly very quietly tells him, "I think I understand. You look so calm. But you are scared. You are that little lonely boy I see in that picture of you as a kid we have on the fireplace. The loneliest boy in the world. You never belonged anywhere. So now here you are with me, the most talkative woman ever, and I overwhelm you. So you just go inside and try to calm yourself down. That's so sad. You must still be very lonely in there somewhere." Rick remembers this as the moment when he suddenly felt seen and understood, that although his wife was angry with him, she loved him.

These moments also occur in our spiritual life. Sam tells his wife, "When I slide into despair and blame myself for not saving my buddy's life in that firefight, I can close my eyes and tell myself, 'Be still and know that God loves you. He knows you tried your best.' It brings me back home."

A major part of keeping your love alive is to recognize these key moments of connection and hold them up where you both can see them, just as we do with family photographs of good times. They remind us of how precious our relationship is and what close connection feels like. They remind us of the simple ways that we can transform our partner's world with the power of our caring.

MARKING MOMENTS OF SEPARATION AND REUNION WITH RITUALS

Rituals are an important part of belonging. They are repeated, intentional ceremonies that recognize a special time or connection. Rituals engage us, emotionally and physically, so that we become riveted to the significance of a particular moment in a positive way. On several occasions in the Old Testament, God instructed His people to stop and create monuments of stone in order to note and remember a key moment. They would then go back, see these stones, and tune in to that moment again.

Religion has used ritual forever in this way. I remember a famous study led by psychologist Alfred Tomatis of a group of clinically depressed monks. After much examination, researchers concluded that the group's depression stemmed from their abandoning a twice-daily ritual of gathering to sing Gregorian chants. They had lost the sense of community and the comfort of singing together in harmony. Creating beautiful music together was a formal recognition of their connection and a shared moment of joy.

Among all primates, meeting and separation are key attachment moments. We recognize this with our children when they are small. We habitually kiss them goodbye and hold and greet them when they return to us. Why not take the time to formally recognize our relationship with our lover in the same way? Regular small gestures that convey the message "You matter to me" go a long way in keeping a relationship safe and sound.

Partners sometimes have a hard time recognizing these separation and reunion rituals. Joel looks blank when I ask him to identify such ceremonies in his marriage to Emma. He tells me, "I know that the dog always flings herself around and greets me when I come home, and I always sit and pat her for a bit. But I guess I go a bit unconscious with Emma. What do I notice and what do I deliberately and regularly do from day to day that kind of keeps us humming along? I'm not sure." As he scratches his head, Emma giggles and then helps him out. "You silly, it's not just the dog! Except when we lost each other for a while, you always walk into the kitchen, you say, real soft, 'How's my sunshine?' and then you pat me, too, usually on my backside. And I like that a lot. I count on it." Joel looks relieved and tells her, "Oh, right. Good. Well, from now on, maybe we should make that two pats and a kiss. For you, I mean, not the dog."

What you don't recognize slips away. Distressed partners sometimes complain bitterly about the loss of these small rituals. Cathy tells Nick, "You don't come and hold me before you leave in the morning. In fact, you don't even say goodbye anymore. It's as if we are roommates. We live in totally separate worlds, and that is fine with you." After a number of A.R.E. conversations, Cathy and Nick decide to reinstate this ritual and to embellish it a little with questions about what the other person is going to do during the day. Sometimes we extend these rituals into family life. I can remember Sunday supper changing from a special twosome meal to a family event when my kids came along. I also remember my son, many years later, complaining, "I'm busy. Why do we have to have these Sunday suppers, anyway?" My small daughter replied witheringly, "'Cause it's Sunday and we are a family and that is special, stupid."

I help couples design their own bonding rituals, especially recognizing moments of meeting and separation or key times of belonging. These are deliberately structured moments that foster ongoing connection. Here are some that come up again and again.

• Regularly and deliberately holding, hugging, and kissing on waking, going to sleep, leaving home, and returning.

• Writing letters and leaving short notes for each other, especially when one person is going away or when a couple has come together after a spat or a time of distance.

• Participating in spiritual or other rituals together, such as formally meeting for special family meals, planting the first spring flowers in a family garden, praying or attending religious events together.

• Habitually calling or texting during the day just to check in and ask after the other person.

• Creating a personal sharing ritual, that is, a time that is just for sharing personal things and connecting, not for problem solving or pragmatic discussions. Pete and Mara have a daily connection ritual that starts when one of them asks, "So how are *you* right now?" or, "So how are *we* doing together?" to shift the conversation away from other issues. Sarah and Ned have set a specific weekly time. On Friday night after supper, they linger over coffee for at least thirty minutes. They call it their "share time."

• Arranging a special time just to be together, for example, having breakfast in bed together on a Saturday morning without the kids, or shifting schedules to eat breakfast together every day.

• Setting up time for a daily devotion to read Scripture and pray together.

• Maintaining a regular date night, even if only once a month.

• Once a year, taking a class together, learning something new, even doing a project together.

• Recognizing special days, anniversaries, and birthdays in very personal ways. When I am tempted to play down these kinds of acknowledgments with my loved ones, I always remember they are concrete symbols of the fact that they exist in my mind and that this is what secure attachment is all about.

• Deliberately deciding to attend to your partner's daily struggles and victories and validating them on a regular basis. As we discussed earlier, small comments such as "That was hard for you to do, but you went for it," "You worked so hard on that project, no one could have tried harder," or "I really saw you struggling to be a good parent there" are nearly always more effective than concrete advice. We often give our children this validation but forget to give it to our partner.

• Taking opportunities to publicly recognize your partner and your relationship. This can take the form of a ceremony, such as a renewal of vows, or it can be a simple thank-you to your partner in front of friends for making a wonderful supper or helping you reach a personal goal.

Some partners need these kinds of formal structured arrangements to shake up a habitual lifestyle that makes any kind of close connection almost impossible. Sean and Amy, working hard to move from mutual withdrawal into a much closer connection, realized that they had created lives so consumed by career demands, long commutes, and kids' activities that, even on weekends, they were hardly ever together in the same room for more than ten minutes.

Chronic obsessive overwork and burnout have become part of our culture. We think it's normal. Juliet Schor, professor of sociology at Boston College, notes in her book *The Overworked American* that the United States (and Canada is similar) is the "world's standout workaholic nation, leading other countries in the number of days spent on the job and the number of hours worked per day." The Chinese get three weeks of mandated holiday. Most Europeans take six.

But Sean was a typical American. He worked every weekend, was on call for any accounting or fiscal crisis in his company, and took his computer on his annual two-week family holiday. Cecile Andrews, a leader in the Voluntary Simplicity movement, reports in her survey that North American couples spend an average of twelve minutes a day talking together. Sean and Amy estimated that for them five or six minutes was more accurate, and that their talk was mostly about scheduling and chores. Lovemaking was a nonissue. They were always too tired.

They decided to put their relationship first. In Sean's accounting terms, they would take care of their "main investment." This meant cutting back on the kids' activities, setting up a monthly date, creating time on Sunday mornings to make love, and getting up three mornings a week to pray and have breakfast together. Amy works at home, so Sean phones during the day just to say hello, sometimes calling her sexy names. If anyone with Amy asks who is on the phone, Amy says, "It's the Relationship RepairMan." This couple has taken back their time and deliberately found ways to nourish their relationship so it can grow and deepen.

SAFETY FIRST

Sorting out attachment issues from practical problems so that the latter can be easily tackled together is a key part of keeping your love strong. In our very first research study using EFT in the 1980s, we found that the couples who learned to reach for each other and create a more secure bond rapidly became skilled at solving the everyday problems that had plagued their relationship. They were suddenly cooperative, open, and flexible. We understood that this was because mundane problems were now just that. They were no longer the screen on which partners' attachment fears and unmet needs played out.

Jim and Mary can now discuss Jim's deep-sea diving trips without getting caught in Demon Dialogues. But it was not so long ago that just the mention of these trips would spark Mary's rage and anxiety at Jim's "macho distancing" and "crazy risk-taking." Now when the logistical difficulties around Jim going on a long diving trip come up, Jim first asks Mary if she needs some help feeling safe in this conversation. Does she have any feelings that she needs to share?

Mary appreciates being asked, and says that she is a little afraid. She no longer feels deserted when Jim goes on these trips, but she still feels anxious about them. She brings up that one of Jim's diving buddies is well known for being reckless. Jim assures her he will absolutely follow the safety rules that they had already agreed on, and he also offers to forgo the trip if the diving team really worries Mary. Mary feels heard and reassured and so can stay open to hearing how this trip is special to her husband. Then together, in about ten minutes, they solve the significant practical problems involved in Jim taking this trip.

I encourage couples as part of their planning for the future to take an ongoing problem, such as a wife wanting her husband to be a more involved parent, and first have an A.R.E. conversation around the issue, sharing the attachment needs and fears that this topic brings up. Then they can move into defining the pragmatic problem and consider solutions as a team. Janet used to complain to her husband, Morris, that he never helped in setting limits for their son; Morris would promptly dismiss her concerns and withdraw. Now she begins by expressing her vulnerability. "I don't feel like I am being a good mom here," she says. "It is so hard for me to really set limits for the kid. And I feel like I flip between being a harridan and a wimp. I get overwhelmed by it all. It never ends, setting rules, dealing with his evasions, talking to the school, driving him to all these appointments. I get angry, but it is because I really need your help here. I can't do this all by myself. I know you withdraw in frustration but when you do that, it leaves me alone and overwhelmed. Can we please find a way to do this together?"

Morris, who now generally feels reassured that his wife values and depends on him, hears her and responds to her distress. They acknowledge that they both get overwhelmed by the demands of parenting and need each other's support. They define the problem as their son's over-involvement with a fast-living set of friends, and they decide jointly to set some limits. They talk specifically about how to support each other in conversations with their son when he does not respect these limits.

A conversation about how to parent together is manageable. A dialogue that slips into desperate abandonment, rage, or hopeless evasiveness will never end in workable solutions. The essence of good problem solving is being able to stay focused and flexible. Emotional safety promotes a team approach and creative problem solving. Countless studies link emotional safety and secure connection to our ability to assert our needs, empathize with others, tolerate ambiguity, and think clearly and coherently. It makes sense to take care of the hot bonding issues hiding out in pragmatic problems first, before trying to find workable solutions. Sometimes just clarifying the emotional music playing when a topic comes up changes the problem itself.

When Halley pressures Don to commit to infertility procedures, he balks. They frame the problem in a number of ways, as a power struggle, a difference in the desire for children, Don's selfishness, Halley's neediness, and their lack of fit as a couple. This is indeed an overwhelming problem! In an A.R.E. conversation, the problem shifts and shrinks. Don is able to talk about how Halley's obsession with having a child leaves him feeling superfluous. "Sometimes I get scared that I am just a sperm bank to you," he says. "I need to know that I matter to you just for me." Once Halley and Don can talk about this and Don is reassured that her desire for a child is part of her love for him, the problem shrinks down to an issue of timing. Don realizes that if they could be together for another year to solidify their relationship, he would feel more willing to go through medical procedures to conceive a child. Halley agrees.

CREATING A RESILIENT RELATIONSHIP STORY

When couples are caught in Demon Dialogues, there is often no coherent story, only a kind of "What is happening to us?" confusion. Partners' stories can be garbled and one-sided. Partners will tell me that everything is fine in the relationship and then slip into raging at each other's insensitive blaming. They say they want caring, but then tell a story of rejecting each other's caring overtures. The emotional volatility destroys their sense of their history and their ability to create a consistent story line. But when partners tune in to each other and "feel felt," it helps them reach a state of balance, physiologically and emotionally, so that they can order information in their minds and create coherent stories of their emotions and relationship.

We use stories to make sense of our lives. And we use stories as models to guide us in the future. We shape stories, and then stories shape us. Once partners feel safe with each other, they can create a clear story of their relationship and figure out how to recover from disconnections and make their bond stronger. This not only sums up their past in a way that makes sense, it gives them a blueprint for the future.

Your Resilient Relationship Story should recap how you both have been stuck in insecurity and then found ways to move out of those mires together.

Nicole and Bert described such wildly different versions of their relationship when they came to see me that neither of them recognized the other's version as having any validity at all. They were each living in a different marriage, and neither of their accounts made much sense. But a few months later, with their connection much more secure, they were able to create a clear, logical story of how their problems evolved and how they had reclaimed their marriage. They called it "How N & B Conquered Demons and Distance and Created the Ultimate Cuddle."

"Well, we fell in love instantly," Bert begins, "and even though we didn't know what we were doing, neither of us having experienced a real good relationship, even with our parents, we did pretty well. We loved each other. But then when our three girls came along, things got pretty stale and cold between us. Nicole's territory was the home, and mine was work and sports. Then when she had those medical problems and we stopped making love, we really lost touch with each other. I guess it was my fault in a way—I didn't support her enough and retreated into my job and my buddies."

"It wasn't all you, though," Nicole pipes up. "I got pretty lost and started getting on your case about everything. Then we got caught in that 'Nicole attack' and 'Bert zone out' polka till all we could see was how nasty the other one was. Finally we realized we were losing each other and worked really hard to risk sharing our hurts and our needs. We realized that both of us felt desperately lonely."

Bert picks up their story. "I think the big thing that helped us was understanding how we really weren't that different after all. We were just expressing our upset differently. I had to learn how my distance really made Nicole feel vulnerable and scared. When she risked telling me that, I felt a whole new set of feelings for her."

Nicole smiles at her husband and adds, "The turning point for me was when you told me that you were exhausted from hearing all the faults I had found in you and that you were just grieving and giving up on me loving you. I didn't want you to do that. So we both found a way to talk about our raw spots, reach for each other, and give each other another chance. When we went back and talked about the night our last baby was born, you helped me let go of all that old hurt and resentment. You accepted that you didn't stand up to that doctor for me like I thought you should. That was so important for me. I was able to start to trust you again."

Bert turns to me and laughs. "I guess we sound pretty satisfied with ourselves, but it feels like we've accomplished a lot. I feel like I have my wife back. We found our way back to being close, and I like that we can talk and say how we did it. It gives me confidence."

Bert and Nicole didn't need much help putting this story together. Sometimes I prompt couples a little to articulate the elements of their story. If you need aid, I suggest that you help each other to come up with the following:

- Three adjectives or images that describe your relationship when it was stalled in insecurity and negative spirals. For example, *dead-ended, exhausted, a minefield.*

- Two verbs that capture how each of you moved in your negative dance and how you were able to change the pattern. *I pushed, you turned away. But we learned to talk about how scared we were and reach out for each other.*

- One key moment when you saw each other differently, felt new emotions, and were able to reach for each other. *I remember that Saturday afternoon when I had walked out. I came back into the room and you were weeping. The look on your face really got to me. I just felt our sadness and came over and told you I wanted us to be close again and I needed your help. We had to help each other get there.*

- Three adjectives, emotions, or images that express your relationship right now. *Playful, contented, delighted, blessed, hand in hand.*

- One thing you are doing to keep your connection with each other open and growing. *Cuddling before we fall asleep, kissing when we wake up.*

- Two ways in which this new sense of connection has translated into your spiritual life—your relationship with God.

Marion and Steve, after successfully taking their relationship from endless bickering to safe emotional connection, come up with the following story. "In the beginning our relationship was cold, tight, and lonely," says Marion. "Steve pushed and banged on the door; I just turned away and hid. We both saw the other person as the problem. But that day when we found ourselves talking about divorce, we realized that both of us were terrified of losing the other. So we started to help each other out and take little risks to learn to trust each other."

Steve now chimes in. "Talking about the times when things really turned around was the most interesting. For me, a key moment was when Marion cried and told me that she had always believed that she wasn't pretty, clever, or sexy enough for me, and she was so sorry that I had ended up feeling lonely. That she wanted to come out and be with me, but she was afraid. I don't think I have ever felt closer to her than in that moment. I never understood how she felt inside. That she wasn't trying to hurt me when she got all distant. And I never understood the impact of my angry comments on her, how small she felt."

I ask, "How about for you, Marion? Do you remember a time when new emotions came in, a time that moved you into a different place with Steve?" "Oh, yes," she replies. "It was one night when we were talking about his pushing me till I blow. And he suddenly looked so sad. He told me, 'Well, I'd rather have you mad at me than just not care at all. At least if you're mad, I know I matter to you.' And I got that. Now when I start to doubt everything again, I go back to that moment in my head. It calms me down. My big, powerful husband needs that from me. Amazing, isn't it?" She tips her head to one side and smiles as if she has just discovered the most exquisite secret. It's a secret that changes her universe.

Steve and Marion have no trouble coming up with positive images of their present relationship. They agree that the image that captures how they are with each other now is the image of how they greet each other in the evening and hold each other. Marion says that she feels more "confident" as a person since they have been able to turn their relationship around. She now feels "close" to Steve in a way that moves her into "calm happiness." Steve chooses his words carefully. "When she risks and comes close, I melt," he says. "And I feel high. We have a new level of trust here. Will *melt, high,* and *trust* do?" I tell him that it seems to me that they will do very nicely. I get him to ask Marion, and she replies with a broad, open smile.

Then we talk about how there will be times when they miss each other's signals, find it hard to respond, and spin out into their negative cycle. They recap exactly how they can now stop the "spin" of negative feelings in their Demon Dialogues. At those times, Steve says to Marion, "We are losing it here and we are both hurting." Marion tells me, "The only way I can really do it is to take a deep breath and leap. I say to Steve, 'This is scary. We need to slow down.'" They agree that they now also take time to listen and comfort each other when those feelings of hurt come up.

I ask them to tell me one thing that they are doing to keep the positive cycle of reaching and connecting strong. Marion shares that their daily devotions and quiet times together have become more joyful and fulfilling, and they are sending each other more messages of encouragement and notes from Scripture. They also tell me that they write loving notes to each other every few days and stick them on pillows, in briefcases, or on dashboards. Neat! I do that for my kids sometimes. How come I never thought to do that for my husband? They also tell me that after making love they always tell each other one thing the other did that they really liked. With all the fighting, they had both lost confidence in their sexual attractiveness and abilities; this was a way to support each other and get their confidence back.

CREATING A FUTURE LOVE STORY

I ask partners to make up their Future Love Story. We talk about what their personal dreams are for the next five to ten years. The more of a safe haven we have with our loved one, the more assured, assertive, and adventurous we can be. When our loved one is by our side, we tend to have more faith in ourselves and can dream in a new, expansive way. In this story, partners relate their vision of their future relationship. They then ask each other for support and discuss how they can make it a reality together.

"Personally, I want my own company," Steve tells Marion. "Even if it's small. But I can't do it without your support. And I want to do it in a way that has you feeling included, not neglected. The ideas you have are really useful to me." When it is Marion's turn, she tells him that she is thinking maybe she can finish her degree after all. And she appreciates him offering to look after the kids during her evening classes. She then mentions how in about five years, they might have another child. Steve rolls his eyes and pretends to fall off his chair at the mention of another baby. But he agrees that they can talk about this, although he has some fears around it. She stays engaged with him and agrees to listen to his reservations.

Then we talk about how they envision their future relationship. Both want to keep the newfound closeness between them and commit to holding on to the ways they have developed to safeguard their time together. Marion tells Steve that she wants their sex life to improve and wants him to read some books on sex with her. He agrees. He wants them to spend more time together with their kids and less time with her extended family. This is hard for her, but she is able to listen to his points and move into being more open to the idea. She tells him her limits. She "just cannot give up" holidays with her family, and he respects this. She looks at me and tells me, "Not bad, huh? A few months ago we couldn't agree on when to go grocery shopping, let alone deal with these kinds of changes and planning for the future." A safe emotional connection makes all the difference.

Finally, I ask them, when they are very old, what would they like to be able to tell their great-grandchildren about their relationship? Steve says, "I'd like to tell them that I was a good husband and I really tried to make my wife happy. That she was the light of my life. Like she is now." Marion can't speak at this point. With tears in her eyes, she murmurs, "Ditto."

The story that Bobby Joe and Frank tell me reflects their belief that marriage is a spiritual journey. She comments, "Now that we are closer, we are beginning to serve God together in a new way, and we see this growing in the future. We will help each other become more of who God wants us to be. We are planning a mission trip next summer with our church and starting a small group in our home to help other couples grow together. As we learn to come together, we will find new ways to serve the Lord."

HOLDING ON TO POSITIVE CHANGES: CREATING NEW MODELS

After Marion and Steve leave, I find myself remembering that in the early days of EFT, we didn't pay much attention to asking couples how they planned to hold on to their positive changes. I used to think that if you understood love, accepted your attachment needs, and found ways into A.R.E. conversations, these moments would be so intoxicating that couples would naturally just keep doing them. You did not need to actively plan how to keep your love alive. But my couples have taught me differently. When you move into new ways of connecting with your partner, it is useful to take the new emotions, perceptions, and responses and integrate them into a narrative that captures all these changes. The Resilient Relationship Story gives you a coherent way of reflecting on your relationship drama, a drama that is always unfolding no matter how clear your focus. Couples tell me that this makes it easier for them to hold on to the positive changes they've made and gives them a model of their relationship as a safe haven that they have built together and can rebuild again and again.

Partners can also call up these positive models to help them deal with moment-to-moment interactions, especially when raw spots get rubbed. They help us contain the fallout when we get hurt, deal with our doubts, and remain connected. When I am flying through turbulent skies and getting panicky, it calms me to remember how I dealt with this situation at other times and how I landed safely.

A Resilient Relationship Story is a little like that. Marion tells me at one point, "Sometimes my whole body screams at me to run, tells me that this is just like my relationship with my dad and my first husband. Then I remember times I have taken risks with Steve and it was good. This helps me turn and take risks again rather than lock him out. Sometimes my head tells me that it's up to him to respond, that I shouldn't have to ask. But then I remember him telling me that he doesn't know what to do unless I help him out and confide in him. It's like part of my brain says, 'I am in shark-infested waters here.' But I bring up these positive pictures and they remind me that I am just in a little pool. And that I am safe with Steve."

New models of positive connection challenge not just our customary ways of seeing and responding to our partner, but also the templates for relationships that develop from our thousands of interactions with parents and past relationships. They change our view of close relationships and what is possible in them. They change who we are as people. I am talking about the cynical, untrusting thoughts prompted by our pasts that we aren't even aware of until they pop up when we are in a panic and cannot safely connect with our lover.

Steve tells me, "Sometimes, when I can't reach her, I can flip into this real negative place and my mind tells me that all relationships are baloney. That you can't trust or depend on anyone and you are a fool to even try. That watching your back and being in control is the only way to live. Then I can be real hostile, and Marion has to be the enemy. But these days Marion and I can connect, and when these ideas come up, there is another part of me that is calm and has this Resilient Relationship Story. Or maybe it's like a movie rather than a story. I think of the images in the story we created, and that old bitterness seems to go away. I think this helps me stay more open to my wife and to other people, too."

John Bowlby believed that we generalize from thousands of small interactions with those we've loved and build models of love and loving in our minds. These models guide our expectations and reactions in the present. This is fine if our models from the past are clear, coherent, and positive, but not if they are negative, confusing, and chaotic. We always have a bias in favor of what we already know. If this bias is negative, it can trap us in the habits of the past and make it difficult to stay open to positive possibilities with loved ones. Negative models tell us that closeness is dangerous and that depending on someone is foolish, or that we are unworthy and cannot expect to be loved. Positive models tell us that others are basically trustworthy, that we are lovable and entitled to caring. When we learn to foster safe, loving interactions with our partners and can integrate new experiences into models that affirm our connections with others, we step into a new world. Old hurts and negative perceptions from past relationships can then be put away and not allowed to orchestrate our way of responding to our lovers.

If we look at research, like that of psychologist Mary Main at the University of California, on adults who have an inner sense of trust and security with others, the key quality of these folks is not that they always had happy relationships with parents and caregivers in the past. It is that they can be emotionally open, lucidly describe past relationships, reflect on the good and bad experiences, and make sense of them. When I encourage partners to work on integrating their new dance into a view of what it means to love and be loved, I am encouraging them to positively reshape their unconscious blueprints for close connection with others. The new blueprint helps them to be truly present with their partner rather than fight echoes from past relationships.

In a counseling session, I might say, "I know your amygdala, the emotional part of your brain, is listening to new messages and responding differently here, but would you please also take this new information, and order, tabulate, and store it in your prefrontal cortex, the reasoning part of your brain, for future reference?" New research in neuroscience tells us that I would not just be using metaphors here. Dan Siegel, a main proponent of incorporating the new findings in brain science into our understanding of relationships, suggests in his book *Parenting from the Inside Out* that mental models are ingrained in our brains in patterns of neural firing. Neurons send messages to one another, and when messages are repeated over and over again, as Canadian psychologist Donald Hebb tells us, neurons fire together and then wire together. New experiences, if they are reflected on and assimilated, can actually reshape our brains.

Thus, Marion and Steve are busy translating new interactions into new pathways in their brains, pathways that reinforce their positive ways of seeing and engaging with each other. I think all the ways of keeping your love alive described in this conversation help neurons wire together and create a neural net of hope and faith that will help a couple hold on to their connection in the future.

In the end, all of this review, ritual, and story making are simply ways of encouraging couples to continuously pay attention to their relationships. This attention is the oxygen that keeps a relationship alive and well. Psychologist Robert Karen, in his book *Becoming Attached*, reminds us that to have a strong and lasting love that helps lovers thrive emotionally and intellectually, we don't need to be rich or smart or funny. We just have to "be there," in all senses of the phrase. If we can do this, love can do more than last—it can flower again and again.

PLAY AND PRACTICE

• Are there any emerging danger points in your relationship right now, echoes of raw spots or anxieties that are just starting up? Can you pinpoint the last time you were aware of this? Your body will give you the message "Now, that doesn't feel good," and you will get a sudden flood of emotion. Can you name the emotion? How can your lover help you with that? What would calm and reassure you, and halt a developing negative cycle? Can you share this with your lover?

• Can you identify small positive moments in your relationship? These can be very small. As long as they stir your heart and bring a smile to your lips, they count. Does your partner know about these moments? Tell him or her.

• Can you single out the key moments in your relationship, when it shifted to another level or you or your partner took the risk of becoming more open and responsive? How did this happen? What was it that you or your partner did that allowed this to happen? Sometimes we remember a first kiss, a coming together after a big fight, reaching for each other in prayer, or a moment when our lover moved in close and gave us just what we needed.

• Do you now have rituals marking belonging, separation, or reunion? Do you consciously say hello and goodbye? See if you can list these rituals with your partner. Can you create a new daily bonding ritual that will help you move into being more open, responsive, and engaged with each other?

• Think of a problem-solving discussion that always ends up in frustration for you and your partner. See if you can write down your attachment needs and fears that are operating just under the surface during this discussion. How could you express these to your partner? What could he or she do to help you with them? If you got this help, how do you think this would affect your discussion?

• With your partner, craft the beginnings of a Resilient Relationship Story. Include how you once got stuck in a Demon Dialogue, and how you exited the dialogue, created an A.R.E. conversation, and renewed your sense of connection. What did you both learn from the experience? If you have a hard time building the story, discuss this with your partner and use the elements mentioned earlier in this conversation—for example, find three adjectives to describe your bond—to help you. Discussing the examples in this conversation can also help.

• Together, create a Future Love Story, a description of the relationship you intend to have in five or ten years. Decide on one thing you as an individual can do right now to bring this dream a little nearer, and share it with your partner. How can your partner help you achieve your own personal dreams?

• What one small thing might you do every day to make your lover feel that you want to "be there" with him or her? Ask your partner what impact this would have on your relationship.

You have just taken a journey through the new science of love. This science tells us that love is even more important than the sappiest love songs insist. But love is not a mystical, mysterious force that sweeps us off our feet, as those love songs suggest. It is our survival code and contains an exquisite logic that we are now able to understand. We have a new lexicon for a truth written into our very DNA as humans made in the image of a loving God. This means that a resilient, deeply satisfying love relationship is not a dream, but an attainable goal for us all. And that changes everything.

PART THREE

The Power of Hold Me Tight

Our Bond with God

"Whoever dwells in the shelter of the Most High will rest in the shadow of the Almighty. I will say of the Lord, 'He is my refuge and my fortress, my God, in whom I trust.'"

—*Psalm 91:1-2*

The core of bonding theory and science is the assertion that we are built for relationship, for connection, and that this is our most basic instinct and compelling need. As the Christian writer Henri Nouwen tells us, "God loved you before you were born, and God will love you after you die. In Scripture, God says, 'I have loved you with an everlasting love.' This is the fundamental truth of your identity. This is who you are, whether you feel it or not. You belong to God from eternity to eternity. Life is just a little opportunity for you during a few years to say, 'I love you too.'"

For people of faith, this connection with God is a primary source of comfort, safety, and equilibrium in an ever-changing and ever-challenging world. From the earliest moments of the Christian church, as described in the writings of Saint Augustine, who died in 430 CE, this faith was not simply a system of rituals and doctrines but a personal encounter with the transcendence we call God, and the experience of the bond that unites us to the divine.

Contemporary writer Max Lucado describes his personal relationship with God this way: "If God had a refrigerator, your picture would be on it. If He had a wallet, your photo would be in it. He sends you flowers every spring and a sunrise every morning... Face it, friend. He is crazy about you!"

Again and again in Scripture, God is referred to as a refuge— a source of safety and comfort. In Psalm 59:16 we read, "I will sing of your strength, in the morning I will sing of your love; for you are my fortress, my refuge in times of trouble." We are explicitly invited to trust our heavenly father and to come "home" to him (John 14:23). Scripture refers to God as parent, friend, and lover (Isa. 66:13; Luke 13:34; John 15:5; Isa. 62:5; Isa. 54:5). Love, attachment, trust, and comfort are all woven into the fabric of Scripture and into the everyday language of our communities of faith.

In our relationship with God, we see the same key elements that are outlined by bonding science as core factors in our earthly attachments.

LONGING FOR CONNECTION

Tim makes an appointment to talk to his pastor about his feelings of emptiness. He says, "I have so much going for me in my life— great job, wonderful family—but I feel this emptiness inside. I feel disconnected at a deeper level. It's kind of like a hunger. Like there is something missing inside of me."

Mary tells her therapist, "I am less depressed now, but I still have this longing. I want to belong, to feel close to God again. I pray, but I feel I have lost the connection to Him as well as my spiritual connection to my friends at church."

The first principle of attachment science is that we all have a built-in *longing* for connection with someone who will respond to us and keep us safe. This longing is wired in and designed to keep us close to those we can depend on. We are born helpless and stay that way for longer than any other animal on this planet; this need for connection shapes our nervous system and the mass of neurons we call our brain. We see this longing when children reach for their mothers, in the loving touch between longtime partners, and in the fellowship of faith communities as they unite together in praise and worship. I love what Nouwen writes about this topic in his book *Words of Hope and Healing: 99 Sayings:* "The mystery of God's presence can be touched only by a deep awareness of His absence. It is in the center of our longing for the absent God that we discover His footprints and realize that our desire to love God is born out of the love with which He has touched us."

Attachment theory teaches us that this longing is not for an abstract "knowledge" of connection; it is for a "felt sense" of belonging. We feel this connection when we are *moved* by the majesty of the natural world, the spiritual truths found in Scripture, and the music of hymn and chorus.

This *longing* becomes most tangible when the uncertainty and transient nature of life hijack us and remind us of our limitations and our vulnerability. As Bowlby stated, in the moment when mind-bending doubt, trouble, and fear come for us, we naturally turn to and reach for a figure who can offer stability and comfort, who can calm our confusion and anxiety. Military chaplains always told me how, under fire, their men would all be calling for their mother, their partner, but most of all to God for help.

All through history, Christians have also spoken of this longing for connection with God in terms of a personal spiritual journey, a seeking for union with God. The Bible promises us, "You will seek me and find me when you seek me with all your heart" (Jer. 29:13). This journey can be framed as a search for peace, for wisdom, for release from shame or sin, and as a returning to wholeness. Indeed, the word *holy* originally signified that which must be preserved whole and intact. Attachment scholars also talk of how, when a child has a secure connection with a parent, he or she is able to put his or her inner world together into a coherent whole in which everything makes sense, rather than being pulled in many directions by random ideas and reactive emotions.

A SAFE HAVEN

The second principle from attachment science that fits so perfectly with the Christian faith is that closeness to a loved one offers us a safe haven—a place of peace, comfort, and consolation. The conviction that our connection with God is our ultimate source of safety is found everywhere in Christian texts, songs, and prayers. Every Christmas, I thrill as I listen to Handel's *Messiah* and the tenor sings, " 'Comfort ye, comfort ye my people,' saith the Lord. Saith the Lord." We know from hundreds of studies on human bonding that connection with a loving attachment figure calms our nervous system, turns off our amygdala—the fear center in our brain—and takes us to a place of emotional balance. In this place, the most flexible, centered, and adaptive part of ourselves can emerge.

In one of the most recent studies in my lab, we invited women who felt disconnected and distressed in their relationship to undergo a brain scan. We found that whether they lay alone in the machine, had a stranger hold their hand, or had their partner hold their hand, when they saw a red X that signaled a shock might be coming, their brain lit up in alarm, and if they were shocked on their ankles they reported that it was indeed very painful. We then gave these women and their partners couple therapy sessions, in which they specifically learned how to reach toward each other and offer each other safe, reassuring connection. After therapy, the red X still set their brain on fire when they lay in the brain scan alone or holding the hand of a stranger, but when their partner held their hand, their brain remained still and calm, and they reported that the shocks they received were simply "uncomfortable" rather than "painful." And they were not simply controlling their fear better—the control center of their brain remained inactive. Their partner's touch was a powerful safety cue, a signal that our human brain has been programmed to tune in to and trust. We believe that this study shows the power of loving connection to transform how we perceive and respond to threats.

My all-time-favorite hymn, "Abide with Me," is all about how the felt presence of God offers us safe haven and release from fear:

Abide with me; fast falls the eventide;
The darkness deepens; Lord, with me abide;
When other helpers fail and comforts flee,
Help of the helpless, Oh, abide with me.

A SECURE BASE

The third key principle of attachment is that loving connection makes us stronger. It offers us a secure base from which to go out into the world, explore, and grow so that, empowered, we can thrive and face whatever demons come for us. In attachment theory, this concept came from the observation that when children knew that they had a safe haven to return to and someone to call on for care, they were more adventurous. Released from worry and the need to scan for danger, they took risks, found their confidence, and actively engaged with their world.

Paradoxically, the fact that they could rely on a loved one, that they could effectively depend on this person, made them stronger and more independent. This reflects the way in which acknowledging our dependence on God also makes us stronger. We read in Psalm 138:3, "On the day I called, You answered me; You made me bold with strength in my soul" (NASB).

Perhaps the best-known example of our relationship with God as the ultimate source of strength is the 23rd Psalm. It reads, "Yea, though I walk through the valley of the shadow of death, I will fear no evil: for thou art with me; thy rod and thy staff they comfort me" (KJV). Elsewhere in Psalms, God is described as "my rock, and my fortress" (Ps. 18:2, KJV) and the "strength of my life" (Ps. 27:1, KJV). A sense of secure connection with an omnipresent and loving God has always been a powerful way to deal with our ultimate vulnerability—our fear of loss and death.

Psychologist Linda McLean at the Princess Margaret Cancer Centre in Toronto worked with forty-two couples in which one partner was facing terminal cancer, helping them move into a Hold Me Tight conversation so that they could deal with their grief and end of life issues together. Her study showed that the loving connection they created helped the dying partner to face death with serenity and lessened the anguish of the partner who was left behind. She concluded that a sense of deep connection helps us deal more positively with the helplessness of grief associated with the loss of a spouse or loved one.

Bestselling author and pastor Rick Warren and his wife, Kay, spoke recently of dealing with grief together after losing their twenty-seven-year-old son to suicide in 2013. "When Matthew was alive, we were worried that should he take his own life, then it would tear our marriage apart," Kay said. "We knew we wouldn't divorce, but we thought it would ruin our relationship. But we made the decision that, though we may grieve differently, we would grieve together and show grace to one another."

Bonding science now offers strong evidence that those who have secure bonds with others react to reminders of death with positive strategies. They take these reminders as calls to help others, create a legacy, and find meaning in their everyday lives. When we feel that we belong in and are part of a loving, benevolent world and have strong bonds with others, we seem to be able to transcend our absorption with the self. We can then live with our vulnerability, rather than being constrained or controlled by it. Once again, this understanding of human bonding reflects the wisdom of Christian teaching and the Christian understanding of the power of a secure bond with God, the one who declares, "Surely I am with you always, to the very end of the age" (Matt. 28:20).

The life plan that Robert had envisioned for his wife and himself did not include her getting cancer in her fifties. After months of being torn between the hope that she would get better and the reality that her health continued to decline, together they chose to face the reality of her impending death. The last few months were hard but sweet. "We spent every waking moment together," he said. "We cried, we laughed, we prayed together. It was a sweet time. She was in my dreams before I met her, and she is in my dreams now that she's gone. She passed away so content and peaceful. It still hurts, but I know I'll be okay. That's what she would want."

For the Christian, however, God is not simply a bastion of hope and confidence when facing distress and danger, or even a resource that empowers us to explore and engage with our world. Understanding the power of secure attachment shows us how trust in God, the ultimate attachment figure, can be a powerful source of positive fulfillment and personal growth throughout life. Those who know and live with a sense of secure connection to special loved ones have been shown to be more able to tune in to and be compassionate toward others, deal with anger constructively, cope with distress, stay open to and forgive others, show more generosity and tolerance, and shape a positive sense of self as one who is worthy of love and care. These qualities go a long way in exemplifying the human virtues laid out in Christ's teachings. It is no wonder, then, that secure bonds with others seem to be linked to greater commitment to religious beliefs and measures of mature spirituality.

Feeling for and with others seems to be a crucial step on every spiritual path. In 1 Peter 3:8 we are admonished to "be like-minded, be sympathetic, love one another, be compassionate and humble." Some years ago, in the middle of a bustling spice market in the old city of Meknes, in Morocco, I noticed a tiny, elderly lady sitting cross-legged on the stone pathway. I remember the scene vividly. Her head is down, her scarf almost covering her small face, a face lined and wrinkled by a life full of more hardship than I will ever know.

She holds her hands up, cupped above her head in a silent plea for alms. We tourists, who have been told to ignore beggars, pass her by. But somehow I cannot just walk away. I tell my husband, "I must go back," and turn toward her. Placing all the coins I have in my pocket in her hands, I murmur, in Arabic, "For you, mother." She looks up at me, and the world suddenly shifts so that there is only the two of us. The noise of the souk is lost to me. The differences between us disappear. But what happens next shocks me, pierces my heart, and leaves me suddenly weeping. In perfect English, the little lady whispers to me, "Bless you, my child." I do not remember what happened next. I think my husband came and took my arm, guiding me back to the tourist van. All I know is that, even now, I think of her and weep. Perhaps this is simply sentimentality, or perhaps it is what we mean when we talk of being touched by the Spirit.

THE PAIN OF SEPARATION

The fourth attachment principle is that, since we are designed for connection, losing this connection profoundly hurts. We know that the pain of rejection registers in the same part of the brain and is coded in the same way as physical pain. Pain alerts us to danger, and separation from others is a danger cue for human beings. When we cannot connect with those we love and depend on, including God, we suffer. But as psychologists Pehr Granqvist and Lee Kirkpatrick playfully suggest, "God does not die, sail off to fight wars, move away, or file for divorce." Nevertheless, in the Bible and in classic Christian literature, separateness from God is referred to as "a dark night of the soul." Even Jesus was not exempt from primal panic and suffering when separated from the one He loved most. He cried out from the cross, *"Eloi, Eloi, lema sabach-thani?"* (Mark 15:34) — "My God, my God, why have you forsaken me?" This is one of the clearest demonstrations, in fact, of His humanity within His divinity.

The diaries of Mother Teresa, in the period of her life when she felt cut off from God, are full of anguish. She grieved and struggled with this loss of felt connection with Christ. In 1956, she confided to Archbishop Périer, "I am longing — with a painful longing to be all for God — to be holy in such a way that Jesus can live His life to the full in me. The more I want Him, the less I am wanted. I want to love Him as He has not been loved, and yet there is that terrible separation, that terrible emptiness, the feeling of the absence of God....Please, Your Grace, pray for me—that I may draw very close to God." She also spoke of the "agony of desolation" that comes from her longing to be with "the Absent One" (in *Come Be My Light: The Private Writings of the Saint of Calcutta*).

All these laws of love and bonding describe what is normal and general about human beings, but we are also different in the ways we deal with our vulnerability and our need for connection. We learn different connection strategies in the relationship with our parents, and some of these strategies can foster and others can disrupt our connection with God. The next section outlines these strategies.

WAYS OF ENGAGING WITH LOVED ONES— EFFECTIVE AND LESS EFFECTIVE

There are really only three basic ways of engaging with those we depend on in our moments of emotional need: reaching, anxiously demanding, and trying to stay more distant—relating but avoiding vulnerability. All through this book you have read of people learning to tune in to their emotions, pinpoint their longings, and reach for a loved one, asking openly and clearly for what they need. This is the best way to shape a strong bond with another, the kind of bond that makes us stronger as human beings and builds loving, lifelong connection. But when this reaching triggers too much uncertainty, we use less effective, insecure strategies. Bonding scientists call these insecure strategies anxious and avoidant. When we are caught in agitated anxious mode, we scan for rejection and become demanding and desperate, but we find it hard to trust or take in any caring we receive. When we feel threatened by the risk involved in depending on another, we tend to turn away, avoid, and deny our need for connection. We can see these three strategies in all our close relationships, including our relationship with God.

Amy's voice is calm as she describes to her pastor her secure connection with God: "I know I can reach for Him and find that still moment of peace. I don't always get what I pray for, but it helps keep me steady. That I can ask and be heard."

Kate does not speak this way. She does not feel confident in her faith. She tells her husband, "I know I shouldn't feel this way, but these days I almost get angry when I try to pray. I felt so sure when I began coming to church, but now I just want to stand and yell, 'Are you listening to me at all?' I ask, 'Do you care that I hurt? I don't think so. If you did, you would help me now.' But then maybe I don't deserve His comfort. I am just not that important to Him." She cries, "It's not fair. Not when I pray so hard every day, asking Him to help me." Kate is caught in her anxiety and agitation.

On the way home from church, Pete asks his friend Tom about his faith. Tom looks out the window and replies in an offhand way, "Look, I was brought up religious and I go to church, but, well, I think you have to stand on your own two feet. The truth is that no one is looking out for you in the end. There is no point in spending your life on your knees praying. It doesn't get you anywhere. I am fine just living from day to day. It's like I say to my wife, 'If something bothers you, the best thing is to just try to forget it.'" Tom is dismissing his need for connection with God. He avoids depending on God.

The secure strategy of owning our need and reaching for connection that we see in Amy's response is the most positive and effective way of dealing with our attachment needs. It is the one most likely to gain us the closeness we desire. Those of us who use this as our main approach have usually experienced at least one relationship, often with a parent, in which a loved one consistently responded to our emotional cues and offered us a safe haven of love. As noted in an earlier chapter, in such relationships we learn to expect that those we depend on will be accessible, responsive, and engaged (A.R.E.). We expect the answer to the key bonding question "Are you there for me?" to be positive. This makes our world a safer place and we are usually more balanced emotionally; we can tolerate vulnerability, trust our own emotions and the caring nature of others. Moreover, there is evidence (from the work of Swedish attachment researcher Pehr Granqvist and others) that children who are cared for in a sensitive, loving way, and who are introduced to the love of God by their parents, report being more religious. Those who have this sense of security in their most important relationships also report that bonding moments in romantic relationships tune them in to their sense of connection to God. Sarah tells Harold, "In the last few months, we have been so close, and I feel so held and cared for. And this morning, in my quiet time with God, this same feeling of being held was there. I felt the warmth of God like I have never felt it before."

When our most important love relationships, those with parents and life partners, are positive, they open us up to the love of God. When we feel precious, held, and protected by loved ones, it appears to be easier for us to feel comfortable seeking closeness to God, have confidence in His benevolence, and open ourselves up to faith. Our experience of having a secure base with others also translates into the ability to explore religious possibilities. We can deal with doubts and ambiguities and struggle through a personal "quest" during which we can truly explore our inner spiritual life. According to Indiana psychologist Kevin Byrd, more secure attachment, with its accompanying emotional balance and positive expectations, often leads to more meditative and conversational forms of prayer, rather than prayer that is focused on petitioning God for help.

When the bonds of human love are positive, one secure connection cascades into another. Sometimes, in my practice, I ask my clients, "When you were small and you cried, did you know that someone would come to comfort you and hold you?" A positive answer here usually leads to a positive assertion that people are basically trustworthy and likely to respond when others need care. For people of faith, the natural next step is a heartfelt affirmative response to the question, "Do you feel that God is there for you and will respond if you ask for help?" For a Christian, experiencing the sensitive soothing care of a parent, a partner, or a Christian community bolsters faith in a benevolent universe infused with a loving God. This sense of connection with God then leads back to an appreciation for and trust in this person's family and life partner. Enrico tells his wife, "I went to the worship service this morning, and as the music lifted me up and I listened to God's message, I was swept into such a sense of thankfulness for your love and what a blessing you are to me."

Even in a monastery, this link appears between devotion to a partner and devotion to God. At Sant'Antimo Abbey in the Tuscan hills, built some nine hundred years ago on the Via Francigena—the ancient pilgrims' path to Rome—the monks' chant echoes out from the soft stone at lauds, terce, sext, and vespers. They sing in joy, "O God, you are my God, at dawn and dusk, I search for you." It is not accidental, surely, that the bell calling them to prayer is named "the spouse."

In this *sacred circle,* where a sense of closeness to the divine and a loving connection with important others work in tandem, love is the gift that keeps on giving. Love for the divine guides and enhances bonding between partners, and the daily practice of love between partners helps to strengthen a sense of secure connection with God. The sacred circle is illustrated in this verse from 1 John 4:7: "Dear friends, let us love one another, for love comes from God. Everyone who loves has been born of God and knows God."

Unsurprisingly, things are a little different when we look at anxious or avoidant ways of engaging with loved ones. A sense of unsafe connection with specific loved ones often generalizes to the way we see the world and the one who shaped that world. We develop anxious perspectives and strategies when we perceive others as having been inconsistent in their support for us. This kind of "Now you see me, now you don't" experience leaves us constantly scanning for signs that we will be deserted or rejected. Anxiously connected partners are quicker to pick up changes in their lover's facial expressions, and faster to assume the worst and attribute negative intentions to others. We intensify our emotions to try to ensure that others will pay attention and respond, but, lost in the flood of feelings, we often become confused and subsequently send confusing messages. We often mix hostile anger (*Why don't you ever...*) with intense pleas for reassurance. It is hard for us then to relax into the care of others or tolerate any perceived lack of response from those we depend on. This drama also plays out in our connection with God. Anxiously attached people often tell me that they feel abandoned by God.

Claire tears up as she tells me, "Peter and I fight about going to church. He says to make up my mind and get into a routine, but there are times when I really *have* to go and times when I just kind of feel like God doesn't care, so why bother? I guess I never quite feel safe, never sure that God really loves me, or even that Peter loves me. If we have a fight and I feel alone, then I really need to go to church and kind of turn to God for comfort, if you know what I mean. But then sometimes I feel just as alone when I pray. I ask and ask and ask, but it's like He isn't listening. Doesn't care. Sometimes I think He is just angry at me and is punishing me." Claire turns to God to compensate for her lack of safe connection in her life, to answer her emotional and spiritual hunger. But she reaches for God in the same way she reaches for her husband, sometimes pleading with Him and sometimes angrily blaming Him. As research studies on the nature of prayer predict, Claire's anxious style of prayer takes the form of intense petitioning and reactivity to God's apparent lack of response to her requests. When she does receive blessings, she can't quite relax and take them in.

The positive side of this is that studies tell us that if Claire can have new experiences of reaching and receiving loving responsiveness from her partner, or find a safer, more reliable sense of connection with God, she can shift into a more secure style of bonding in both the romantic and faith-based aspects of her life. As she does this, she will begin to see God as a more stable and accepting figure and as a less controlling one. In fact, later in therapy she tells me of a religious retreat she went on and also of a positive experience of closeness with Peter. She notes, "For the first time, I really saw the delight in his eyes. And I got that it was for *me!* I was delightful to him! Somehow that helped me feel that God had forgiven me for my failings. And if God has forgiven me, loves me even, well, then that changes everything."

Adopting avoidant strategies is a way of protecting ourselves in a world in which those closest to us seem unresponsive to our needs or even punishing and cruel when we are most vulnerable. We then blunt our need for belonging and try to dial down our expectations. We cannot totally expunge our longings, though, so this blunting takes constant *effort*. When we feel vulnerable or when others show need, we tend to shut down our emotions and turn away. And while this avoidance tends to go along with a lack of belief in a caring God, it also appears in committed Christians. Stuck in avoidance, we tend to see others as unloving, even dangerous, and God as distant and harsh. Nevertheless, our innate craving for safe attachment breaks through, so we try to reach for Him and protect ourselves at the same time. Often then we cannot accept and take in love and grace, even when it is given.

Theo, referred to me for his post-traumatic stress problems, grimaces in irritation when I ask if he has been back to church to meet with his pastor. "I don't think I'm going back there. Everyone wants to yap at you. As if they really cared anyway. I asked that pastor, 'Where was God in that firefight then—in all that rawness and murder?' I gave up on my species and on God years before that. Religion is all rules and shoulds. If you are good, then maybe you get to see an angel? It's just like my marriage to Janie, all carrot and stick. I totally messed that up. She was right to leave. In the end, everyone is out for themselves, so you have to just take care of you. So what. I cried at the Easter service when that pastor was kind to me, but I am fine without that sloppy stuff. I don't need it. I am strong enough on my own. I just keep busy." I softly point out that he is shouting but also weeping. "People should give up on me," he whispers. I ask him what it was like to let himself cry at the Easter service. After a long silence, he murmurs, "It was okay—well, it was good. It was that pastor shaking my hand and the hymn, the one I used to sing when I was young." He sighs. "It reminded me of those moments when I felt safe and that God was up there watching me, that He was with me." I ask him if he can close his eyes and try to tell God how much he hurts, and how he struggles to be, as he says, "a rock. So nothing can touch me." For a moment, he is open. He connects with the sense that God accepts his struggles and knows his pain. Now I see a more thoughtful Theo emerging. He decides to go back to talk to the pastor who reached for him and to keep talking to God. He turns again to the ultimate source of safety and comfort, and for the first time in years begins to feel hopeful about his life.

REFLECTIONS

The process of religious conversion has often been likened to falling in love. Bonding studies now offer a solid, scientific scaffolding for the wisdom of the sacred writings that speak of the power of love and mankind's deep need for belonging. The blueprint for connection that is stamped into our nervous system by the Creator is mirrored in all our primary love relationships: those between parent and child, between life partners, and the bond between ourselves and God.

There is no conflict between science and faith here. In fact, the workings of the human heart seem to lead in a straight path directly to our understanding of the nature of the one who shaped it. Sir Arthur Eddington, a dedicated Quaker who was also a scientist, at first fiercely opposed Einstein's scientific theory of relativity, seeing it as sacrilegious. But he was the one who finally proved this theory, showing how the bending of light in the 1919 solar eclipse followed Einstein's predictions. Listening to the truth in his own heart, Eddington finally concluded that Einstein's way of making sense of the universe had to be right: his ideas were so beautiful that, in them, "I can hear God thinking."

Surely in the exquisite architecture of love and loving, in our elemental nature as *Homo vinculum,* the one who bonds, we can see the divine.

PLAY AND PRACTICE

1. When we ask life partners to begin exploring their emotional bond, we often give them a short questionnaire (page 68) to help them pinpoint the key elements that define security in this bond.

If you remember, the key question in a bonding relationship is "Are you there for me?" In secure relationships, we see the one we love as A.R.E.—accessible, responsive to our call, and truly engaged with us. This *presence* is what shapes the moments of connection that we remember, the moments when we truly know what it is to love and be loved.

If you apply this kind of exploration to your connection with God, you can ask yourself the following three questions. If you wish, you can use the lettered statements, deciding if, at this time, they are true, somewhat true, or not true for you, to help you formulate your response to the three main questions.

From your viewpoint, do you experience that God is accessible to you?
a) I know that I can call on God when I need Him.
b) I have the sense that I matter to God on a personal level.
c) I know I can pray and share my deepest feelings with Him and He will listen.
d) I trust that I can find Him when I need him. He will not turn away from me.
e) I have a sense of His presence in my life. He is there in my joy and my pain.

From your viewpoint, do you experience that God is responsive to you?
a) If I need comfort or guidance, my sense is that God is there for me.

b) I can lean on God when I am anxious and unsure and most need Him.

c) If I call on Him in prayer, He hears and answers me.

d) When I am lost and need reassurance, I can call out to Him and He will be there for me.

e) Even when I make mistakes and fail, I can turn to God to find comfort and acceptance.

From your point of view, do you experience your connection with God as close? Do you feel a sense of meeting and engagement?

a) I know God cares about my joys, hurts, and fears. They are worth His attention.

b) I feel close and safe enough to confide in God — to risk showing Him my innermost self.

c) Even when I feel cut off from God, I trust that on a deeper level He is still there, watching over me.

d) There are moments when I feel God's presence.

e) In prayer, in church services, and in moments of love and service with others, I feel the closeness of God and that He is with me.

Nobody will answer these questions positively all the time. Our bonds seem to vary naturally across moments of more secure connection, increasing distance, and then reconnection. I've offered these questions to simply help you explore your ongoing bond with God. If it feels right, you can share your responses with your partner or even with your pastor and fellow Christians, to draw closer to them.

2. We can reflect on the sacred circle described in this chapter. This is where a positive sense of connection with God fosters more loving bonds with special others, and in turn, these

loving bonds help us to tune in to and turn toward the love of God.

Can you think of times when your grounding in your faith helps you keep your emotional balance and be more open, responsive, and engaged with your partner and with others? If you can, please share these with this person or these people.

Can you think of times when your sense of connection to your partner moves you into a sense of closeness with God and the infinite? If you can, please share these with your partner.

3. Do you see similarities between how you relate to your partner, especially in times of doubt or stress, and the way you pray to God when you are upset?

Mary reflects, "I realize now that when I get scared or feel alone, I deal with these feelings by giving ultimatums to Jim. I make threats in the hope that he will pay me more attention. The other day, I suddenly heard myself doing the same thing while praying, and this helped me begin to talk to God from a more vulnerable place."

Can you share your discoveries with your partner?

4. When do you feel most open and responsive to God? Can you share this with your partner?

5. We can connect deeply with our partner by moving into a Hold Me Tight conversation in which we share our fears and our emotional needs. How can your partner help you offer up these needs to God in prayer? Your partner may help you simply formulate these needs or join with you in prayer.

6. How does your Christian faith help you move into the steps in the forgiveness conversations? Does this faith help you take responsibility when you hurt your partner? Does your Christian perspective help you forgive your partner

when he or she hurts you? Are there Scriptures that particularly help you with this, and if so, could you share those with your partner?

7. Can you read the Song of Solomon and share a few passages that speak to you about healthy sexuality and your sexual connection with your partner?

8. Christian couples can often outline many ways in which their faith helps them to shape and keep loving bonds. Tick off any of the folllowing examples that are true for you.

- Tim says, "I can turn to the Lord for comfort and support when I am angry or upset. This calms me and helps me slow down and take my wife's feelings into account. I am a better husband when I can turn to Him for support."

- Anne says, "When I feel mean, like I want to lash out at Sam, my commitment to my faith, my desire to truly follow Christ, turns me around. The image of the Lord and His kindness and caring reminds me that this is how I want to be. So I try a different, kinder way."

- Steve says, "My colleague tells me that you have to show your partner what they can do and cannot do. Maybe, but I have been taught to show forgiveness: to forgive my partner and to be compassionate. So that is what I try to do. After all, I make mistakes and I feel forgiven by the Lord. I feel loved by God, so it's easier to pass the love on."

- Aimee says, "I didn't get married just to be happy. It's a journey for me. It's part of my journey toward God, toward being the best Christian I can be. So my husband and I have a commitment to help each other grow.

This helps us hang in when we get stuck and hurt each other."
- Pat says, "Our faith brings us together. Praying together, moving into worship together, and praising the Lord together takes our relationship to a whole new level of closeness."

Ultimate Connection — Love as the Final Frontier

"And did you get what you wanted from this life, even so?
I did.
And what did you want?
To call myself beloved, to feel myself
Beloved on the Earth."

—*Raymond Carver*

"I have loved you with an everlasting love; I have drawn you with unfailing kindness."

—*Jeremiah 31:3*

"Truly religious people are ambitious. They want to live lives overflowing with significance...to retain their peace and serenity in the midst of their pain...to live generously, large-heartedly...to transform themselves into a beautiful ritual vessel brimful of the sanctity that they are learning to see in life."

—*Karen Armstrong,* The Case for God

Learning how to nurture the bonds of love is an urgent task. Loving connection provides the dependable web of intimacy that allows us to cope with life and to live life well. And that is what gives our life its meaning. For most of us, on our deathbeds, it is the quality of our connection with our precious ones that will matter most.

Instinctively, we know that those who grasp the imperatives of attachment live better lives. Yet our culture encourages us to compete rather than connect. Even though we are created by God to relentlessly seek out belonging and intimate connection, we persist in defining healthy people as those who do not need others. This is especially dangerous at a time when our sense of community is daily being eroded by an endless preoccupation with getting more done in less time and filling our lives with more and more goods. This erosion squeezes out our quality time with God, loved ones, and our church family.

We are building a culture of separateness that is at odds with our own God-given nature. We know, as Thomas Lewis and his colleagues state so well in their book *A General Theory of Love,* that if we "feed and clothe a human infant but deprive him of emotional contact he will die." But we have been taught to believe that adults are different. However did we get here?

Psychiatrist Jonathan Shay, in his book on the trauma of combat, *Odysseus in America,* reminds us that there are "two momentous human universals": that we are all born helpless and dependent, and that we are all mortal and we know it. For a Christian, the only healthy way to deal with this vulnerability is to reach out and be held by both Him and each other. Then, calmed and strengthened, we can walk out into the world.

The attachment perspective recognizes that our need for emotional connection with others is absolute. Thousands of studies in developmental psychology with mother and child, research on adult bonding, and the investigations of modern neuroscience confirm that when we are in close relationships, we are truly interdependent. We are not like separate little planets revolving around each other.

This *healthy* dependence is the essence of romantic love. The bodies of lovers are linked in a "neural duet." One person sends out signals that alter the hormone levels, cardiovascular function, body rhythms, and even immune system of the other. In loving connection, the cuddle hormone oxytocin floods lovers' bodies, bringing a calm joy and the sense that everything is right with the world. Our bodies are set up for this kind of connection. In Mark 10:7–8 we read, "For this reason a man will leave his father and mother and be united to his wife, and the two will become one flesh."

Even our identity is a kind of duet with those closest to us. A loving relationship expands our sense of who we are and our confidence in ourselves. You wouldn't be reading this book had I not found a way to plug into my husband's belief that I could write it, and my ability to hold on to his reassuring words kept me writing rather than walking away. Our loved ones do indeed come into our hearts and minds, and when they do, they transform us.

The quality of the love we receive puts us on a certain track. Assess how safely connected to Mom one-year-olds are when put in the Strange Situation, and you can predict how socially competent these children will be in elementary school and how close their friendships will be in adolescence, according to Jeff Simpson of the University of Minnesota. A secure connection to Mom and the closeness of these early friendships also forecast the quality of these individuals' love relationships at age twenty-five. We are our relationship history.

HOW DOES LOVE WORK?

To achieve a lasting loving bond, we have to be able to tune in to our deepest needs and longings and translate them into clear signals that help our lover respond to us. We have to be able to accept love and to reciprocate. Above all, we have to recognize and accept the predesigned code of attachment rather than attempting to dismiss and bypass it. In many love relationships, attachment needs and fears are hidden agendas, directing the action but never being acknowledged. It is time to acknowledge these agendas so that we can actively shape the love we so badly need.

To shape love, we have to be open and responsive, emotionally as well as physically. We can see what love encompasses in studies of the fluffy little titi monkey conducted by Bill Mason and Sally Mendoza of the University of California. Females nurse their babies but don't offer any other maternal responses. They do not groom or touch their infants. The true nurturer is the male, who assumes 80 percent of the infant care. It's the male who holds and carries the baby, who is emotionally engaged and is the safe haven. Baby titis don't seem to mind at all when the mother is removed from the family for a while, but when the father is taken away, the infants' levels of the stress hormone cortisol soar.

In my office, more emotionally distant partners sometimes tell me, "I do all kinds of things to show I care. I mow the lawn, bring in a good salary, solve problems, and I don't play around. Why is it that, in the end, these things don't seem to matter, and all that counts with my wife is that we don't 'talk about emotional stuff and cuddle'?" I tell them, "Because that's just the way we are made. We need someone to pay real attention, to hold us tight, to come very close sometimes and respond to us in an emotional way that moves us, connects with us. Nothing compares with that. You need that, too. Have you forgotten?" Connection is sweet, holding is deeply calming and satisfying, whether we are receiving or giving. Most of us love to hold a baby. It feels so good, just as it feels good to hold our lover.

But is attachment and bonding the whole ball of wax? Adult

love also involves sexuality and caretaking, or serving the other's needs. Attachment is the bottom line, the scaffold on which these other elements are built. The interconnections are obvious. Sexuality is best when there is safe connection. The risk that is essential to eroticism does not come from constant superficial novelty, but from the ability to stay open to your partner in the moment.

Caretaking and pragmatic support come naturally when we feel close and connected. "When you love, you wish to do things for," Ernest Hemingway wrote. "You wish to sacrifice for. You wish to serve." We know from research that secure partners are more sensitive to each other's needs for care.

Rose and Bill, a grad-school couple, fought about everything, but especially emotional connection and pragmatic supportiveness. Even at the conclusion of therapy, after they've made considerable progress, they get into a fight about the fact that he doesn't keep the pediatrician's number on his cell phone although she has asked him to do just that. When the baby gets ill, she can't use his phone to call the doctor. They finally find a way to step out of the argument. "When I can't find that number, I get scared," Rose says to Bill. "I need you to listen when I ask for stuff like that." Bill now offers support. "I hear you," he says. "It's like you are saying to me, 'Do you have my back?' You need to depend on me here. And you are a great mother to our kids. I have put the number on my phone and ordered you your own cell phone so this won't happen again. Maybe there are other ways I can support you here." In a later session, Rose tells Bill that she no longer resents taking care of the kids in the evenings when he needs to study. Now that she feels closer to him, she actually enjoys bringing him coffee and listening to how he is doing with his courses. Being able to create a more secure bond frees up our attention so that we can tune in to and actively support our loved one.

In a romantic relationship, secure attachment, sexuality, and supportiveness all come together. Partners create a positive loop of closeness, responsiveness, caring, and desire. In his first counseling session, Charlie solemnly announced that, although he didn't believe in divorce, he had decided to contact a divorce lawyer. Now, a few months later, he tells me, as his wife, Sharon, nods happily in agreement, "We are a lot closer. I don't think we have ever been this close. Somehow I just don't get so uptight and jealous anymore. I trust her. I can tell her when I need her help to set my mind at ease, and she can turn to me, too. We feel closer in bed. Sex is so much easier. I think we both feel desired and that we can ask for what we want. When we feel close like this, I like taking care of her. I like helping when her back hurts. I went and found her a little heating pad. And she is helping me with my weight-loss plan. This is like a whole new relationship here."

But making love work is also accepting that, even when it's good, it is always a work in progress. Just when you get it right, one of you changes! Ursula Le Guin, the novelist, reminds us that love "does not sit there like a stone. It has to be made like bread, remade all the time, made new." The intention behind EFT is to offer couples a way to do just that.

Thirty years of research tells us that we have helped many different kinds of couples "make" their love, newlyweds and long-married folks, the basically happy and the seriously distressed, traditional and unconventional, highly educated and blue-collar, reticent and effusive. We have found that the bonding moments in EFT not only help heal relationships, they create relationships that heal. Partners who are depressed and anxious benefit enormously from the experience of supportive connection that a more loving relationship offers.

If I had to summarize the lessons I've learned from all these couples, they would look like this:

- Our need for others to come close when we call — to offer us safe haven — is absolute.
- Emotional starvation is a reality. Feeling emotionally deserted, rejected, or abandoned sparks physical and emotional pain and panic.
- There are very few ways to cope with our pain when our primary needs for connection are not met.
- Emotional balance, calm, and vibrant joy are the rewards of love. Sentimental infatuation is the booby prize.
- There is no perfect performance in love or sex. Obsession with performance is a dead end. It is emotional presence that matters.
- In relationships there is no simple cause and effect, no straight lines, only circles that partners create together. We pull each other into loops and spirals of connection and disconnection.
- Emotion tells us exactly what we need, if we can listen to it and use it as a guide.
- We all hit the panic button at times. We lose our balance and slip into anxious controlling or numbing and avoiding modes. The secret is to not stay in these positions. It's too hard for your lover to meet you there.
- Key moments of bonding, when one person reaches for another and the other responds, take courage but they are magical and transforming.
- Forgiving injuries is essential and only happens when partners can make sense of their own hurt and know that their lover connects and feels that hurt with them.
- Lasting passion is entirely possible in love. The erratic heat of infatuation is just the prelude; an attuned loving bond is the symphony. Emotional safety enhances erotic exploration and relaxed absorption in lovemaking.

- Neglect will kill love. Love needs attention. Knowing your attachment needs and responding to those of your lover can make a bond last until "death us do part."
- All the clichés about love—when people feel loved they are freer, more alive, and more powerful—are truer than we ever imagined.

Knowing all this, I still have to relearn these lessons every time I lose connection with a loved one. I still have to face that nanosecond of choice: to blame, to try to grab control, to dismiss, to get revenge, to shut down and shut out, or to breathe deep and tune in to my own and my loved one's emotions, to risk, to reach, to confide, to hold.

Working with Christian couples, I have also learned how, as mentioned in the last chapter, Christian faith and loving bonds with others come together to form a sacred circle in which faith shapes love for another and love for a precious other enhances faith. More specifically, these couples have taught me that:

- When we are secure and connected with God, we worry less about who is in control. Flexibility prevails. Both partners can lead and follow because God is at the helm.
- Partners who can turn to God as "the comforter" and find safe haven are more able to turn to their loved one from an open and vulnerable place.
- Acknowledging our human vulnerability with our partner frees us up to turn to God with more open hearts.
- Knowing we are precious in the sight of God neutralizes our shame so we can more easily reveal ourselves to our loved ones.
- Rituals such as praying together and sharing daily devotions bring us closer to our partner by enhancing our spiritual and emotional intimacy.

- The sense of connection with a loving God calms us and helps us tune in to our partner's world so that we can respond more compassionately and sensitively to his or her needs.
- Bonding moments with loved ones seem to generally enhance our faith in the goodness of creation and the Creator.

A WIDER CIRCLE

When lovers are united in a strong and secure bond, it does more than enhance their connection to each other. The circle of loving responsiveness widens like the ripple from a stone dropped in a pool. Being in a loving relationship augments our caring and compassion for others, in our family, our churches, and our community. Loving relationships offer a model of the service to others that has always been an inherent part of the Christian faith, as exemplified by Christ Himself.

In the early research on attachment, Mary Ainsworth found that as early as three years of age, kids who are secure with their moms show more empathy to others. When we don't have to worry about safety with our loved ones, we naturally have more energy to give to others. We see others more positively and are more willing to emotionally engage with them. Feeling loved and secure makes us kinder and more tolerant people.

Psychologists Phil Shaver and Mario Mikulincer have shown in their studies that simply pausing and recalling times when someone cared for you instantly reduces your hostility to people who are different from you, if only for a brief period. Christians have always known this, though. Father Anthony Storey, a Catholic priest and one of my life mentors whom I spoke about in the introduction, always reminded me that meditating on religious images or sayings was not simply a religious ritual but also a way of connecting with the best part of ourselves — the part that naturally believes in and resonates with the best in others.

LOVE BETWEEN LOVERS, LOVE IN FAMILIES

We have known for decades that happy families start with happy relationships between partners. When we are stressed-out and constantly fighting with our partner, it spills over into our relationships with our children. It is clear beyond all doubt that conflict between parents is bad for kids. When we are frustrated and anxious, the way we discipline our kids suffers. Mostly we become harsher and more inconsistent. But it is more than just an issue of discipline. If we are struggling in an unhappy relationship, we are often off balance emotionally and find it harder to be open and really tuned in to our youngsters. Because we are not emotionally present for them, they miss out on our nurturing and guidance. Alice tells me, "I am turning into this irritable, harsh person. I am so drained by what Frank and I are going through, I just don't have the energy for the kids. When my youngest started to cry about being scared to go to school, I shouted at him. I feel awful about this. I've become a harridan, and Frank is distant with everyone. We have to solve this, for everyone's sake."

High levels of conflict in a marriage often precipitate behavioral and emotional problems in children, including depression. But conflict is not the only factor affecting youngsters. Partners' emotional distancing from each other also frequently leads to distancing from the kids. Psychologist Melissa Sturge-Apple of the University of Rochester confirms this is especially true of fathers and their offspring. Her studies find that when men withdraw from their wives, they also often become unavailable to their children.

If we think in positive terms, when we feel securely attached to our partner, we tend to find it easier to be good parents, to provide a safe haven and secure base for our youngsters. Our kids then learn positive ways to deal with their emotions and move into constructive dependency with others. There is a mountain of scientific evidence that securely attached children are happier, more socially competent, and more resilient in the face of stress. The idea that one of the best things you can do for your child is to create a loving relationship with your partner is not sentimental, it's a scientific fact.

But then therapists have been telling us for years that if we want to be really good parents, we must either have had secure, loving childhoods or counseling to deal with less-than-loving childhoods. My experience is that even if we have childhoods that have left us with lots of emotional difficulties and we never go to see a therapist, creating a better marriage can turn us into better parents. Psychologist Deborah Cohn from the University of Virginia agrees. She finds that moms who are anxious and insecure about closeness, if they are married to responsive men who provide them with a safe connection, are able to be positive and loving with their kids. When we love each other well, we help each other parent well.

When you have a safe connection in your relationship, you can pass that quality on, not just to your kid but to your kid's future partners. Psychologist Rand Conger and colleagues from Iowa State University observed 193 families with adolescent children over a period of four years and found that the degree of warmth and supportiveness between parents and the quality of their parenting predicted how the children would relate to romantic partners five years later. The children of warmer and more supportive parents were warmer and more supportive with their partners, and their relationships were happier. When we love our partner well, we offer a blueprint for a loving relationship to our children and their partners.

Better relationships between love partners are not just a personal preference, they are a social good. Better love relationships mean better families. And better, more loving families mean better, more responsive communities.

SOCIETY

Loving families are the basis of a humane society. As the poet Roberto Sosa writes, "Blessed are the lovers, for theirs is the grain of sand that sustains the center of the seas." The widening circle of engagement with and responsiveness to others does not stop with our immediate loved ones or even with the future families they create. It continues to spread out, to help create more caring communities and, ultimately, a more caring world. The great commission found in Matthew 28:16–20, where he tells Christians to take the Word out into the world, is surely not just about spreading a set of beliefs; it's also about spreading the essence of Christianity, which is that God so loved the world that He gave His son to mankind to teach us to love each other (John 3:16).

Understanding our longing for love and how love works is crucial if we want to shape a world that allows those longings to be answered and reflects the best of our nature. A human being longs for, is wired for, connection with others. Our nature is to bond intimately with a precious few, but then, having learned the lessons of belonging, to connect with others, our friends and colleagues, our tribe, and our communities of faith. When we are at our best, we offer support and caring to others because we recognize that they are just like us, human and vulnerable. In fact, we rejoice in the fellowship that takes us out of our own small world and makes us part of the greater whole.

I grew up in a small, less-than-affluent British town after World War II, where the sense that we all needed to pull together to survive was tangible. Everyone came to my parents' pub — the clergyman, the commodore, the paper seller, the judge, the doctor, the clerk, the housewife, and the whore. Elderly villagers would spend all evening in one corner playing cards and discussing politics. Tramps who wandered from town to town would be given shelter, a beer, and a huge plate of my mother's bacon and eggs before they wandered on. Soldiers who broke down, overwhelmed with the memories of war, were taken into a back room, held, and comforted. Mourners were given a hug, a whiskey, and maybe a cheery out-of-tune song on the piano, courtesy of my grandmother. Of course, there was also fighting and dissension, prejudice and cruelty. But in the end, there was a sense that we all stood together. We knew that we needed each other. And most of the time, there were at least one or two of us who could manage to be compassionate.

Interestingly enough, it is this kind of community that I still long for. This is my understanding of what Christ intended His church to be—a place where everyone is welcomed and accepted, where it is okay to need and be needed, and where uniqueness, rather than uniformity, is celebrated. One opportunity to create this kind of kinship may rest in community groups and home fellowships in our churches.

For centuries poets and prophets have assured us that we would all be better off if we loved each other more and that we should do just that. Most often this message is given as a set of moral rules and abstract ideas. Trouble is that it doesn't seem to have that much impact unless we are also emotionally touched, that is, unless we personally experience a connection to a loving God and another human being. Then we can tune in to the hurt and sadness of others as if it were our own.

Like many of us, I find myself giving a little money to the relief funds for victims of earthquakes and other disasters. But it is hard to really respond to huge overwhelming problems or to faceless crowds. For me, it is easier and much more satisfying to give money every month to the families of two little girls in India who are registered with the foster parents plan of the international relief agency Plan Canada. I have pictures of them. I know their names and the names of their villages. I know that one family now has a goat and that the other has clean water for the first time. I dream of going to visit them. I feel a connection to the stoic-looking mothers who stand beside these children in the photos that arrive in the mail every few months. Modern technology makes these links possible and allows someone like me, on the other side of the world, to connect and to care. Many of us have had this kind of connection through groups such as Compassion International, World Vision, and other nonprofit mission organizations.

Ten years ago, in a small, picturesque community of old wooden houses on a beautiful river in the hills outside Ottawa, an organization called the Wakefield Grannies sprang up. It started with one person, Rose Letwaba, a South African nurse, giving a Sunday morning talk in the church by the river. She spoke of the grandmothers in a Johannesburg slum who are raising their grandchildren, all AIDS orphans, in poverty so crippling that the kids' toothbrushes are always locked up, they are that valuable. A dozen Wakefield grandmothers got together and each connected with one South African granny and began to contribute money to that family. There are now more than 150 Grandmother-to-Grandmother groups in Canada and the U.S.

A large nondenominational church in Nashville, Tennessee, has adopted a small, poverty-stricken Appalachian community. For over a decade, groups of seventy-five to a hundred church members have visited the community two or three times each year, deepening their relationships with the people there. They provide typical ministry aid, such as school supplies, medical and dental services, and gifts and food at Christmas. But what sets them apart is the focus on getting to know the people on an individual basis and coming alongside them on their life journey. They've provided prom dresses, hairstylists, and manicurists in the spring, allowing teenage girls to experience a special occasion that they ordinarily would not be able to. When church members became aware of a woman with Stage IV cancer who wanted to get married, they purchased a beautiful dress, shoes, and jewelry for her wedding day. There are no hidden agendas here—just a ministry and outpouring of Christ's love.

These stories of love in action give me hope that we can learn about love, nurture it with our partners and family, and then, with the empathy and courage it teaches us, find ways to take it out into the world and make a difference. Writer Judith Campbell suggests, "When your heart speaks, take good notes." These stories began with people being open and responding from their heart to the plight of others. They speak to the power of emotional responsiveness and personal connection to shape our world for the better.

It seems to me that if we, as a species, are to not only survive *but thrive together* on this fragile blue and green planet, we have to learn to step past the illusion of separateness and grasp the depth of our need for secure connection with others. We must learn how to shape the constructive dependency that offers us not only an emotional home but the promise of a safe and collaborative world. The wisdom found in our own souls, in Scripture, and in science is now coming together to guide us forward. We are created for connection—something Christians have always known. Much of the Bible is, in essence, a love story. It is all about the restoration of loving connection with God. At last, we are finding our way to shape the story of secure and lasting love with life partners. Christians have always known that we are *Homo vinculum* — the one who bonds — and that we are all the stronger for it. As is written in John 15:9–17, the most priceless and pertinent commandment of all is "This is my commandment, that you love one another as I have loved you."

For more information on EFT or the Hold Me Tight®: Conversations for Connection relationship education program based on this book, or to find a therapist trained in EFT, go to www.iceeft.com.

Acknowledgments

First, I wish to thank all the couples I have had the honor to work with over the last twenty-five years. You have fascinated, enthralled, and educated me. In the drama of separateness and togetherness that is a couple therapy session, I have explored with you the reality of what it means to love, to be heartbroken, and to find a way to deep, nurturing connectedness.

Second, I wish to thank my dear colleagues at the Ottawa Couple and Family Institute and International Center for Excellence in EFT, especially Dr. Alison Lee and Gail Palmer. Without them, the Institute and Center would not exist; with them, I've been able to create a professional family.

I would like to thank all my wonderful graduate students at the University of Ottawa, School of Psychology, who have hurled themselves at outcome and change process studies in couple therapy with a passion and commitment that match my own. They have watched thousands of tapes of therapy sessions with me.

I thank my colleagues at the School of Psychology at the University of Ottawa and at Alliant International University in San Diego, who have collaborated with and supported me. Also, I thank the amazing colleagues who teach EFT with me, especially the almost fifty members of the trainers group from the International Center for Excellence in Emotionally Focused Therapy (ICEEFT), who have taken this way of understanding relationships and helping couples and families all over the world. I also acknowledge the constant validation and support given to me by the members of the more than forty EFT communities and centers all over the world and the more than four thousand active members of ICEEFT.

A special thank-you goes to my colleagues in social psychology, particularly Dr. Phil Shaver, Dr. Mario Mikulincer, and others who have been pioneers in applying attachment theory to adult relationships and who have tolerated a crazy clinician in their midst. Over the past twenty years, they have produced an explosion of research studies and rich insights — knowledge that I have taken into my couple sessions and used to make a difference in people's lives. I also thank my dear colleague John Gottman for all the debates and discussions and the wonderful validation and encouragement he has given me over the years.

I would like to thank Tracy Behar, my editor at Little, Brown, for her unflagging enthusiasm and outrageous confidence in me and this project; my agent, Miriam Altshuler, for her total professionalism and expert guidance; freelance editor Anastasia Toufexis, who waded through rough drafts of the original version of this book and saved the reader from having to do the same; and my amazing, conscientious assistant, Jackie Evans. In particular, I would like to honor my wonderful partner and colleague in this Christian edition of *Hold Me Tight,* Kenny Sanderfer, for inspiring me and guiding me back to my Christian roots. He gracefully educated me about how the faith community has changed since the nuns of St. Joseph taught me my catechism. He also connected me again to the spirit behind the songs of praise that thrilled my soul as a young chorister in the small Norman cathedral in Rochester, England. Without his support and thoughtful contributions, this book would never have seen the light of day.

I must thank my three children, Tim, Emma, and Sarah, for tolerating my obsession with this book and my desire to revisit it in order to offer it to the Christian community. I appreciate all the friends in Ottawa, across the USA, and in other parts of the world who continue to believe in me and to support my mission, which is to make loving relationships available to all people everywhere. I have been most fortunate to find exactly what it was that I was meant to do, as a researcher, teacher, writer, and therapist, but my real learning about love and relationships has been done, of course, in my own family. Most of all and always, I must thank my incredible partner, John Palmer Douglas, who is my safe haven, my secure base, my inspiration.

Sue Johnson

Special thanks to all the wonderful teams and people who have made my contribution to this book possible: Trevecca Nazarene University; Dr. Don Harvey; Robin Gould, D.R.E., LMFT; Christie Eastman; Pete Wilson, pastor and friend; all the couples who participated in the small-group research; Kentucky/Tennessee EFT community; and ICEEFT EFT trainers.

Special thanks also to Robin Pippin, who was a great source of encouragement, advice, and editorial contributions, and to my faith community, which stood behind me with encouragement and prayers.

Kenny Sanderfer

Glossary

amygdala An almond-shaped area in the midbrain associated with rapid emotional responses, especially the processing of fear. It appears to play a crucial role in "fight-or-flight" responses. When you leap out of the path of a suddenly approaching car, your amygdala has just saved your life.

A.R.E. An acronym for a conversation that positively addresses the question "Are you there for me?" Attachment theory and research tell us that emotional accessibility (Can I reach you? Will you pay attention to me?), responsiveness (Can I rely on you to respond and care about my feelings?), and engagement (Will you value me, put me first, and stay close?) characterize secure bonding interactions between intimates.

attachment cue Any sign—from an inner-felt sense, a loved one, or a situation—that turns on the attachment system, our attachment-oriented emotions, or our sense that we need others. A sudden sense of doubt that a partner cares, a dismissive comment from a partner, or a threat from a situation makes us focus on how available and responsive our loved ones are.

attachment figure A person we love or are emotionally attached to whom we see as a potential safe haven and source of comfort. Usually a parent, sibling, romantic partner, or lifelong friend. On a spiritual level, God can also be an attachment figure.

attachment injury A sense of betrayal and/or abandonment at a key moment of need that, if not addressed and healed, undermines trust and connection and triggers or fuels relationship distress and partner insecurity.

attachment protest A reaction to perceived separation from an attachment figure. It is often the first response to emotional and physical disconnection. Protest is designed to signal distress to attachment figures and get them to respond. It is characterized by anger and anxiety.

codependent A term applied to a person who facilitates, albeit often unintentionally, the dysfunctional behavior of a loved one. For example, the partner of an alcoholic who wants the drinking to stop but does not insist that this problem be confronted. The implication is that this partner's dependence on the relationship prevents him or her from confronting the alcoholic.

contact comfort A phrase used by psychological researcher Harry Harlow to describe the response of infant monkeys to physical contact with a "soft" mother, made of squashy cloth. Contact comfort is, in Harlow's view, essential to help infants soothe themselves in times of stress and anxiety. In his studies, infant monkeys sought contact comfort before food. He concluded that, in primates, contact comfort is a primary need.

conversation In this book, a deliberate attempt to talk with a partner in a way that each learns about the relationship. The seven transforming conversations illuminate how you interact, not only what you talk about.

cortisol A key stress hormone released by the adrenal glands to mobilize the body, particularly the amygdala, to deal with emergencies. Hostile critical reactions from others trigger especially high levels of cortisol. If produced constantly or in excess, the hormone can damage the body, notably the heart and immune system. There is also evidence suggesting that it destroys neurons in the hippocampus section of the brain, impairing memory and learning and facilitating overgeneralization of danger cues. For example, we know that dark streets late at night are potentially dangerous, but under prolonged stress, we may begin thinking that all streets, even early in the evening, hold danger.

Demon Dialogues The three patterns of interaction that form self-perpetuating feedback loops and make secure connection more and more difficult. These patterns are: Find the Bad Guy, or mutual blaming and criticism; the Protest Polka, wherein one person protests lack of safe emotional connection and the other defends and withdraws (the polka is also known as the demand-withdraw cycle); and Freeze and Flee, in which both partners withdraw in self-protection.

earned security The concept that our attachment expectations and responses can be revised as we gain experience in relationships. Even if we have a negative history, for example, with a parent, if we have a loving partner we can "earn" a secure feeling in our relationship.

effective dependency A positive state of secure attachment that enables us to tune in to our need for others and successfully ask for support and comfort. This state promotes connection with others and helps us handle stress as well as explore and deal with the world.

emotion From the Latin *emovere,* to move. Emotion is a physiological process that orients us to important cues in our world and gets us ready to act. It is best understood as a process. It consists of a very rapid perception that something is important, followed by a body response, an effort to understand the meaning of the cue, and a move into action. Emotions, expressed mostly in voice and face, also send rapid signals to others. In this book the word is used interchangeably with the word *feelings*.

enmeshed Extreme closeness that impedes separate functioning and autonomy. In the past, lack of separateness, rather than lack of secure, positive connection, was considered the core problem in conflicted families and couple relationships. Health was defined as being able to separate from others, to stay objective and in control of emotions, and to not allow loved ones to strongly influence one's decisions.

handles Descriptive images, words, or phrases that capture and distill your innermost feelings and vulnerabilities. Once we find our handles, we can use them to open the door to and explore our inner world.

mirror neurons Nerve cells that activate in sympathy with and in the same brain location as the nerve cells of the person whose actions we are watching. This seems to be the physiological basis of imitation, our ability to participate in another's actions. These neurons help us sense what others intend and help us connect with what the other feels. We grasp the minds of others; we resonate with their state. Scientists suggest that the more active a person's mirror neuron system, the stronger his or her empathy will be.

oxytocin The neurotransmitter most associated with bonding between mother and infants and between sexual partners. Dubbed the "cuddle hormone," oxytocin is synthesized in the hypothalamus region of the brain and is found only in mammals. It plays an important role during nursing (helping to eject milk), labor (helping the uterus to contract), and orgasm. It also seems to promote close contact and affiliative behaviors with attachment figures as well as overall positive social interaction. The higher our levels of oxytocin, the more we want to approach and engage with others. Oxytocin appears to inhibit aggressive and defensive behaviors. It also depresses production of stress hormones like cortisol. Skin-on-skin touch and warmth prime oxytocin manufacture.

primal panic The feeling often induced by separation from a key attachment figure. This panic mobilizes us to call to, reach for, and renew contact with the loved one who provides protection and a sense of safety. Emotion theorist Jaak Panksepp, who coined the term, views primal panic as a specific anxiety system in the brain that is especially honed in mammals. He refers to it as an "ancestral neural code" that sparks our brains to produce stress hormones like cortisol upon separation and the calming hormone oxytocin when we are again in close contact with the loved one.

resonance A term in physics that denotes a sympathetic vibration between two elements that leads them to suddenly synchronize signals and match pace and vibration. This creates a prolonged response. In relationships, we resonate with each other when we are tuned in to each other physiologically. Then emotional states converge. We are on the same wavelength, so that we literally share in the experience of others. It is this resonance that triggers a wave of emotion in a crowd—for example, at weddings when the vows are said and the happy couple march out together, or at soldiers' funerals when the bugler sounds a final goodbye.

Strange Situation The renowned and pivotal experiment created by Mary Ainsworth and John Bowlby to study attachment between mothers and toddlers. It involves separating a child from its mother in an unfamiliar environment where the child is likely to feel uncertain or anxious, and coding the child's emotional response when the mother returns.

symbiosis In psychological theory, a state in which one person is mentally and emotionally fused with another. Originally, for example, it was believed that a baby experienced himself or herself as part of the mother's body. Growing up was thought to be primarily a process of becoming more and more separate and autonomous. Inability to separate could lead to mental illness. For example, schizophrenia once was seen as the result of being symbiotically fused, usually with one's mother. The idea is part of the "dependency and closeness are dangerous for your mental health" school of thought. More recent theories question the validity of this concept.

synchrony A state of mutual emotional attunement and responsiveness.

2 Ds A term used to refer to two universal relationship sensitivities or raw spots, namely the sense of being *deprived* of connection or emotionally starved, and the feeling of being *deserted* or rejected as unlovable by loved ones. Both result in our feeling alone and vulnerable.

undifferentiated A concept used in family therapy indicating that a person cannot distinguish between feelings and rational thought and is reactive in relationships rather than able to make self-directed choices. The implication is that this person is too dependent on others for his or her sense of self-worth. If a therapist believes that a lack of differentiation is the problem in a distressed relationship, then improvement involves helping the partners to create clear boundaries with each other and focus on making independent decisions.

vasopressin A hormone produced in the brain, closely related to oxytocin, which has similar effects. In research with male prairie voles, vasopressin peaks during arousal and oxytocin peaks during ejaculation. Vasopressin seems to trigger a preference for a particular partner and a tendency to aggressively guard that partner from other suitors. It also appears to trigger more intense parental care.

References

General

Blum, Deborah. *Love at Goon Park: Harry Harlow and the science of affection.* Berkley Books, 2002.

Coontz, Stephanie. *Marriage, a History: From obedience to intimacy or how love conquered marriage.* Viking Press, 2005.

Ekman, Paul. *Emotions Revealed.* Henry Holt, 2003.

Goleman, Daniel. *Social Intelligence: The new science of human relationships.* Bantam Press, 2006.

Gottman, John. *The Seven Principles for Making Marriage Work.* Crown Publishers, 1999.

Johnson, Susan M. *The Practice of Emotionally Focused Couple Therapy: Creating connection.* Brunner/Routledge, 2004.

Jong, Erica. *O, The Oprah Magazine,* February 2004.

Karen, Robert. *Becoming Attached.* Oxford University Press, 1998.

Lewis, Thomas, Amini, Fari, and Lannon, Richard. *A General Theory of Love.* Vintage Books, 2000.

Mikulincer, Mario, and Shaver, Phil. *Attachment in Adulthood: Structure, dynamics and change.* Guilford Press, 2007.

Siegel, Daniel, and Hartzell, Mary. *Parenting from the Inside Out.* Putnam, 2003.

Love — A Revolutionary New View

Barich, Rachel, and Bielby, Denise. "Rethinking marriage: Change and stability in expectations 1967–1994." *Journal of Family Issues,* 1996, vol. 17, pp. 139–169.

Bowlby, John. *Attachment and Loss,* Volume 1: *Attachment.* Basic Books, 1969.

———. *Attachment and Loss,* Volume 2: *Separation.* Basic Books, 1973.

———. *Attachment and Loss,* Volume 3: *Loss.* Basic Books, 1981.

Buss, David, Shackelford, Todd, Kirkpatrick, Lee, and Larsen, Randy. "A half century of mate preferences: The cultural evolution of values." *Journal of Marriage and Family,* 2001, vol. 63, pp. 491–503.

Campbell, A., Converse, P. E., and Rodgers, W. L. *The Quality of American Life.* Russell Sage Publications, 1976.

Coan, J., Schaefer, H., and Davidson, R. "Lending a hand." *Psychological Science,* 2006, vol. 17, pp. 1–8.

Coyne, James, Rohrbaugh, Michael J., Shoham, Varda, Sonnega, John, Nicklas, John M., and Cranford, James. "Prognostic importance of marital quality for survival of congestive heart failure." *American Journal of Cardiology,* 2001, vol. 88, pp. 526–529.

Dimsdale, Joel E. *Survivors, Victims and Perpetrators: Essays on the Nazi Holocaust.* Hemisphere, 1980.

Eisenberger, Naomi I., Lieberman, Matthew D., and Williams, Kipling. "Why rejection hurts: A common neural alarm system for physical and social pain." *Trends in Cognitive Science,* 2004, vol. 8, pp. 294–300.

Feeney, Brooke C. "The dependency paradox in close relationships: Accepting dependence promotes independence." *Journal of Personality and Social Psychology,* 2007, vol. 92, pp. 268–285.

Finegold, Brie. "Confiding in No One." *Scientific American Mind,* 2006, vol. 17, p. 11.

Hardy, Alister. *The Spiritual Nature of Man: A study of contemporary religious experience.* Clarendon, 1979.

Hawkley, Louise, Masi, Christopher M., Berry, Jarett, and Cacioppo, John. "Loneliness is a unique predictor of age-related differences in systolic blood pressure." *Psychology and Aging,* 2006, vol. 21, pp. 152–164.

House, James, Landis, Karl R., and Umberson, Debra. "Social relationships and health." *Science,* 1988, vol. 241, pp. 540–545.

Kiecolt-Glaser, Janice K., Loving, Timothy J., Stowell, J. R., Malarkey, William B., Lemeshow, Stanley, Dickinson, Stephanie, and Glaser, Ronald. "Hostile marital interactions, pro-inflammatory cytokine production and wound healing." *Archives of General Psychiatry,* 2005, vol. 62, pp. 1377–1384.

Kiecolt-Glaser, Janice K., Malarkey, William B., Chee, Marie-Anne, Newton, Tamara, Cacioppo, John T., Mao, Hsiao-Yin, and Glaser, Ronald. "Negative behavior during marital conflict is associated with immunological down-regulation." *Psychosomatic Medicine,* 1993, vol. 55, pp. 395–409.

Kiecolt-Glaser, Janice K., Newton, Tamara, Cacioppo, John T., MacCallum, Robert C., and Glaser, Ronald. "Marital conflict and endocrine function: Are men really more physiologically affected than women?" *Journal of Consulting and Clinical Psychology,* 1996, vol. 64, pp. 324–332.

Kirkpatrick, Lee. "An attachment theory approach to the psychology of religion." *International Journal for the Psychology of Religion,* 1992, vol. 2(1), pp. 3–28.

———. "A longitudinal study of changes in religious belief and behavior as a function of individual differences in adult attachment style." *Journal for the Scientific Study of Religion,* 1997, vol. 36(2), pp. 207–217.

———. "Attachment and religious representations and behavior." In *Handbook of Attachment: Theory, research, and clinical applications,*

Jude Cassidy and Phillip R. Shaver (eds.). Guilford Press, 1999, pp. 803–822.

Levy, David. "Primary affect hunger." *American Journal of Psychiatry,* 1937, vol. 94, pp. 643–652.

Medalie, Jack H., and Goldbourt, Uri. "Angina pectoris among 10,000 men." *American Journal of Medicine,* 1976, vol. 60, pp. 910–921.

Mikulincer, Mario. "Attachment style and the mental representation of the self." *Journal of Personality and Social Psychology,* 1995, vol. 69, pp. 1203–1215.

———. "Adult attachment style and information processing: Individual differences in curiosity and cognitive closure."*Journal of Personality and Social Psychology,* 1997, vol. 72, pp. 1217–1230.

———. "Adult attachment style and individual differences in functional versus dysfunctional experiences of anger." *Journal of Personality and Social Psychology,* 1998, vol. 74, pp. 513–524.

Mikulincer, Mario, Florian, Victor, and Weller, Aron. "Attachment styles, coping strategies, and post-traumatic psychological distress: The impact of the Gulf War in Israel." *Journal of Personality and Social Psychology,* 1993, vol. 64, pp. 817–826.

Mikulincer, Mario, Gurwitz, Vera, and Shaver, Phil. "Attachment security and the use of God as a safe haven: New experimental findings." Paper presented at the 115th Annual Convention of the American Psychological Association, San Francisco, 2007.

Morell, Marie A., and Apple, Robin. F. "Affect expression, marital satisfaction and stress reactivity among premenopausal women during a conflictual marital discussion." *Psychology of Women Quarterly,* 1990, vol. 14, pp. 387–402.

O'Leary, K. D., Christian, J. L., and Mendell, N. R. "A closer look at the link between marital discord and depressive symptomatology." *Journal of Social and Clinical Psychology,* 1994, vol. 13, pp. 33–41.

Orth-Gomér, Kristina, Wamala, Sarah, Horsten, Myriam, Schenck-Gustafsson, Karin, Schneiderman, Neil, and Mittleman, Murray.

"Marital stress worsens prognosis in women with coronary heart disease." *Journal of the American Medical Association,* 2000, vol. 284, pp. 3008–3014.

Putnam, Robert D. *Bowling Alone: The collapse and revival of American community.* Simon and Schuster, 2000.

Roberts, Brent W., and Robins, Richard W. "Broad dispositions, broad aspirations: The intersection of personality and major life goals." *Personality and Social Psychology Bulletin,* 2000, vol. 26, pp. 1284–1296.

Simpson, Jeffry, Rholes, William, and Nelligan, Julia. "Support seeking and support giving within couples in an anxiety provoking situation: The role of attachment styles." *Journal of Personality and Social Psychology,* 1992, vol. 62, pp. 434–446.

Twenge, Jean. "The age of anxiety? Birth cohort change in anxiety and neuroticism." *Journal of Personality and Social Psychology,* 2000, vol. 79, pp. 1007–1021.

Uchino, Bert, Cacioppo, John, and Kiecolt-Glaser, Janice. "The relationship between social support and physiological processes." *Psychological Bulletin,* 1996, vol. 119, pp. 488–531.

Yalom, Marilyn. *A History of the Wife.* HarperCollins, 2001.

Where Did Our Love Go? Losing Connection

Gottman, John. *What Predicts Divorce?* Lawrence Erlbaum Associates, 1994.

Huston, Ted, Caughlin, John, Houts, Renate, Smith, Shanna, and George, Laura. "The connubial crucible: Newlywed years as predictors of marital delight, distress and divorce." *Journal of Personality and Social Psychology,* 2001, vol. 80, pp. 237–252.

LeDoux, Joseph. *The Emotional Brain: The mysterious underpinnings of emotional life.* Simon and Schuster, 1996.

Lewis, C. S. *The Four Loves.* Mariner Books, 1971.

Panksepp, Jaak. *Affective Neuroscience: The foundations of human and animal emotions.* Oxford University Press, 1998.

Conversation 2: Finding the Raw Spots

Davila, Joanne, Burge, Dorli, and Hammen, Constance. "Why does attachment style change?" *Journal of Personality and Social Psychology,* 1997, vol. 73, pp. 826–838.

LeDoux, Joseph. *The Emotional Brain: The mysterious underpinnings of emotional life.* Simon and Schuster, 1996.

Manning, Brennan. *Abba's Child: The cry of the heart for intimate belonging.* NavPress, 2002.

Conversation 4: Hold Me Tight — Engaging and Connecting

Carter, Sue. "Neuroendocrine perspectives on social attachment and love." *Psychoneuroendocrinology,* 1998, vol. 23, pp. 779–818.

di Pellegrino, Giuseppe, Fadiga, Luciano, Fogassi, Leonardo, Gallese, Vittorio, and Rizzolatti, Giacomo. "Understanding motor events: A neurophysiological study." *Experimental Brain Research,* 1992, vol. 91, pp. 176–180.

Gallese, Vittorio. "The shared manifold hypothesis: From mirror neurons to empathy." *Journal of Consciousness Studies,* 2001, vol. 8, pp. 33–50.

Insel, Thomas. "A neurobiological basis of social attachment." *American Journal of Psychiatry,* 1997, vol. 154, pp. 726–735.

Johnson, Sue, and Greenberg, Leslie. "Relating process to outcome in marital therapy." *Journal of Marital and Family Therapy,* 1988, vol. 14, pp. 175–183.

Keller, Timothy. *Prayer: Experiencing awe and intimacy with God.* Dutton, 2014.

Kosfeld, Michael, Heinrichs, Markus, Zak, Paul, Fischbacher, Urs, and Fehr, Ernst. "Oxytocin increases trust in humans." *Nature,* 2005, vol. 435, pp. 673–676.

Stern, Daniel. *The Present Moment in Psychotherapy and Everyday Life.* Norton, 2004.

Uvnäs Moberg, Kerstin. "Oxytocin may mediate the benefits of positive social interaction and emotions." *Psychoneuroendocrinology,* 1998, vol. 23, pp. 819–835.

Varela, Francisco, Lachaux, Jean-Philippe, Rodriguez, Eugenio, and Martinerie, Jacques. "The Brainweb: Phase synchronization and large-scale integration." *Nature Reviews. Neuroscience,* 2001, vol. 2, pp. 229–239.

Conversation 5: Forgiving Injuries

Herman, Judith. *Trauma and Recovery.* Basic Books, 1992.

Simpson, Jeffry, and Rholes, William. "Stress and secure base relationships in adulthood." In *Attachment Processes in Adulthood,* Kim Bartholomew and Dan Perlman (eds.). Jessica Kingsley Publishers, 1994, pp. 181–204.

Conversation 6: Bonding Through Sex and Touch

Davis, Deborah, Shaver, Phillip, and Vernon, Michael. "Attachment style and subjective motivations for sex." *Personality and Social Psychology Bulletin,* 2004, vol. 30, pp. 1076–1090.

Field, Tiffany. *Touch.* MIT Press, 2003.

Gillath, Omri, and Schachner, Dory. "How do sexuality and attachment interrelate?" In *Dynamics of Romantic Love: Attachment, caregiving and sex,* Mario Mikulincer and Gail Goodman (eds.). Guilford Press, 2006, pp. 337–355.

Harlow, Harry. *Learning to Love.* Jason Aronson, 1978.

Hazan, Cindy, Zeifman, D., and Middleton, K. "Adult romantic attachment, affection and sex." Paper presented at the International Conference on Personal Relationships, Groningen, Netherlands, 1994.

Johnson, Susan M. *Love Sense: The revolutionary new science of romantic relationships.* Little, Brown and Company, 2013.

McCarthy, Barry, and McCarthy, Emily. *Rekindling Desire.* Brunner/Routledge, 2003.

Michael, Robert, Gagnon, John, Laumann, Edward, and Kolata,

Gina. *Sex in America: A definitive survey.* Little, Brown and Company, 1995.

Montagu, Ashley. *Touching.* Harper and Row, 1978.

Simpson, Jeffry, and Gangestad, S. "Individual differences in sociosexuality: Evidence for convergent and discriminant validity." *Journal of Personality and Social Psychology,* 1991, vol. 60, pp. 870–883.

Stern, Daniel. *The Present Moment in Psychotherapy and Everyday Life.* Norton, 2004.

Conversation 7: Keeping Your Love Alive

Johnson, Susan, and Greenberg, Leslie. "The differential effects of experiential and problem solving interventions in resolving marital conflict." *Journal of Consulting and Clinical Psychology,* 1985, vol. 53, pp. 175–184.

Main, Mary. "Metacognitive knowledge, metacognitive monitoring and singular (coherent) vs. multiple (incoherent) models of attachment." In *Attachment Across the Life Cycle,* Colin Murray Parkes, Joan Stevenson-Hinde, and Peter Marris (eds.). Routledge, 1991, pp. 127–159.

Schor, Juliet. *The Overworked American.* Basic Books, 1992.

Our Bond with God

Armstrong, Karen. *The Case for God.* Knopf, 2009.
———. *Fields of Blood: Religion and the history of violence.* Knopf, 2014.

Byrd, Kevin, and Boe, AnnDrea. "The correspondence between attachment dimensions and prayer in college students." *International Journal for the Psychology of Religion,* 2001, vol. 11, pp. 9–24.

Eddington, Sir Arthur S. Extract from speech Eddington gave to the Royal Astronomical Society, Cambridge, 1919.

Granqvist, Pehr, and Hagekull, Berit. "Longitudinal predictions of religious change in adolescents." *Journal of Social and Personal Relationships,* 2003, vol. 20, pp. 793–817.

Granqvist, Pehr, and Kirkpatrick, Lee. "Attachment and religious representations and behavior." In *Handbook of Attachment,* Jude Cassidy and Phillip R. Shaver (eds.). Guilford Press, 2008, pp. 906–933.

Granqvist, Pehr, Mikulincer, Mario, Gewirtz, Vered, and Shaver, Phillip R. "Experimental findings on God as an attachment figure: Normative processes and moderating effects of internal working models." *Journal of Personality and Social Psychology,* 2012, vol. 103, pp. 804–818.

John of the Cross, Saint. *Dark Night of the Soul.* Dover Publications, 2003.

Johnson, Susan, Burgess Moser, Melissa, Beckes, Lane, Smith, Andra, Dalgleish, Tracy, Halchuk, Rebecca, Hasselmo, Karen, Greenman, Paul, Merali, Zul, and Coan, James. "Soothing the Threatened Brain: Leveraging contact comfort with Emotionally Focused Therapy." *PLOS One,* 2013, 8(11): e79314 doi:10.1371/journal.pone.0079314.

Lucado, Max. http://www.goodreads.com/author/quotes/2737.

Lyte, Henry F. "Abide with Me," 1847. https://en.wikipedia.org/wiki/Abide_with_Me.

McLean, L., Walton, T., Rodin, G., Esplen, M., and Jones, J. M. "A couple-based intervention for patients and caregivers facing end-stage cancer: Outcomes of a randomized controlled trial." *Psycho-Oncology,* 2013, vol. 22(1), pp. 28–38.

Mikulincer, Mario, and Shaver, Phillip. *Attachment in Adulthood: Structure, dynamics and change.* Guilford Press, 2007.

Nouwen, Henri, and Imbach, Jeff (eds.). *Words of Hope and Healing: 99 sayings by Henri Nouwen.* New City Press of the Focolare, 2005.

Ten Elshof, Judith, and Furrow, James. "The role of secure attachment in predicting spiritual maturity of students at a conservative seminary." *Journal of Psychology and Theology,* 2000, vol. 28, pp. 99–108.

Teresa, Mother. *Come Be My Light: The private writings of the Saint of Calcutta.* Doubleday, 2007.

Ullman, Chana. *The Transformed Self: The psychology of religious conversion.* Plenum Press, 1989.

Warren, Rick, and Warren, Kay. http://www.christiantoday.com /article/htb.leadership.conference.2014.rick.and.kay.warren.we.must .hold.onto.hope/37221.htm

Ultimate Connection — Love as the Final Frontier

Cohn, D. A., Silver, D. H., Cowan, C. P., Cowan, P. A., and Pearson, J. "Working models of childhood attachment and couple relationships." *Journal of Family Issues,* 1992, vol. 13(4), pp. 432–449.

Conger, R. D., Cui, M., Bryant, C. M., and Elder, G. H., Jr. "Competence in early adult relationships: A developmental perspective on family influences." *Journal of Personality and Social Psychology,* 2000, vol. 79(2), pp. 224–237.

Mason, B., and Mendoza, S. "Generic aspects of primate attachments: Parents, offspring and mates." *Psychoneuroendocrinology,* 1998, vol. 23, pp. 765–778.

Mikulincer, M., Shaver, P., Gillath, O., and Nitzberg, R. "Attachment, caregiving and altruism: Boosting attachment security increases compassion and helping." *Journal of Personality and Social Psychology,* 2005, vol. 89, pp. 817–839.

Simpson, J., Collins, A., Tran, S., and Haydon, K. "Attachment and the experience and expression of emotions in romantic relationships: A developmental perspective." *Journal of Personality and Social Psychology,* 2007, vol. 92, pp. 355–367.

Sturge-Apple, M., Davies, P., and Cummings, M. "Impact of hostility and withdrawal in interparental conflict on parental emotional unavailability and children's adjustment difficulties." *Child Development,* 2006, vol. 77, pp. 1623–1641.

Copyright Acknowledgments

Index

abandonment, 45, 48, 91, 99, 125, 184, 277, 294

Abba's Child (Manning), 109

"Abide with Me" (hymn), 253

accessibility, 29, 47, 125, 127, 137, 145, 152–53, 184
    Hold Me Tight conversation and, 65, 67, 156, 162, 169
    See also A.R.E.

Adam (Bible), 7, 55, 78, 83, 176

adequacy, 48, 92–93, 125

affairs, 187, 194, 195

aggressiveness, 26, 31, 47, 117, 297
    Demon Dialogues and, 57, 62, 78–80, 90, 101

Ainsworth, Mary, 25, 279, 297

ambiguity, 32, 43, 95, 134, 137, 184, 231, 260

American Psychological Association, 9

Amini, Fari, 109

amygdala, 40, 111, 117, 124, 242, 252, 293, 295

Andrews, Cecile, 229

anger, 29, 31, 40–41, 44, 116–17, 122, 137, 214, 256, 262, 294

Demon Dialogues and, 79, 91–92, 112, 150, 157

anxiety, 26, 29, 31, 34–35, 71, 179, 185, 190, 276–77, 294, 297
    attachment needs and, 251, 258–59, 262–63
    Demon Dialogues and, 77, 134, 150
    parenting and, 280–81
    sexual intimacy and, 205, 208
    See also fears, attachment

apologies, 192–93, 196–97, 199

A.R.E. (Accessibility, Responsiveness, and Engagement), 60–61, 153, 239, 260, 293
    Hold Me Tight conversation and, 65, 156, 169, 172, 177, 193
    Play and Practice, 68–71, 106, 243–44, 266–68
    sexual intimacy and, 201, 207, 213, 218
    strengthening bonds and, 220, 223–24, 226, 231–32, 244
    See also accessibility; engagement; responsiveness

Sanderfer, Kenny, 3–5, 7–8, 9–10
Sant'Antimo Abbey (Tuscany), 261
Schor, Juliet, 229
Scriptures. *See* Bible
self-protection, 41, 77–79, 101, 122,
    156, 196, 198, 263–64, 295
separateness, 91, 193, 257, 272, 285,
    296
sexual intimacy, 30, 72, 103, 200–
    218, 275–76
    A.R.E. and, 201, 207, 213, 218
    Christianity and, 201, 204
    culture and, 200–201, 204
    Demon Dialogues and, 206, 211
    emotional connection and, 41,
        201–2, 203–4, 208–9, 211, 277
    gender and, 90, 203–4, 211
    openness and, 209, 212, 217
    Play and Practice, 216–18
    responsiveness and, 208–9, 211
    safety and, 202, 209, 210, 216,
        218, 275, 277
    Sealed-Off Sex, 202–4, 216
    Solace Sex, 202, 205–8, 216
    Synchrony Sex, 202, 208–11, 216
shame, 53–54, 112, 117, 125, 139,
    165, 191–93, 197, 278
sharing, 105, 122–32, 138–39,
    151, 165
    of attachment fears, 53–55, 63,
        139
    benefits of, 124, 162
    trauma and, 190–92
    of vulnerability, 122–24, 127,
        129–30, 132, 139, 166, 278,
        282
Shaver, Phil, 29–30, 279
Shay, Jonathan, 272
siblings, 95, 110, 121
Siegel, Dan, 242
Simpson, Jeff, 30–31, 183, 203, 273
Sistine Chapel, 176

Sosa, Roberto, 282
spiritual wisdom, 4, 11, 201, 265
Spitz, René, 23
Stern, Dan, 208
Storey, Anthony, 7, 279–80
stories, creating, 193–94, 199, 242
    Future Love Story, 221–22,
        237–39, 244
    Resilient Relationship Story,
        221, 232–37, 239–40, 241,
        244
Strange Situation experiment,
    25–26, 273, 297–98
Sturge-Apple, Melissa, 280
support, 28, 30–31, 276
survival mechanism, connection as,
    6, 22, 24, 57, 117, 244
Su Tung-p'o, 220
symbiosis, 28, 298
synchrony, 175–76, 208–9, 215, 297,
    298

Taj Mahal, 19
Teacher Man (McCourt), 83
Teresa, Mother, 257–58
testosterone, 204
therapy
    couples, 4–6, 8–9, 11, 13–14, 20,
        52–53, 55–56
    EFT, 3–6, 8–10, 14, 55–56, 239,
        276
    family, 24
Tomatis, Alfred, 225
touch, 23, 27, 31, 35–36, 61, 206–8,
    252–53, 297
    comfort and, 26, 125, 206–7, 216,
        294
Touching (Montagu), 207
traumas, relationship, 29, 181–99
    forgiveness and, 187–99, 277
    Play and Practice, 195–99
    recognition of, 187–91, 195–96

321

ABOUT THE AUTHORS

DR. SUE JOHNSON is the developer of Emotionally Focused Couple and Family Therapy (EFT), a cutting-edge intervention that is empirically validated with thirty years of research. She is also director of the Ottawa (Canada) Couple and Family Institute and the International Center for Excellence in Emotionally Focused Therapy, as well as Professor Emeritus of Clinical Psychology at the University of Ottawa and Distinguished Research Professor at Alliant University in San Diego, California. Sue is a fellow of the American Psychological Association and has received numerous honors for her work, including the Outstanding Contribution to the Field of Couple and Family Therapy Award from the American Association for Marriage and Family Therapy and the Research in Family Therapy Award from the American Family Therapy Academy. She trains mental health professionals in EFT worldwide. Sue lives in Ottawa, Canada, with her husband and family. Please visit www.drsuejohnson.com and www.iceeft.com for further information on EFT and Dr. Sue Johnson.

KENNETH SANDERFER is a licensed marriage and family therapist, providing couple and family therapy at his private practice in Nashville, Tennessee. He has received training in Emotionally Focused Couple Therapy (EFT) and is a certified EFT therapist, supervisor, and trainer, as well as an AAMFT (American Association for Marriage and Family Therapy) approved supervisor. Kenny grew up in Texas, where he received his undergraduate degree in agriculture, and spent several years in West Africa as an agricultural missionary. After returning to the United States, he received his master's in marriage and family therapy from Trevecca Nazarene University, where he is now an adjunct professor. Kenny has written articles for several major Christian magazines. When away from work, he enjoys fly-fishing, farming, training horses, and spending time with his wife, Suzette, and their five grandchildren.